Global Perspectives on International Joint and Double Degree Programs

Global Perspectives on International Joint and Double Degree Programs

EDITED BY MATTHIAS KUDER, NINA LEMMENS AND DANIEL OBST

DAAD Deutscher Akademischer Austausch Dienst
German Academic Exchange Service

This publication was funded, in part, by the German Federal Ministry of Education and Research.

New York

IIE publications can be purchased at: www.iiebooks.org

The Institute of International Education
809 United Nations Plaza, New York, New York 10017

© 2013 by the Institute of International Education
All rights reserved. Published 2013
Printed in the United States of America
ISBN-13: 978-0-87206-363-1

Library of Congress Cataloging-in-Publication Data

Global perspectives on international joint and double degree programs / edited by Matthias Kuder,
Nina Lemmens, and Daniel Obst.
    pages cm
  ISBN 978-0-87206-363-1
  1. Joint academic degree programs. 2. University cooperation. 3. Education and globalization.
  I. Kuder, Matthias, editor of compilation. II. Lemmens, Nina, editor of compilation. III. Obst,
Daniel, editor of compilation.
  LB2381.G56 2013
  378.2--dc23
                                    2013033891

The views expressed in these chapters are solely those of the authors.
They do not necessarily represent the official positions of the
Institute of International Education or the German Academic Exchange Service (DAAD).

Copy Editor: Teresa Barensfeld
Editorial Support: Stacy Asch, Shepherd Laughlin, Jon Grosh
Cover Design and Layout: Pat Scully

Table of Contents

Institutional Perspectives

Regional Perspectives

The Student Perspective

Accreditation and Quality Assurance

Figures and Tables

Figures

Tables

The Road Less Traveled is the Road to the Future

Allan E. Goodman, President and CEO, Institute of International Education (IIE)

Dorothea Rüland, Secretary General, German Academic Exchange Service (DAAD)

The terms "international joint degree" and "international double degree," while nowadays common among educators all over the globe, have not always been in our lexicon. Hailing from the tradition of singular institutions of higher education, until recently colleges and universities around the world have typically granted one degree, and from one institution only. Bearing a degree from that institution elicited school-specific pride; the decades of tradition became a part of a student's identity. To be sure, this is still the case for the majority of higher education experiences today.

However, in the 1990s, a new trend began, spearheaded primarily by higher education institutions in Europe. Universities started collaborating on curriculum, coordinating credits, and offering a combined degree from two different schools. Like many revolutionary ideas before, these few initial programs were seen as avant-garde by some—and completely impractical by others. Indeed, it took more than a decade for a broader section of the international higher education community to come around to the idea and begin to initiate new joint or double degree programs at their own institutions.

Joint and double degree programs arguably are not in the center of international engagement activities, largely because of the complexity involved in setting them up and operating them. But these collaborative degree programs continue to gain traction, because they offer an opportunity to build strong institutional partnerships between higher education institutions. Additionally, they provide particularly deep and meaningful international experiences to students. Instead of seeking solely to be a product of a single institution, students are beginning to seek out the international competency currency that such collaborative degrees have to offer.

A recent report published by the Institute of International Education and the Freie Universität Berlin, *Joint and Double Degree Programs in the Global Context*, confirms that the efforts made by those pioneering institutions in the 1990s were not in vain. According to that report, 95 percent of the nearly 250 respondents in 28 countries want to develop more joint and double degree programs. Nearly two-thirds of the responding institutions that had already initiated programs had done so in the last decade. Where joint and double degree programs have historically been characterized as too complex and too expensive to implement, institutions are realizing that—when done right—the benefits can outweigh the costs.

On an institutional level, forward-looking colleges and universities are motivated to develop joint or double degree programs because they can be an effective tool to broaden educational offerings, strengthen research collaboration, advance internationalization, and raise the international visibility or prestige of the institution. In some cases, they might even result in increased revenue for the institutions involved. On a global level, they provide a chance to build particularly strong strategic academic partnerships between higher education networks around the world, and they have become an increasingly important element of the educational exchange relationship between countries.

This book, the first in a series of joint publications by the Institute of International Education (IIE) and the German Academic Exchange Service (DAAD) that will look into "global perspectives" on pressing issues in our field, is therefore particularly important. It not only highlights the current trends and recent developments in defining, developing and sustaining international joint and double degree programs. It also provides regional and institutional perspectives from Europe, North America, Africa, the Middle East, South America and Asia. It describes both the policy frameworks—especially around accreditation, quality assurance, and student exchange—in different countries, and individual program examples that serve as illustrative case studies of institutional internationalization. We thank the authors for their important contributions.

DAAD and IIE have a long and fruitful shared history. IIE was established in 1919 in the aftermath of World War I to catalyze educational exchange. IIE's founders—Nobel Peace Prize winners Nicholas Murray Butler, president of Columbia University, and Elihu Root, former U.S. secretary of state, and Stephen Duggan, Sr., professor of political science at the College of the City of New York and IIE's first president—believed that we could not achieve lasting peace without greater understanding between nations, and that international educational exchange formed the strongest basis for fostering such understanding. The Institute met the need for a central point of contact and source of information for both U.S. higher education and foreign nations interested in developing educational ties with the United States.

In the early 1920s, Carl Joachim Friedrich, a student of political science at the University of Heidelberg in Germany, came to study in the United States. He persuaded IIE to create fellowships for 13 other German students of social and political science. In 1925, this vision was greatly expanded: the Akademische Austauschdienst (AAD) (Academic Exchange Service) was founded at that time, and has expanded to become what is now DAAD. Today, DAAD and IIE provide international exchange opportunities for nearly 100,000 students, scholars and professionals each year. Both organizations are at the forefront of supporting and promoting the development of closer institutional ties between colleges and universities on all continents.

In today's rapidly expanding international education sector and in the increasingly competitive world our students face upon graduating, higher education institutions are pulled in many directions. They are asked to prepare global citizens, perform cutting-edge research, develop innovative teaching methods, maintain active alumni networks, and fulfill a host of other requirements—all on diminishing budgets. Understanding that counterparts in other countries share similar challenges and have complementary ways of addressing them, higher education institutions are increasingly braving the still relatively uncharted waters of innovations like joint and double degree programs as a promising path into the future. Building upon the models of those first trail-blazers from decades past, the joint and double degree programs created today are proof that, when done collaboratively, great things are possible.

Introduction

Global Perspectives on International Joint and Double Degree Programs

Matthias Kuder, Freie Universität Berlin; Nina Lemmens,
German Academic Exchange Service (DAAD); and Daniel Obst,
Institute of International Education (IIE)

Collaborative degree programs have become a popular form of higher education internationalization around the world, but they are complex and challenging to implement. National and international organizations, higher education associations, and funding agencies have undertaken efforts to study the dynamics and frameworks of joint and double degree programs in their particular contexts. Some of these efforts have culminated in full-fledged studies, some have led to the formulation of best practices, and yet others have produced overviews that assess specific regional or national collaborative degree landscapes.

The *Survey on Master Degrees and Joint Degrees in Europe* by Tauch and Rauhvargers (2002) was one of the first efforts to map the experiences with joint programs in Europe. In 2009, a consortium led by the Institute of International Education (IIE) and Freie Universität Berlin produced the first transatlantic survey and a subsequent publication (Kuder & Obst, 2009). In 2011, a follow-on survey extended the original publication's scope beyond the transatlantic sphere, resulting in the report *Joint and Double Degree Programs in the Global Context* (Obst, Kuder, & Banks, 2011). There are analyses of collaborative degree programs in particular contexts, including on graduate education, published by the Council of Graduate Schools (2010), or on the employability of graduates of collaborative degree programs, published by the Franco-German University (2012). A variety of other studies and monitoring exercises have addressed joint and double degree programs in particular countries or regions, including Thailand (Office of the Higher Education Commission, 2011), Latin America (Gacel-Avila, 2009), UK–Russia (SQW Consulting, 2010), and Germany–Netherlands (Nickel, Zdebel, & Westerheijden, 2009). Institutions promoting the development of joint and double degree programs, such as the German Academic Exchange Service or the European Commission, have supported various initiatives aiming to evaluate such programs (Culver, Puri, Spinelli, DePauw, & Dooley, 2011). And a growing number of international associations, including the International Association of Universities, now include joint and double degree programs in their frequent efforts to map internationalization (International Association of Universities, 2010). Increasing interest in joint and double degree programs is also seen on the agendas of international higher education conferences, working groups, and expert seminars specifically devoted to this format of internationalization.

These developments clearly illustrate the need for reflection on these complex forms of international collaboration. In response, this publication aims to provide a concise information source on joint and double degree programs by drawing on a broad range of expertise from individuals, institutions, and organizations. It is the first book on collaborative degree programs that pools existing knowledge from different regional contexts and features a collection of articles on experiences, concepts, and policies. We hope that the book at hand will offer orientation to higher education institutions, government agencies, and other related organizations that engage in developing approaches and formulating policies aimed at joint and double degree programs.

The book's first section builds a basis for understanding the nature of collaborative degree programs, overarching trends, and challenges. By offering a conceptual framework for terminology, Jane Knight's article addresses confusion about different forms of collaborative degree programs. The article further provides an overview of recent research on joint and double degree programs, analyzes developments and innovations in this context, and addresses factors that influence the operationalization of collaborative degree programs. Finally, it identifies and discusses various issues that continue to raise critical questions in the context of joint and double degree programs. Based on the results of a global survey conducted by IIE in 2011, Matthias Kuder formulates a plea for a more strategic approach to developing joint and double degree programs. Addressing a select set of challenges, the article argues that they often result from a mix of unbalanced expectations and underdeveloped institutional policies. The article by Tabea Mager, Svend Poller, and Francesco Girotti presents essential ingredients for the successful development and management of joint programs. The authors feature an overview of findings assembled in the course of the JOIMAN and JOI.CON initiatives, with hands-on recommendations for institutions that plan to establish joint and double degree programs. The articles by

Mareike Tarazona and Diana Yefanova are both based on doctoral theses. Tarazona shows factors influencing the sustainability of joint and double degree programs involving German higher education institutions. Based on two case studies at Japanese universities, Yefanova examines faculty and administrators' role in the process of implementation of double degree programs at the graduate level. The article also explores issues around stakeholder access to decision-making processes related to program implementation at those institutions. Though both studies are set in particular country contexts, their findings arguably transcend regional borders.

The book's second section focuses on institutional perspectives. It introduces examples of approaches and experiences in program development and delivery at higher education institutions in Africa, Asia, Europe, the Middle East, North America, and South America. Alessia Lefébure explains a holistic approach to developing collaborative degree programs based on the example of the Alliance Program, a joint venture by New York's Columbia University and three Paris-based institutions—École Polytechnique, Sciences Po, and Sorbonne University (Paris-1). Using the metaphor of a router, Lefébure shows how the Alliance Program serves as a laboratory for the promotion of innovative forms of international collaborations, including joint and double degree programs in a variety of academic fields and levels. The article by Christoph Steber discusses the Technical University of Munich's (TUM) experience with collaborative degree programs. With 46 such arrangements currently in existence, the TUM article looks back at over 20 years of experience in this field, outlining rationales for collaborative degree programs and their impact on students and institutions. In the case of Stellenbosch University, Dorothy Stevens presents her institution's relatively young history of promoting joint and double degree programs, discussing specific challenges, policies, and regulations. The article by National University of Singapore (NUS) also discusses policies and approval processes for collaborative programs. Bernard Tan illustrates how NUS has made collaborative programs, both within the institution and in cooperation with partner universities abroad, a centerpiece of its institutional strategy to attract high-quality students and produce talent for Singapore. In the article featuring the case of Unicamp, Leandro Tessler and José Pissolato Filho present their institution's experience in building collaborative degree programs, starting with a focus on French–Brazilian joint ventures, and outline opportunities as well as challenges specific to the Brazilian context. Finally, Lars Ribbe, Manar Fayyad, and Joern Trappe describe their institutions' take on building collaborative programs. With the example of the German–Jordanian Master's Program in Integrated Water Resources Management, the authors give us a micro-level glimpse at the structure of a particular program, including the advantages it offers to both sides and as well as specific problems the authors encountered.

The third section focuses on regional perspectives and country-specific experiences. The article by Xavier Prats Monné and Claire Morel presents the European Commission's rich experience with promoting joint programs through Erasmus Mundus and other specific programs such as Atlantis, and underlines the high priority that joint programs enjoy in the context of EU higher education policies. Furthermore, Prats Monné and Morel outline the impact these programs have had on the European Higher Education Area and offer an outlook on current developments, specifically the new Erasmus+ funding program, which will take the promotion of joint programs to an even higher level. The article by Christian Thimme offers deep insight into the experience of funding joint and double degree programs, explaining why the German Academic Exchange Service (DAAD) chose to promote collaborative degree programs and outlining DAAD funding programs and procedures. China's experience with collaborative degree programs is the focus of Liu Jinghui's article, which features a concise overview of current policies and legislation governing the establishment of such programs. Liu discusses models and formats together with the impact they have had in the Chinese context, as well as challenges that need to be addressed in the future.

Stephen Conelly and James Garton shift the focus to Australia. Their article argues that these relatively new formats of collaboration are part of a third wave of internationalization in Australia, which is more focused on building international collaborations. Conelly and Garton provide examples that illustrate issues and challenges specific to the Australian context and discuss where this development is heading at the country's universities. Elena Karpukhina's contribution discusses the Russian experience with collaborative degree programs. Based on an earlier study, the article looks at the experience of Russian institutions with joint programs in the European context, including an overview of trends and specific features, driving forces, and challenges that can complicate further development. The Japan International Cooperation Agency (JICA) Research Institute has issued surveys and papers studying joint and double degree programs in the Asian context. Takako Yuki's article provides a condensed version of a number of survey findings and explores the patterns of joint and double degree programs in this part of the world. Jocelyn Gacel-Ávila looks at the current state of collaborative degree programs in Latin America, presenting the results of a small survey she conducted among higher education institutions in Latin America specifically for this publication. Diana Carlin's article reviews the current status of collaborative degree programs in the United States. Carlin analyses U.S.-specific trends based on a number of studies that have been conducted in recent years, points to challenges in the American context and suggests some best practices that can help U.S. institutions in developing collaborative degree programs. Fred Hall turns our attention to Canada with his article focusing on joint and double degree programs at the graduate level. Hall's contribution is also based on a recent study, the first to provide a comprehensive overview of joint and double degree programs and respective policies in graduate education at Canadian higher education institutions.

The book's last two sections focus on topics that frequently emerge in discussions about collaborative degree programs: student demand, employability of graduates, and quality assurance issues. The article by Jochen Hellmann and Patricia Rohland builds on the extensive experience of the Franco-German University (FGU), an institution that has been promoting collaborative degree programs between French and German higher education institutions since 1999. Hellmann and Rohland present the results of a recent survey among graduates of FGU-funded programs regarding employability—an issue often discussed in the context of collaborative programs but not yet sufficiently researched. Another important issue that has received little attention to date is student demand for collaborative degree programs. To assess student interest and the current landscape of collaborative degree programs in Europe, Megan Brenn-White and Elias Faethe analyze Europe's largest internet portal for education programs, including joint and double degree arrangements, with a particular focus on visitor behavior. The results indicate that such programs do receive more attention from students, or at least from those who are internationally mobile. Finally, the last two articles of the book are devoted to quality assurance in joint and double degree programs. Mark Frederiks' contribution addresses the accreditation of joint programs in the European context and provides an overview of respective accreditation procedures, challenges, and future perspectives. Nadia Badrawi's article focuses on quality assurance in the Arab region. Badrawi first investigates the joint and double degree program landscape in Arab countries and then discusses quality assurance in this context.

Different authors may use different terms when discussing collaborative degree programs. The basic definition used in this book refers to the qualification that is awarded upon graduation from a collaborative degree program. A joint degree program thus awards a single qualification (one degree certificate signed by all participating institutions) and a double degree program awards two (or more) qualifications, one from each of the participating institutions. At the same time, authors of the articles were also invited to indicate their definition of collaborative degree programs and to stick to the terms they are familiar with in their regional contexts.

We would like to thank all authors for their contributions. This book is truly a global publication and will no doubt contribute to creating a better understanding of joint and double degree programs around the world.

REFERENCES

Council of Graduate Schools. (2010). Joint degrees, dual degrees, & international research collaborations. Washington, DC: Council of Graduate Schools. Retrieved from http://www.cgsnet.org/joint-degrees-dual-degrees-international-research-collaborations-2010

Culver, S. M., Puri, I. K., Spinelli, G., DePauw, K. P. K., & Dooley, J. E. (2011). *Collaborative dual degree programs and value added for students: Lessons learned through the Evaluate-E project.* Retrieved from http://jsi.sagepub.com/content/16/1/40.full.pdf+html

Franco-German University. (2012). Enquête auprès des diplômés 2011. Retrieved from http://www.dfh-ufa.org/uploads/media/UFA_Enquete_Diplomes_2011.pdf

Gacel-Avila, J. (2009). *Joint and double degree programmes in Latin America: Patterns and trends.* London: OBHE. Retrieved from http://www.obhe.ac.uk/documents/view_details?id=776

International Association of Universities. (2010). *Internationalization of higher education: Global trends regional perspectives – The IAU 3rd global survey report.* Paris: International Association of Universities.

Kuder, M. & Obst, D. (2009). *Joint and double degree programs in the transatlantic context: A survey report.* New York, NY: Institute of International Education. Retrieved from http://www.iie.org/en/Research-and-Publications/Publications-and-Reports/IIE-Bookstore/Joint-Degree-Survey-Report-2009

Nickel, S., Zdebel, T., & Westerheijden, D.F. (2009). Joint degrees in European higher education: Obstacles and opportunities for transnational programme partnerships based on the example of the German-Dutch EUREGIO. Retrieved from http://www.jointdegree.eu/uploads/media/Che_Joint_Degrees_in_European_Higher_Education.pdf

Obst, D., Kuder, M., & Banks, C. (2011). *Joint and double degree programs in the global context: Report on an international survey.* New York, NY: Institute of International Education. Retrieved from http://www.iie.org/Research-and-Publications/Publications-and-Reports/IIE-Bookstore/Joint-Degree-Survey-Report-2011

Office of the Higher Education Commission. (2011). *Collaborative degree programs between Thai and foreign higher education institutions.* Retrieved from http://www.inter.mua.go.th/main2/files/file/collaborative%20degree%20program%202011.pdf

SQW Consulting. (2010). *Evaluation of the UK–Russia BRIDGE programme: Final report.* Retrieved from https://www.gov.uk/government/uploads/system/uploads/attachment_data/file/31922/10-989-bridge-report.pdf

Tauch, C. & Rauhvargers, A. (2002). *Survey on masters degrees and joint degrees in Europe.* European University Association. Retrieved from http://www.eua.be/eua/jsp/en/upload/Survey_Master_Joint_degrees_en.1068806054837.pdf

Chapter One

Joint, Double, and Consecutive Degree Programs: Definitions, Doubts, and Dilemmas

JANE KNIGHT, UNIVERSITY OF TORONTO[1]

Introduction

The number and types of international joint, double, and consecutive degree (JDCD) programs have skyrocketed in the last five years, demonstrating that they clearly have a role in the current landscape of higher education. As an internationalization strategy, they address the heartland of academia—the teaching/learning process and the production of new knowledge between and among countries. These programs are built on the principle of international academic collaboration and can bring important benefits to individuals, institutions, and national and regional education systems. The interest in them is increasing, but so is concern about the necessary academic requirements and the validity of a double or multiple degree qualification.

The major drivers for stimulating the interest in joint and double degree programs include the increased demand for higher education and particularly international education especially for job-seeking graduates; greater emphasis on academic mobility for students and professors; improved information and communication technologies that permit more virtual collaboration among higher education institutions (HEIs); and, finally, the rather tenuous perception by many institutions that greater international involvement can only elevate one's reputation and status.

For many academics and policymakers, double and joint degree programs are welcomed as a natural extension of exchange and mobility programs. For others, they are perceived as a troublesome development leading to double counting of academic work and the thin edge of academic fraud. A broad range of reactions exist due to the diversity of program models; the involvement of new (bona fide and rogue) and traditional providers; the uncertainty related to quality assurance and qualifications recognition; and, finally, the ethics involved in deciding what academic workload or new competencies are required for the granting of joint, double, multiple, or consecutive degrees.

This chapter aims to clarify the confusion about the differences between a joint, a double, and a consecutive degree program by providing a conceptual framework of definitions. It provides highlights from recent research surveys and studies, and looks at new developments and innovations in establishing these types of collaborative programs. Finally, it examines the factors that challenge the operationalization of the programs and explores issues that raise doubts and dilemmas and require further debate and analysis.

Terminology: Diversity, Misunderstandings, and Confusion

A review of the literature, university web pages, survey reports, and research articles shows a plethora of terms used to describe international collaborative programs, such as double and joint degrees. These terms include double, multiple, tri-national, joint, integrated, collaborative, international, consecutive, concurrent, cotutelle, overlapping, conjoint, parallel, simultaneous, and common degrees. They mean different things to different people within and across countries, thereby causing mass confusion about the real meaning and use of these terms.

To deal with the confusion of so many terms, organizations, governmental bodies and institutions have tried to provide a definition to clarify what they mean. Different regions of the world—indeed each country active in this aspect of international education—have proposed definitions that relate to the concepts integral to their native languages and to their policy frameworks. This has resulted in a multitude of definitions and another layer of complexity. An analysis of these definitions shows a variety of core concepts or elements used to describe double and joint degrees. They include (1) number of collaborating institutions, (2) number of qualifications or certificates awarded, (3) completion time, (4) organization of the program, (5) recognition bodies, and (6) number of countries involved. Together, these concepts illustrate the myriad of ways that definitions can differ. While it is not the intention of this chapter to propose a universal set of definitions, it is necessary to have some common understanding of what is meant in order to facilitate the collaborative agreements and mutual understanding that underpin these programs and degrees and to ensure that the qualifications awarded are recognized.

Proposed Working Definitions

This section differentiates and defines three primary types of international collaborative programs: joint degree program, double degree program/multiple degree program, and consecutive degree program (Knight, 2008b).

Joint Degree Program

A joint degree program awards one joint qualification upon completion of the collaborative program requirements established by the partner institutions.

The distinguishing feature of this type of international collaborative program is that only one qualification is awarded jointly by the cooperating institutions. The duration of the program is normally not extended, and thus students have the advantage of completing a joint program in the same time period as an individual program from one of the institutions. The design and integration of the course of study varies from program to program, but it usually involves the mobility (physical or virtual) of students, professors, and/or course content. It is important to emphasize that students traveling to the partner country for research or course work is not a requirement in all joint degree programs. Visiting professors, distance courses, and joint virtual research projects are options that provide valuable alternatives to student mobility.

Awarding a joint qualification can face many legal issues. National regulations often do not allow for a university to jointly confer a qualification, especially in association with a foreign institution. In this case, if both names of the collaborating institutions appear on the degree certificate, there is a risk that the joint degree will not be recognized by either of the host countries, meaning that the student does not have a legitimate qualification even though all program requirements have been completed. The situation becomes more complicated when one looks for an international body that will recognize a joint degree from two bona fide institutions. At this point, the Lisbon Recognition Convention (officially, The Convention on the Recognition of Qualifications concerning Higher Education in the European Region) is the only one of six UNESCO regional conventions that does so. Innovative ways to circumvent this problem have been developed by the organizers of joint degree programs.

Overall, the most important features of a joint degree program are the strengths that each institution brings to the program and the opportunities for students to benefit from a program that draws on the teaching, curricular, and research expertise of two or more institutions located in different countries. The major drawbacks at the current time are the issues related to the legality and recognition of a jointly conferred qualification.

Double Degree Program/Multiple Degree Program

A double degree program awards two individual qualifications at equivalent levels upon completion of the collaborative program requirements established by the two partner institutions.

A multiple degree program is essentially the same as a double degree program, except for the number of institutions involved and qualifications offered:

A multiple degree program awards three or more individual qualifications at equivalent levels upon completion of the collaborative program requirements established by the three or more partner institutions.

As titles of bachelor's and master's degrees and doctorates often differ across countries, the term *equivalent level* is used to indicate that the double or multiple degrees conferred are of the same standing.

The duration of a double or multiple degree program can be extended beyond the length of a single degree program to meet the requirements of all partners participating in the collaborative program. The legality and recognition of the qualifications awarded by a double/multiple degree program are more straightforward than for joint degrees. It is assumed that each partner institution is officially registered or licensed in its respective country. Thus, awards offered by the enrolling institution in a collaborative program should be recognized in that country, while the other or double awards would be treated like any other foreign credential.

The major hurdles facing double/multiple degree programs involve the design of the curriculum and the establishment of completion requirements. There is no standard way to establish completion requirements due to the variety of disciplines, fields of study, and national regulations involved. Each partnership does it according to the practices and legalities of the collaborating institutions. However, the double/multiple counting of the same student workload or of learning outcomes can put the academic integrity of the program in jeopardy. The idea of having two degrees from two different institutions in two different countries is attractive to students, but careful attention needs to be given to ensuring that the value and recognition of the qualifications are valid and do not violate the premise and academic purpose of the collaborative degree program. This is especially true for multiple degree programs.

Consecutive Degree Program

A consecutive degree program awards two different qualifications at consecutive levels upon completion of the collaborative program requirements established by the partner institutions.

Consecutive degree programs are becoming more popular both nationally and internationally. This kind of program basically involves two consecutive qualifications (usually bachelor's and master's degrees or master's degree and doctorate) awarded when program requirements for each degree, as stipulated by the awarding institutions, are completed. For the international consecutive degree program, the two awarding institutions are located in different countries. In this case, it is usual for a student to be mobile and complete the course work and research requirements for the first degree in one country and the requirements for the second degree in the partner institution located in another country. The duration of the program is usually longer than a single program, but shorter than if the two degrees were taken separately.

Major Surveys and Research Studies

Due to the relatively short history of international joint, double, and consecutive degree programs compared to other types of academic partnerships, research on these programs remains limited. However, several large-scale regional surveys and other reports show a distinct increase in international collaborative programs in the last few years and forecast further growth, even if the definitions of the terms *joint*, *double*, and *consecutive* are not consistently used among researchers, policymakers, and practitioners.

In Europe, the European University Association (EUA) highlighted the growth of JDCD programs in several survey reports as early as 2002 (Tauch & Rauhvargers, 2002). It is important to note that the term *joint degree* is commonly used in Europe to include both joint and double degrees. The *Trends V* report documents the growth of joint degree programs, particularly at master's degree level (Crosier, Purser, & Smidt, 2007). However, this report also cautions that the additional financial cost required by these programs could ultimately limit their development and impact on institutional and regional goals for internationalization. The *Trends 2010* report also surveys institutions on the types of joint degree programs (bachelor's, master's, and doctorate), new developments, and legislative changes in permitting joint degrees. *Trends 2010* indicates that many institutions are developing joint degree programs as a response to an increasingly global job market (Sursock & Smidt, 2010). EUA's 2009 *Survey of Master Degrees in Europe* confirms further growth in joint degree programs but modest progress in legislative changes to allow the awarding of joint degrees (Davies, 2009).

In the United States, the Council of Graduate Schools (CGS) documented the diversity and growth of collaborative degree programs between American and international HEIs in its annual *International Graduate Admissions Survey* in 2007 and 2008 (CGS, 2007, 2008). These initial efforts at investigating international JDCD programs reveal significant growth in double compared to joint degree programs, an increasing number of institutions with one or more JDCD programs, and partnerships with institutions mostly in Europe, China, India, and South Korea (Redd, 2008).

In 2009, the Institute of International Education and Freie Universität Berlin produced a survey report on trans-Atlantic joint and double degree programs based on responses from 180 American and European HEIs (Kuder & Obst, 2009). The data show that American institutions are more likely to offer joint and double degrees at the undergraduate level, while European institutions prefer the graduate level. Interestingly, American institutions are more likely to use student fees to cover the cost of these programs, while European institutions rely on institutional budgets and external funding, such as governments and foundations.

In Latin America, a recent survey (Gacel-Avila, 2009) confirms the growth of double degree programs compared to joint ones and indicates that private institutions are using JDCD programs to recruit fee-paying students, while public ones view these programs as capacity-building tools to strengthen graduate education. Unlike the European case, graduate employability ranks low as a rationale for developing these programs. Instead, the top rationales are the internationalization of the curriculum and the provision of innovative programs.

Data on JDCD programs in Asia, Africa, and the Middle East are not widely available. However, the EU-Asia Higher Education Platform (EAHEP) met in 2009 to discuss the use of joint degree programs to promote student and staff mobility and cultural exchanges between the two regions. This symposium also examined the benefits and challenges of international JDCD programs and recommended best practices for such collaborations given some of the challenges and dilemmas facing these initiatives.

Several other national or institutional reports also address the growth of international JDCD programs. At national level, the German Academic Exchange Service (DAAD) completed a regional survey report, with most respondents coming from Germany (Maiworm, 2006); another study examined German–Dutch joint degree programs (Nickel, Zdebel, & Westerheijden, 2009); and the Finnish Ministry of Education made several recommendations for the development of joint and double degree programs (Ministry of Education, 2004). At the institutional level, there are reports from the University of Graz, Austria (Maierhofer & Kriebernegg, 2009), and the National University of Singapore (Kong, 2008). The European Consortium for Accreditation recently published a report on quality assurance and accreditation issues related to international joint degree programs (Aerden & Reczulska, 2010).

New Developments and Trends

These reports illustrate several new trends evident in the landscape of joint, double, consecutive degree programs around the world. While it is difficult to assume that these trends apply to all countries and institutions promoting JDCD programs, they do illustrate some general trends worthy of serious consideration (Knight & Lee 2012).

- Double degree programs are far more common than joint degree programs. This is most likely due to legal barriers and administrative challenges in granting a joint diploma. Yet double degree programs raise the most doubts and dilemmas about completion requirements and legitimacy of the qualifications. Consecutive degree programs appear to be the least common and are more controversial.

- Most joint degree programs involve two rather than multiple institutions. Joint degree programs in most disciplines are commonly intraregional rather than interregional. In contrast, double degree programs exhibit more interregional pairings that are remarkably international in scope.

- Joint and double degree programs are mostly at master's degree level, but there is increasing interest in developing collaborative doctorate programs that draw on expertise such as teaching, thesis supervision, and the research specialties of different institutions. The short length and flexibility of many master's degree programs compared to bachelor's degree and doctorate programs probably facilitate international collaborative programming.

- Many JDCD programs are in business or engineering disciplines, two areas that are often considered highly mobile and international in nature, and for which there is a market demand. MBA double degree programs are probably the most numerous and varied type of JDCD programs. As such, they also raise many questions and issues.

- JDCD programs are now incorporating an overseas internship component, especially in professional fields such as nursing and journalism. In some cases this is how student mobility is introduced into the program.

- Online JDCD programs are being developed to facilitate program mobility. Some collaborative programs rely on faculty mobility rather than student mobility, or require student mobility only for the internship component. Conceivably, a student could complete an entire international JDCD program without ever leaving his or her home country. Although online programs may be more accessible to students with demanding schedules and/or limited resources, these students are deprived of the cultural immersion that characterizes many JDCD programs.

- A new development is the creation of large consortia to provide a wide range of learning opportunities for students. For example, in 2010, Europe launched the Erasmus Mundus joint doctorate program in astrophysics, with the collaboration of 13 institutions. This international consortium includes both traditional universities in Europe and advanced research institutes worldwide. The research institutes provide cutting-edge scientific equipment and a community of highly skilled scientists to complement the academic environment of universities.

- Another innovative measure is the consecutive degree program that offers two degrees at separate levels from two different countries. Some of these programs appear to act as new channels for graduate schools to recruit international students rather than as a collaborative program designed for both local and international students. Some double degree programs also offer diplomas in two very different disciplines (e.g., science and philosophy) in a time frame that is equivalent to a standard single-discipline degree.

Issues and Challenges

The benefits of JDCD programs are many and diverse, but so are the challenges that face the collaborating institutions involved in establishing these types of initiatives. Different regulatory systems, academic calendars, credit systems, tuition and scholarship schemes, teaching approaches, and examination requirements are only a few of the more technical challenges that need to be surmounted. This section identifies several academic issues that institutions and higher education authorities need to address in order to move ahead in the development and recognition of these programs and qualifications.

Alignment of Regulations and Customs

National and institutional regulations and customs differ from country to country, and present many challenges for the design and implementation of international collaborative programs. For instance, there are often regulations preventing students from enrolling at more than one university at a time, or laws requiring students to spend their last year or semester at the home university, or mandatory practices regarding the recruitment and selection of students. Nonrecognition or limitations on the number of courses or credits taken at a partner university are additional barriers. Different academic years can present problems for JDCD programs, in particular, student mobility. However, they provide more opportunities for faculty exchange. Examination or evaluation requirements and procedures often present obstacles to double degree programs.

Quality Assurance and Accreditation

Quality assurance and accreditation are of fundamental importance but pose significant challenges for JDCD programs. When institutions have internal quality assurance procedures in place, quality review requirements for their own components can be met. But, it is more difficult to assure the quality of courses offered by a partner university. Common entrance and exit requirements are often used as quality proxies, but it would be helpful if mutual recognition of respective quality assurance programs (where they exist) were included in the agreement for a collaborative program.

Accreditation is even more of a challenge, as national systems do not exist in all countries around the world. Where they do exist, an added challenge is that accreditation agencies differ enormously; some focus on programs and others on institutions, some focus on inputs and others on processes or outputs. Furthermore, the establishment of procedures for accrediting international collaborative programs is relatively new territory for many agencies.

For the time being, the best case scenario is that accreditation is completed by each partner institution involved in a JDCD program. For professional programs, there are international accreditation agencies like ABET or EQUIS, which may be appropriate for joint or double degree programs. However, more institutions have their home programs accredited by these professional accreditation bodies than their double or joint degree programs. An important question is whether regional, national, or international accreditation is the best route for international collaborative programs.

Language

The language of instruction for joint and double degree programs introduces new complexities. Each partner usually offers its programs in the home teaching language and, in some cases, in English. This means that courses may be offered in at least three different languages, or more if multiple partners are involved. Students need to be at least bilingual—usually their native language(s) plus English. There are two issues at play here. The first is the dominance of English in cases where English is not the native language of any of the partners. This underscores the Anglicization trend, or what some call "language imperialism" in the higher education sector (and many other sectors as well). Are international collaborative programs encouraging the overuse of English and the standardization of the curriculum? The second issue relates to the required proficiency level of students and professors in the second language of instruction or research, and the training needed to help students and academics meet language proficiency requirements. The positive side of the language issue is that students are required to be bilingual or multilingual, which helps their communication skills, employability, and understanding of another culture. However, the establishment of language requirements and the availability of improvement courses need to be made crystal clear by each partner in the collaborative agreement. It is imperative that teaching and learning standards remain high, even when nonnative language is being used by all the institutions and students involved in the program.

Fees and Financing

Financial issues such as tuition fees and funding can be quite complex. It is clear that revenue generation is not usually the primary motive for these kinds of programs, as they often require extra investments by the institutions or higher tuition fees charged to students

(Maierhofer & Kriebernegg, 2009). In countries that do not charge tuition fees per se, or have limited autonomy to set fees, the extra costs must be borne by the institutions or external funders. However, the sustainability of a program can often be at risk when it is dependent on external funds. The development of a program becomes more complicated when multiple partners with different tuition fees are involved, or when there are extra costs for the professors' physical and virtual mobility. Arrangements for joint costs regarding marketing, recruiting, assessments, and administration also need to be negotiated. In those cases where revenue is generated, an agreement for income distribution is necessary.

Doubts and Dilemmas

In addition to paying attention to academic alignment and technical questions, there are other macro issues that also need to be considered, as they are often expressed as doubts and dilemmas. These revolve around the questions such as: What is really driving the growth of JDCD programs? Are they sustainable without external funding sources? What are the certification processes? Are qualifications being recognized as legitimate ones? And, finally, how are completion requirements and standards being established and met?

Student Rationales—Quality Experience or Two Degrees for the Price of One?

Students are attracted to JDCD programs for a number of reasons. The opportunity to be part of a program that offers two degrees from two universities located in different countries is seen to enhance their employability prospects and career path. Some students believe that a collaborative program will be of higher quality, given that the expertise of two universities has shaped the academic program. This is especially true for joint degrees. Other students are not as interested in enhanced quality but are attracted to the opportunity to obtain two degrees for the price of one, so to speak. They argue that the duration is shorter for a double or consecutive degree program, the workload is definitely less than for two single degrees, and there is less of a financial burden. This argument is not valid for all programs of this type, but there is an element of truth in these claims. Double degree programs are being presented by a leading European international education organization as "a lot easier to achieve and not necessarily less valid" and "two degrees for the price of one." Finally, the status factor cannot be ignored. There is a certain sense of elitism attached to having academic credentials from universities in different countries, even if the student never studied abroad but benefited from distance education and visiting foreign professors.

Institutional Drivers—Capacity Building or Status Building?

JDCD degree programs can lead to a deeper, more sustainable type of relationship than other internationalization program strategies, such as twinning and franchising.

Academic benefits in terms of curriculum innovation, exchanges of professors and researchers, and access to expertise and networks of the partner university make joint degrees especially attractive. Consecutive degrees allow institutions to work with partners that may offer a master's degree, doctorate program, or specialty that is not available at their own university.

For other institutions, the primary rationale is to increase their reputation and ranking as an international university. This is accomplished by deliberately collaborating with partners of equal or greater status. This type of status building applies to institutions in both developed and developing countries. For instance, institutions in developing countries seek double degree programs with developed country partners so that they can indirectly verify the quality of the program, because the courses must be determined to be equivalent in order to count toward a double or multiple degree. Examples exist of institutions that believe that a collaborative program with a partner of greater status will also help or even bypass their national accreditation processes. Finally, collaborative programs are perceived by some universities as a way to attract talented students who may want to stay for work experience after graduation and perhaps immigrate permanently. These issues present enduring questions and doubts about what is truly driving institutions to promote more and more JDCD programs.

Sustainability

The financial investment required to launch these kinds of programs is a subject worthy of further investigation. In some cases, the bulk of the extra costs can be borne by increasing student tuition fees, which in turn makes the program quite elitist and only available to financially independent or supported students. In other situations, costs are absorbed by the institutions. So far, the driving force for collaborative programs does not appear to have been income generation, unlike cross-border programs (e.g., franchise and twinning programs and the recruitment of foreign students). All in all, the sustainability of JDCD programs that are reliant on external funding from governments, businesses, or foundations is vulnerable, as are programs that are totally dependent on student fees.

Certification

The granting of legal certification for the award and the subsequent recognition of the qualifications awarded are by far the most vexing issues. As already discussed, there are only a few countries—although the number is increasing—that legally allow one of its universities to confer a joint qualification in partnership with an institution in another country. This means that the student often gets a formal diploma from one university and an unofficial certificate from the other(s), indicating that it was a joint collaborative program. For some students, this is not a problem, because it is the international nature of the academic program that is most important, and not the qualification. For others, this is not the case, as credentialism is an increasingly important concern to students.

Recognition and Legitimacy of Qualifications

Employers, academic institutions, and credential evaluation agencies all need to be cognizant of what is entailed in the granting and recognition of double or multiple qualifications. There is a perception that some double, multiple, and consecutive degrees are more legitimate than others, but this is merely a perception, and one that is difficult to prove. The recognition process raises legitimacy or misrepresentation issues often associated with double/multiple degree qualifications—more than with joint or consecutive qualifications. Part of the concern rests with the double counting of course credits or workload for two or more qualifications. This has led to the "two for the price of one" label for double degrees. In this case, price is measured not only in monetary terms, but also in student workload terms.

Completion Requirements

The diversity of models used to determine the completion requirements for double/multiple degree programs is extremely varied. There is no single explanation or standard framework used to set program completion requirements. This raises the critical question of whether the framework is based on (1) the number of completed courses or credits, (2) the student workload, or (3) required outcomes or competencies. These three approaches lead to different explanations and doubts regarding the legitimacy of the double/multiple degrees awarded. The value of a qualification or credential is at the root of the murkiness surrounding the acceptability or legitimacy of double/multiple degrees emanating from a collaborative program. Many would argue that attributing the same courses or workload toward two or more degrees from two or more institutions devalues the validity of a qualification. Others believe that if students meet the stated learning outcomes or competencies required to obtain a qualification, regardless of where or how the competencies are acquired, the credential is legitimate. This logic infers that double and multiple degrees, based on a set of core courses or competencies and augmented by the additional requirements of collaborating institutions, are academically sound and legitimate; it is the process for recognizing these qualifications that requires more attention, and not the completion requirements per se. Both arguments are valid, but the variety of models used prevents a clear resolution to the question of legitimacy. Doubt remains.

Final Words

Interesting new questions are being raised as the volume, scope, and types of JDCD programs increase. Several of these questions are included in this section to stimulate further reflection, research, and debate about enhancing the benefits of these types of programs and minimizing risks and unintended consequences (Knight & Lee, 2012).

- Is national, binational, or international accreditation the best route for JDCD programs?

- Are international collaborative programs encouraging the overuse of English and the standardization of curriculum?

- Are JDCD programs sustainable without additional internal or external funding?

- Can one thesis or dissertation fulfill the requirements of two graduate programs that are research based?

- Can international JDCD programs be integrated into national and regional qualification frameworks?

- What role might prior learning assessment recognition play in double or consecutive degree programs?

- Will the status-building and credentialism motives eventually jeopardize the quality and academic objectives of these international collaborative degree programs?

Clearly, the debate is nuanced and complicated by national policies, customs, and interpretations of what constitutes the requirements for a qualification. The critical point emanating from the doubts and different interpretations of the legitimacy of double/multiple degrees is that rigorous analysis is required. Stakeholders, including students, HEIs, employers, accreditation and quality assurance agencies, policymakers, academic leaders, and credential recognition bodies, need to address this issue individually and collectively. Similarities and differences among countries and stakeholders need to be acknowledged and respected, but there needs to be some common understanding about what two or more qualifications at the same level emanating from a double or multiple degree collaborative program actually represent and signify.

The challenge facing the higher education sector is to work out a common understanding of what JDCD programs actually mean and involve, and to iron out the academic alignment issues inherent to working in different national regulatory frameworks, cultures, and practices. Most importantly, a robust debate on the vexing questions of accreditation, recognition and legitimacy of qualifications needs to take place to ensure that international collaborative programs and their awards are respected and welcomed by students, HEIs, and employers around the world, and do not lead to undesirable unintended consequences.

NOTES

[1] This chapter is based on Knight (2011).

REFERENCES

Aerden, A., & Reczulska, H. (2010). *The recognition of qualifications awarded by joint programmes: An analysis of current practices by national recognition centres.* European Consortium for Accreditation in Higher Education. Retrieved from http://www.ecaconsortium.net/admin/files/assets/subsites/1/documenten/1270211409_eca—-the-recognition-of-qualifications-awarded-by-joint-programmes—-2010.pdf

Becker, R. (2009). *International branch campuses: Markets and strategies.* London, UK: Observatory on Borderless Higher Education.

Council of Graduate Schools. (CGS). (2007). *2007 CGS international graduate admissions survey: Phase II final applications and initial offers of admission.* Retrieved from http://www.cgsnet.org/ckfinder/userfiles/files/R_IntlAdm07_II.pdf

Council of Graduate Schools (CGS). (2008). *2008 CGS International Graduate Admissions Survey: Phase II Final Applications and Initial Offers of Admission.* Retrieved from http://www.cgsnet.org/ckfinder/userfiles/files/R_IntlAdm08_II.pdf

Crosier, D., Purser, L., & Smidt, H. (2007). *Trends V: Universities shaping the European Higher Education Area.* Brussels, Belgium: European University Association.

Davies, H. (2009). *Survey of master degrees in Europe.* Brussels, Belgium: European University Association. Retrieved from http://www.eua.be/publications/

EAHEP. (2009). *Student mobility, joint degree programmes and institutional development. The second EAHEP workshop outcome report.* Kuala Lumpur, Malaysia, 16–17 February 2009. EU-Asia Higher Education Platform. Retrieved from http://www.eahep.org/images/Malaysia/second%20eahep%20workshop%20final%20outcome%20report%202.pdf

EACEA. (2009). Erasmus Mundus Programme: Action 2: Partnerships with third country higher education institutions and scholarships for mobility. *EACEA* website. Retrieved from http://eacea.ec.europa.eu/erasmus_mundus/programme/action2_en.php

EC/UNESCO. (2004). *Recommendation on the recognition of joint degrees.* Adopted by the Committee of the Convention on the Recognition of Qualifications concerning Higher Education in the European Region. Retrieved from http://www.enic-naric.net/documents/recommendation-joint-degrees-2004.en.pdf

EUA. (2004). *Developing joint masters programmes for Europe: Results of the EUA joint masters project.* Brussels, Belgium: European University Association. Retrieved from http://www.eua.be/publications/

Gacel-Avila, J. (2009). *Joint and double degree programmes in Latin America: Patterns and trends.* London, UK: Observatory on Borderless Higher Education.

Kong, L. (2008). Engaging globally through joint and double degree programmes: A view from Singapore. *GlobalHigherEd* website. Retrieved from http://globalhighered.wordpress.com/2008/02/15/engaging-globally-through-joint-and-double-degree-programmes-a-view-from-singapore/

Knight, J. (2008a). *Higher education in turmoil: The changing world of internationalization.* Rotterdam, The Netherlands: Sense.

Knight, J. (2008b). *Joint and double degree programmes: Vexing questions and issues.* London, UK: Observatory on Borderless Higher Education.

Knight, J. (2005). *Borderless, offshore, transnational and cross-border education: Definition and data dilemmas.* London, UK: Observatory on Borderless Higher Education.

Knight, J. (2011). Doubts and dilemmas with double degree programs. In *Globalization and internationalization of higher education* [Online monograph]. *Revista de Universidad y Sociedad del Concomiento (RUSC),* 8(2):297–312.

Knight J., & Lee, J. (2012). International joint, double, and consecutive degrees: New developments, issues, and challenges. In D. Deardoff, H. De Wit, J. Heyl, and T. Adams (Eds.), *The SAGE handbook of international higher education* (343–58). Thousand Oaks, CA: Sage.

Kuder, M., & Obst, D. (2009). *Joint and double degree programs in the transatlantic context.* Institute of International Education & Freie Universitaet Berlin. Retrieved from http://www.iienetwork.org/file_depot/0–10000000/0–10000/1710/folder/80205/TDP+Report_2009_Final21.pdf

Maierhofer, R., & Kriebernegg, U. (2009). Joint and dual degree programs: New ventures in academic mobility. In R. Bhandari and S. Laughlin (Eds.), *Higher education on the move: New developments in global mobility* (pp. 65–77). New York, NY: Institute of International Education.

Maiworm, F. (2006). *Results of the survey on study programmes awarding double, multiple or joint degrees.* Kassel, Germany: German Academic Exchange Service (DAAD) and German Rector's Conference (HRK). Retrieved from http://www.ehea.info/Uploads/Seminars/Berlin_results_survey.pdf

Ministry of Education, Finland. (2004). *Development of international joint degrees and double degrees: Recommendation of the Ministry of Education.* Helsinki, Finland. Retrieved from http://www.minedu.fi/export/sites/default/OPM/Koulutus/koulutusjaerjestelmae/tutkintojen_tunnustaminen/opetusministerioon_suositus_kansainvaelisten_yhteistutkintojen_ja_kaksoistutkintojen_kehittaemisestae/liitteet/JointDegrees_recommendations.pdf

Nickel, S., Zdebel, T., & Westerheijden, D. (2009). *Joint degrees in European higher education: Obstacles and opportunities for transnational programme partnerships based on the example of the German-Dutch EUREGIO.* Gronau, Germany: Centre for Higher Education Development and Enschede, The Netherlands: Center for Higher Education Policy Studies.

Redd, K. (2008, October). Data sources: International graduate programs—2007 & 2008. *CGS Communicator.* Retrieved from http://www.cgsnet.org/ckfinder/userfiles/files/DataSources_2008_10.pdf

Sackmann, R. (2007). "Internationalization of markets for education: New actors within nations and increasing flows between nations." In K. Martens, A. Rusconi, & K. Leuze (Eds.), *New arenas of education* governance (pp. 155–175). New York, NY: Palgrave Macmillan.

Schneller, C., Lungu, I., & Wächter, B. (2009). *Handbook of international associations in higher education: A practical guide to 100 academic networks world-wide.* Brussels, Belgium: Academic Cooperation Association.

Schüle, U. (2006). *Joint and double degrees within the European higher education area—Towards further internationalization of business degrees.* Paris, France: Consortium of International Double Degrees. Retrieved from www.CIDD.org

Sursock, A., & Smidt, H. (2010). *Trends 2010: A decade of change in European Higher Education.* Brussels, Belgium: European University Association. Retrieved from http://www.eua.be/publications/

Tauch, C., & Rauhvargers, A. (2002). *Survey on master degrees and joint degrees in Europe.* Brussels, Belgium: European University Association. Retrieved from http://www.eua.be/eua/jsp/en/upload/Survey_Master_Joint_degrees_en.1068806054837.pdf

Chapter Two
Balancing Expectations and Realities: A Plea for Strategy

MATTHIAS KUDER, FREIE UNIVERSITÄT BERLIN

While collaborative degree programs have largely developed in Europe, they no longer represent a European niche phenomenon. Instead, they have become a regular part of internationalization portfolios at many higher education institutions around the world. "Dual degree programs are gathering steam" was the headline in a *New York Times* article in 2011, which referred to this worldwide trend among universities to collaboratively offer study programs, whether as joint or double degree arrangements (Guttenplan, 2011). Although there is no accurate global account of the current number of collaborative degree programs, it is safe to say that by now they can be found in the thousands rather than hundreds.[1] Higher education institutions are attracted to developing collaborative degree programs because they can offer a range of opportunities for students, faculty, and entire institutions alike. Using synergies with their international partners, institutions can pool resources and design unique programs, attract additional students, and raise their global profiles.

However, there is evidence that many institutions may enter these complex forms of international collaboration partly based on incorrect expectations and without a clear understanding of how to manage their development. Challenges in developing such programs often result from the lack of a strategic approach and the absence of appropriate institutional policies and guidelines. This can not only hinder the ability of institutions to fully capitalize on the potential offered by collaborative degree programs, but it can also lead to negative effects on program sustainability, which is reported to be one of the biggest challenges for many joint and double degree programs.

In 2005, the International Association of Universities (IAU) global survey report had joint and double degree programs ranked eighth in importance among a list of internationalization growth areas. Five years later, the 2010 edition of this report further confirmed the ascent of collaborative degree programs, now ranking them fifth on the list of internationalization activities given highest priority in institutional internationalization policies among the IAU survey participants. The same report further shows that higher education institutions dedicated, on average, slightly more attention and resources to developing international joint and double degree programs compared to activities such as internationalization at home, hosting international scholars, recruiting fee-paying international graduate students, or delivering distance education and online programs abroad (International Association of Universities, 2010). This finding was based on aggregate results from institutions in a wide sampling of countries, and the percentage differences between the individual measures receiving institutional attention were not dramatic. Still, the picture is clear enough. Joint and double degree programs keep higher education institutions busy—busier even than other forms of internationalization. A global survey on collaborative degree programs conducted by the Institute of International Education (IIE) and Freie Universität Berlin (FUB) in 2011 further confirmed this trend. Ninety-one percent of the 245 participating higher education institutions stated that joint or double degree programs were part and parcel of their institutions' internationalization efforts. Roughly the same percentage of respondents indicated that their institutions are eager to develop more joint and double degree programs in the future (Kuder, Obst, & Banks, 2011).

Where is the Strategy?

At the same time, the IIE/FUB study revealed a striking dichotomy. A surprising 45 percent of the survey respondents indicated that their institutions did not have a particular strategy or policy in place that would guide their faculty and administrators in developing joint and double degree programs. This finding suggests that while growing numbers of higher education institutions embrace the idea of collaborative degree programs and claim that this is part of a strategic reasoning, a large proportion of institutions either lack corresponding policies with articulated requirements and recommendations, or at least are slow in formulating them. This is by no means a phenomenon only found in the context of collaborative degree programs. As the 2012 edition of the *Mapping of Internationalization on U.S. Campuses* report by the American Council of Education demonstrates, campus-wide policies and guidelines for regulating international partnerships are not quite standard yet. Among U.S. higher education institutions showing an increased focus on internationalization, an average of only 40 percent confirmed that respective policies were in place, with only doctoral institutions showing significantly higher rates (American Council on Education, 2012). Notwithstanding the specifics of the higher education landscape in the United States and the fact that one should be careful in extrapolating these findings to other countries, comparable studies in other regional contexts would likely arrive at similar conclusions.

Of course, not all forms of internationalization efforts will require the same degree of sophistication when it comes to formulating institutional policies and respective regulatory frameworks. Joint and double degree programs are complex, and they touch upon a number of core competencies of various academic and administrative units within and between institutions. These include curriculum development, admission regulations, degree completion requirements, awarding of qualifications, legal aspects, and not least quality assurance and accreditation procedures. Given this complexity, a concerted institutional approach with formulated policy and guideline frameworks can prove extremely helpful in managing expectations, and addressing requirements as well as potential challenges early on.

Aligning Expectations with Impact

Most higher education institutions share a similar set of expectations and goals when it comes to developing collaborative degree programs. The results of the 2011 IIE/FUB global survey mirror these expectations (Kuder, Obst, & Banks, 2011). The top five reasons given by the 245 participating institutions for embarking on developing joint or double degree programs were: (1) broadening education offerings, (2) strengthening research collaboration, (3) advancing internationalization, (4) raising their international visibility and prestige, and (5) increasing international student enrollment. The survey's inquiry into perceived effects prompted by collaborative degree programs reveals some striking examples in which expectations and impact diverge.

By far the most common impact of collaborative degree programs cited among survey participants was an increased level of interaction between faculty members.[2] But only one-fifth of respondents also indicated that collaborative degree programs had specifically led to further joint research endeavors, a goal that institutions had reported to be one of the key motivations for developing the programs in the first place. Some of the reported programs might be relatively new, and side effects such as joint research projects need time to evolve. Similarly, joint doctoral programs might yield such results more frequently than, for example, collaborative programs at the undergraduate level. Nonetheless, while collaborative degree programs can surely lead to further joint research endeavors, this finding suggests that, on average, such results are not necessarily the rule, or at least that they do not materialize in a short time.

A similar contrast can be found with regard to the goal of increasing the recruitment of international students, again one of the major motivations given by the survey participants. Only about one-third of the respondents confirmed that their collaborative degree programs resulted in improved recruitment and greater numbers of international students. In fact, several sources show that most joint and double degree programs involve a small number of students, domestic or international. The 2011 IIE/FUB report also confirmed this: about one-quarter of all survey respondents indicated an average enrollment rate of five students or fewer in a given joint or double degree program, and another 30 percent reported average enrollment rates of 6 to 15 students. These numbers suggest that institutions developing collaborative degree programs with the goal of noticeably increasing international recruitment might more effectively pursue this goal by other means.

Who are Collaborative Programs For?

Although joint and double degree programs can be found in almost any discipline, surveys show that business and engineering are the most prevalent academic fields for such programs, and the IIE/FUB report indicates that these disciplines often show above-average success in recruiting students. Collaborative degree programs offered in highly specific or small niche academic fields naturally face a smaller pool of prospective students—which is not to say that they are less attractive or less suitable for collaborative degree arrangements. A number of factors determine the potential pool of students for a given joint or double degree program, including language(s) of tuition, the academic field, the particular setting, and the overall attractiveness of a program, as well as its degree of complexity, both in academic terms and mobility patterns. Regardless of the academic discipline or other specifics, the problem of recruiting a sufficient number of students was ranked among the top five challenges reported by all survey respondents, raising a fundamental question: who is it that the programs are made for?

Three general observations can be suggested to explain why some collaborative degree programs might attract only small student numbers. First, a program might be specifically aimed at a limited student body, in which case small enrollment numbers would not be considered a challenge or disadvantage. Despite small student numbers and perceived recruitment challenges, many of the IIE/FUB survey respondents actually indicated that they were content with the student participation situation in their joint and double degree programs. This was especially true for institutions that had developed a more strategic approach to joint and double degree programs, including respective recruitment policies and guidelines.

Second, some institutions or individuals might embark on developing a collaborative degree program without a thorough consideration of the program's attractiveness and potential student demand. A look at the ranking of top motivations for building such programs reveals two interesting details. Respondents to the IIE/FUB survey ranked potential student demand for a particular program relatively low on the list of institutional motivations. The demand of the labor market for graduates with particular skills and competencies developed by the programs ranked even lower. This is surprising given that such programs are a significant undertaking for all parties involved, and usually more resource intensive than traditional study abroad formats. Some 40 percent of all survey respondents indicated that they established additional administrative structures dedicated to administering joint and double degree programs. Against this backdrop, surely one would expect higher education institutions to regard potential student interest as a key factor to be addressed before a joint and double degree program is developed.

Third, some institutions build a program that is attractive and potentially in demand, but fail to advertise it to prospective students, especially beyond their own campus. In fact, as the IIE/FUB study shows, the challenge to recruit the right number of students for a given program can be traced in part to corresponding institutional recruitment and marketing strategies, or the lack thereof. While the IIE/FUB survey respondents generally articulated the wish to attract international students to their collaborative degree programs, only 45 percent had also developed recruitment measures that would help them achieve this goal. Among institutions reporting fewer than five participants in their programs, 60 percent had no specific recruitment measures in place, and the highest number of these respondents reported that their programs enrolled mostly local students. Without a doubt, the ability to identify which students a joint or double degree program seeks to attract, and to define and execute a suitable recruitment strategy, will have an impact on enrollment rates and, in a larger sense, on the program's sustainability.

From Implementation to Sustainability

Expectations, impact and program sustainability are in many cases strongly intertwined with the question of how joint or double degree programs have been set up. Only 16 percent of the IIE/FUB survey respondents said that their programs were developed mainly from the top down, with the initiative coming from their institution's leadership. Forty-one percent of respondents identified faculty as the major driving force, with some institutional input and support. Finally, 43 percent of the IIE/FUB survey respondents indicated that their programs were developed based on a mix of active involvement by faculty, the institution's leadership, and respective administrative units. A clear majority of the survey respondents also confirmed that they built their joint or double degree programs with existing exchange partner institutions and based on known contacts among faculty. Roughly 40 percent reported that they had made a deliberate strategic decision to pick a new partner institution for developing a collaborative degree program.

Clearly, individual faculty members who champion such initiatives are a key factor in the development of most joint and double degree programs. However, the challenges reported by respondents indicate that the institution can play an equally important role, be it the university at large, or a particular school or department. Ensuring sustainability, securing adequate funding, settling legal issues, securing support from national or international organizations, conducting accreditation procedures, and negotiating fee structures were all reported among the most pressing challenges in the IIE/FUB survey. All of them reach beyond the capacity of one or several faculty members to accomplish. This underlines the fact that successful development and sustained delivery of a given joint and double degree program will be closely linked to the degree of involvement and guidance provided by the respective institution, its leadership and administration.

According to many experts in the field, "sustainability is a priority item in [joint programs] which is obviously disastrously underestimated or even ignored" (JOIMAN Network, 2010). The list of top challenges reported in the IIE/FUB survey supports this statement. While sustainability is identified as the number one challenge, almost all of other reported top challenges have a direct effect on the ability to sustain the delivery of a given program. This is particularly true for program funding, certainly one of the biggest factors in this context. Most of the IIE/FUB survey participants acknowledged that they did not expect their joint and double degree programs to substantially increase levels of revenue via student fees. On the contrary, given the aforementioned relatively small average student numbers and the understanding that operating such endeavors might often cause additional direct or indirect costs, it is likely that institutions relying largely on student fees will either need to subsidize their joint and double degree programs or find external support sources. Of course, this applies even more to institutions in systems that do not rely on tuition fees, or that rely on them only to a limited extent. Close to one-third of the IIE/FUB survey participants reported that they had to discontinue or cancel a joint or double degree program that was under development or already established. Most of these respondents cited lack of students and lack of funding as the main reasons for program cancellation.

Many institutions may benefit from national or international funding programs that specifically support collaborative degree programs, for instance with mobility scholarships for students and funding for administrative costs. While such grants prove extremely helpful in the initial phase of program establishment, most are of limited duration and operate on the understanding that the respective institutions will gradually find other internal or external means to run the program. The level of program funding required will naturally vary depending on certain program characteristics. For instance, institutions developing additional course offerings specifically designed for the delivery of a joint or double degree program will face greater costs than those using only their own and their partner institutions' existing course offerings in a complementary way. Similarly, joint or double degree arrangements relying heavily on the availability of support schemes such as mobility scholarships for students or additional staff positions for program administration will require greater levels of commitment and funding. Regardless of the availability of initial funding schemes, institutions establishing joint and double degree programs are well advised to assess program costs early on and develop a clear understanding of how the funds needed to sustain the program can be secured in the long term.

Each joint and double degree program is a unique undertaking, with specific features determined by its particular setting, mode of delivery, and objectives. While some collaborative degree programs might fare better than others, this will depend on many factors, making it difficult to single out particularly successful formats and simply apply them to all environments. The issues discussed in this chapter, however, clearly suggest that a more structured approach to developing joint or double degree programs can prove beneficial to higher education institutions entering this realm of international collaboration. And there are plenty examples how this can be done. A briefing paper recently published by the Institute of International Education outlines the procedure for screening and authorizing collaborative degree programs developed at Rice University (Chevallier, 2013). The University of Melbourne,[3] Imperial College London,[4] and RWTH Aachen[5] are only a few other examples of institutions that have developed policies and frameworks for creating joint and double degree programs.

In *Borderless 2011: Perspectives on the Future*, a report published by the Observatory on Borderless Higher Education, Amit Chakma of the University of Western Ontario writes that "a future trend will be towards the establishment of institutional partnerships and joint-degree programs that will attract students and researchers alike to the combined strengths of multiple universities working in partnership" (p. 15). It should be added that institutions seeking to effectively capitalize on the opportunities provided by such partnerships should carefully define strategic priorities, communicate respective requirements, offer guidance to initiators of joint and double degree programs, and ensure a clear understanding of responsibilities among the units involved in program development and delivery.

NOTES

[1] For instance, institutions participating in the 2011 IIE/FUB global survey reported 1,300 collaborative degree programs, and in 2009 the Bologna Stocktaking Working Group estimated the number joint programs in the European Higher Education Area at 2,500.

[2] The second and third top impacts cited, respectively, were increased international visibility of the institution and increased internationalization of the campus.

[3] University of Melbourne: http://iro.unimelb.edu.au/internationalcooperation/dualjointprograms

[4] Imperial College London: https://workspace.imperial.ac.uk/registry/public/Procedures%20and%20Regulations/Quality%20Assurance/Guidelines%20for%20Collaborative%20programmes.pdf

[5] RWTH Aachen: http://www.daad-akademie.de/imperia/md/content/internationaledaad-akademie/tagungsdokumentationen/doppelabschluessesept/leitfadenjoint_degrees_-_rwth_aachen.pdf

REFERENCES

American Council on Education. (2012). *Mapping internationalization on U.S. campuses: 2012 edition.* Washington, DC: American Council on Education.

Chevallier, A. (2013). *A process for screening and authorizing joint and double degree programs.* New York, NY: Institute of International Education. Retrieved from http://www.iie.org/~/media/Files/Corporate/Publications/Briefing-Paper-Joint%20-Double-Degrees.ashx

Guttenplan, D. D. (2011, March 28). Dual-degree programs are gathering steam. *New York Times.* Retrieved from http://www.nytimes.com/2011/03/28/world/europe/28iht-educLede28.html?pagewanted=all

International Association of Universities (2010). *Internationalization of higher education: Global trends regional perspectives. The IAU 3rd global survey report.* Paris, France: IAU.

International Association of Universities (2005): *Internationalization of higher education: New directions, new challenges. 2005 IAU global survey report.* Paris, France: IAU.

JOIMAN Network. (2010). *How to manage joint study programmes? Guidelines and good practices from the JOIMAN Network.* Retrieved from https://www.joiman.eu/ProjectResults/PublicDeliverables/Forms/PublicDeliverables.aspx

Kuder, M., Obst, D., & Banks, C. (2011). *Joint and double degree programs in the global context: Report on an international study.* New York, NY: Institute of International Education.

The Observatory on Borderless Higher Education. (2011). *Borderless 2011: Perspectives on the future.* Retrieved from http://www.obhe.ac.uk/documents/view_details?id=864

Chapter Three

How to Manage Joint Programs: Recommendations and Results of JOIMAN and JOI.CON

Tabea Mager and Svend Poller, Leipzig University,
Francesco Girotti, University of Bologna

Joint programs require joint forces. That statement might not come as a surprise. However, its implications cannot be stressed enough. In this chapter, joint programs are understood as international degree programs that are developed and managed in collaboration by at least two higher education institutions (HEIs). Furthermore, the definition includes a double or joint degree being awarded to students graduating from the program. Joint programs are intense in the planning stages and time-consuming in the actual running. Challenges like the development of the joint curriculum and its implementation, followed by the process of mutual degree awarding need to be met. The calculation of program costs and debates about tuition fees often create more questions than answers.

To tackle all the challenges connected to joint programs, several European universities and national structures joined forces in 2008 to establish the JOIMAN network. Funded by the European Union within the Lifelong Learning Program, the network set its agenda in the full project title: Joint Degree Management and Administration Network: Tackling Current Issues and Facing Future Challenges. The members of JOIMAN invested over two years in mapping the situation of joint programs in Europe and beyond.

Cornerstones of the project were detailed questionnaires, interviews with program coordinators, reviews of national legal documents, and, finally, networking and dissemination at conferences. All results and best practices were edited in a final report. A selection of challenges and solutions will be referenced in the chapter at hand.[1]

Joint programs are often perceived as highly unique products. However, the JOIMAN network made some general observations that were common in all programs investigated.

Program models: There are different models of joint programs and their level of integration varies. Currently, the Erasmus Mundus model is the most integrated version. However, especially outside of Erasmus Mundus, other models of joint programs are possible and follow different partners' regulations. That holds true especially for non-European partners because Erasmus Mundus does not foresee equal roles for European and third-country partners.

Role of the institution: Joint programs require joint forces not only at transnational level but also at institutional level. Support from policy and decision makers is needed both in the development and implementation phase. Without institutional support, the program will fall apart.

Awareness and timing: Most coordinators underestimate the complex nature of joint programs and are not aware of all processes involved and questions to be answered. Many of the problems that they encounter could have been eased or even avoided by thinking processes through at the very beginning. Instead, challenges are met with ad hoc solutions that sometimes trigger even more problems in the long run.

Budget and sustainability: The lack of awareness in program details extends to the fundamental question of how to sustain the program. Most programs are managed by few committed individuals but are not integrated sufficiently in the institutions. Usually, there are hardly any reserves available to sustain the programs beyond their confirmed funding period. Policies concerning additional revenues are rather vague or do not exist at all. Even the calculation of full program costs seems to be an enigma.

These observations become all the more vital when non-European countries get on board joint program partnerships. JOIMAN discovered that consortia extending beyond Europe are basically facing the same challenges as intra-European ones. However, the very same challenges become more pressing when distances of location grow and harmonization of study programs is not a declared political objective. Therefore, the motivation to establish a joint program beyond Europe and the early consideration of necessary steps need to be even stronger. JOIMAN identified several main reasons for cooperating with non-European partners. Some of them, like topic-related cooperation and reinforcing already existing cooperation, mirrored the intra-European motifs. Other reasons were more typical for non-European partnerships, for example, capacity building or politically driven collaboration. The latter naturally influences the level of program integration:

Although intra-European programs showed a strong bottom-up approach in the implementation, several non-European partners had started to engage in the field after strategic decisions had been made on the institutional level, and related processes were of a top-down nature. Yet in the end, the implementation of joint programs with non-European partners came down to the same necessary prerequisites like intra-European partnerships: mutual trust and the willingness to compromise.

The challenges and solutions observed within JOIMAN led to a new project initiative in 2011: the JOI.CON network, which was established as a partnership of former JOIMAN members. The project was funded once again by the European Union within the Lifelong Learning Program. JOI.CON built upon the findings of JOIMAN and transferred those findings into a training period for joint program coordinators. The idea was to start from the most challenging condition that those coordinators met or were to meet in reality: to solve highly complex challenges in a very limited time frame. Based on that, Leipzig University, as the JOI.CON coordinator, developed a joint program simulation. International coordinators were to ask the right questions at the right time, supervised by experienced trainers. Such a joint program simulation was meant to create a safe laboratory atmosphere with real international stakeholders planning fictive joint programs and learning about crucial processes on the way.

The following challenges illustrate some main JOIMAN and JOI.CON findings. First, JOIMAN identified the topics that are central in the implementation of joint programs. Subsequently, they were posed as main themes to JOI.CON training teams. Both the JOIMAN recommendations and the JOI.CON team solutions are available on the JOIMAN website.[2] Some of the challenges are, of course, interrelated and have to be met in transversal processes. Needless to say, the list is not exhaustive.

Challenge 1: Select and get to know your partners (and don't forget to get to know yourself).

For a successful joint program, it is crucial to know your partners well. JOIMAN showed that most institutions engage in joint programs with partners they already have some cooperation experience with. A double or joint degree is often seen as an upgrade of mobility projects that are more loosely knit. While mutual trust is a prerequisite for wanting to join forces, the process of getting to know the partner is often underestimated. Challenges or even just peculiarities can arise on various levels. Starting from the individual scientific point of view, up to the national legislation framework, there are a variety of potential misfits and hurdles to be ruled out. One obvious obstacle is national legislation and its impact on degree awarding. Some countries do not yet allow issuing joint degrees, while others do but only under certain circumstances. Even though many EU countries adopted a favorable legislation on joint degrees or joint programs, legislative impediments are still common. Often they even derive from the applicability of those favorable legal frameworks, such as those concerning accreditation procedures. However, JOIMAN found out that much more often the obstacles actually stem from within the partnership. Lack of knowledge of one's own institutional regulations was many times twinned with lack of insights into partners' rules. That led to frustration and stagnating implementation of the program. Again, the role of the institution is crucial to advocate changes at national level and, above all, to adapt institutional regulations to an international education context.

JOIMAN recommended:

When selecting a partner for a joint program, academic criteria are essential but not sufficient. The following recommendations can guide you through the process of selecting and getting to know your partners:

- Define selection criteria for partners beforehand and base programs on trusted partnerships.

- Check the national legal frameworks of your partners in relation to degree awarding and fee policies.

- Check the educational system of your partners' country and institution, especially if they are outside the European Higher Education Area (EHEA).

- Ensure institutional and individual commitment of all parties involved.

JOI.CON teams found out:

Not only is it necessary to get to know your partners but to find out what you actually really know about your *own* regulations. One of the trainees defined his most surprising training experience as "insights I gained about my own university and how different the rules are from country to country." A very useful tool to gather and analyze all crucial information is the comparison table that the JOI.CON teams created.[3] It includes detailed questions on vital issues like financial regulations, national legislation, administrational processes, and degree awarding possibilities. By completing the table with information of all partners involved, you can easily identify possible ways toward a mutual joint program. Also, the colleagues involved already get to know future contact persons within their institutions while researching for the contents of this matrix. (Implementing physical and virtual meetings to get to know your partners will be elaborated on in Challenge 5.)

Challenge 2: Define the level of integration and anticipate degree certification.

The core of each joint program is the jointly developed curriculum with common learning outcomes. Joint programs can be run on various levels of integration. Yet mere mutual mobility does not automatically add up to a joint program. The following elements characterize a truly integrated program:

- A jointly planned curriculum including elements like mutual teaching exchange, mandatory and balanced mobility periods for students, and common summer/winter schools or preparatory courses.

- A common language policy that enables students to study at all partner institutions.

- Full recognition of the periods spent and exams taken at partner institutions.

- Joint certification of the program (double degree with cross-reference or joint degree).

- Joint "ownership" of the program in all its components, including admission and administration of student data.

This, of course, is not a list you need to tick off to make sure you run a truly joint program. However, the more elements you recognize from your program, the more likely you are operating on a high integration level. While both your partnership and students will benefit from a truly integrated program, an intensified integration level takes even more joined forces to consider all the crucial aspects.

A joint degree is often treated synonymously with a joint program. Yet JOIMAN showed that many institutions that faced (mostly legal) difficulties in issuing joint degrees were running successful joint programs. What is finally put down on certification paper is important but should not be the central concern of a joint program consortium. However, the question of options available needs to be raised early enough to avoid misunderstandings and prepare valid documents.

JOIMAN recommended:

Ask yourself why you intend to develop a joint program and define the integration level in accordance to your answer.[4] Different levels of integration will generate different benefits for the institution and for the students. They will also affect the organization and management structure of the program.

JOI.CON teams found out:

The level of integration very much depends on whether your institution identified joint programs in general and the project at hand as added value. Therefore, support on operational and strategic levels needs to be ensured as early as possible. Talking to colleagues about your project is a good way of getting to know relevant key actors and build up a network for later program phases. The certification of a joint program needs to be considered at a very early stage. Legislation frameworks might rule out certain options but they may also render compromises of various degree formats possible. For example, the majority of the consortium might issue a joint degree, while single partners issue double degrees within the same consortium. Rather than relying on the common opinion, consult the legal texts in question to make sure that legislation has not recently changed or others missed loopholes for interpretation.

A joint degree is not necessarily more beneficial than a double degree. True jointness arises from joint program elements, both in curriculum and administration. The "paper at the end" is a result of discussions figuring in regulations and technicalities, not the soul of your project.

Challenge 3: Calculate full program costs and consider tuition fees.

Most coordinators are not aware of the full costs of a joint program. But what exactly are the full costs and how are they calculated? Full costs include both obviously program-related cost items and institutional contributions that might not be visible at first sight, for example:

- Staff expenses for all administrative and academic colleagues involved.
- Rent for rooms and building costs like electricity, and so forth.
- Travel costs for consortia meetings and teaching mobility.
- Expanses for additional curricular activities, for example, summer schools.
- IT costs for joint data administration and internal communication tools.
- Costs for information material and promotion activities.
- Accreditation cost (where applicable).
- Reserves for unforeseen expenses and sustainability.

When going through the program with your partners in detail, you might identify additional cost items. For non-European partners, cost items might be higher than for European ones (e.g., travel), and issues like currency exchange rates come into the picture.

The topic of tuition fees leads the way back to getting to know your partner. Some partners might not be allowed to charge tuition, and others might have to. The picture is not black and white, either, because some partners are allowed to modify the tuition policy in case of international programs or specific funding. Also, European and non-European students may be charged different tuition fee amounts in many institutions. A common understanding needs to be created in order to avoid misinterpretation of terminology, for example, tuition fee versus administrative fees.

JOIMAN recommended:

Try to calculate the full costs as early as possible, and use this calculation for budget negotiations within the consortium. When this is not possible, at least commonly define the additional costs generated by the international collaboration. Decide on transparent management structures of the budget, and monitor the budget constantly. Do not forget to reserve funds for sustainability, and consider involving funding sources outside the academic world. Also, your partner might have other funding access than you do. Especially with non-European partners, funding lines supporting the specific partner regions should be explored on both sides. Again, the support of the institution is crucial and might give access to funding resources.

JOI.CON teams found out:

In terms of finances, the keywords are *transparence* and *compromise*. The full cost calculation[5] of a program might influence the curriculum because mobility periods at institutions that are costly for students need to be carefully planned in duration. Compromises need to go with the smallest common denominator within the consortium. The JOI.CON teams came up with the following solutions:

TABLE 3.1: CONSIDERATIONS FOR CALCULATING PROGRAM COSTS

Possible Solution	PRO	CON
1. Single consortium fee	The consortium remains cohesive. Students are treated equally. Reserves for sustainability can be collected. Fee collection process remains uncomplicated. Joint program marketing is transparent.	Legal framework of partners might pose obstacles. Currency exchange complicates transfers. Fee might be less attractive for students from countries with lower or no tuition fees. Program might profit inappropriately from fees.
2. Fees charged according to actual study location	No currency exchange is involved. There are reliable (consistent) funds for institution that really hosts the students. Fees are matter of students' choice.	Additional costs of managing arise. Students do not pay equal amounts. Funds are not consistent, and additional service fee for consortium might be needed. Not all scholarship schemes are eligible.
3. Fees charged according to home institution	Students benefit from expensive universities at low cost. No currency exchange is involved. Scholarship schemes are eligible.	There is a risk of uneven student flow. Students might pay high fees while studying at low-fee institutions. Funds are not consistent, and additional service fee for consortium might be needed.

Source: JOI.CON, www.joiman.eu

Challenge 4: Discuss procedures and prepare relevant documents.

The soul of a joint program is the cooperation agreement. A good cooperation agreement serves two purposes:

- It functions as legally binding program reference.
- It facilitates the negotiation of processes, responsibilities, and rules between partners.

It is important to reserve time for the cooperation agreement and view it not only as a product but as a trigger of all questions to be answered before running the program. The JOIMAN cooperation agreement template lists all crucial issues to be considered. The main topics to be discussed and put into writing are the following:

- The study program (learning outcomes, learning methodology, structure including mobility and teaching units)
- The program management (admission, selection, examination, certification)
- The kind of qualification and correspondent certificate to award (double/multiple or joint)

Quality assurance and (academic as well as financial) sustainability are two cross-cutting topics. It is also important that some topics like certification (degree awarding) might chronologically take place at the end of the program's first edition, yet they need to be considered in the preparation phase. The agreement already states the nature of future certification for students. Not only does the format have to be decided on but also the content. For some institutions it is mandatory to include certain personal data of students (e.g., birthdate). Other nations or institutions do not allow the same data to be put into writing due to data protection. The question of preparing relevant documents goes as far as the paper it is printed on, which has to have a certain quality in some countries.

Once the degree format is decided on as double, multiple, joint, or a combination of several, some detailed questions concerning the degree awarding itself include:

- In case of double degrees, how will the "jointness" be communicated on paper?
- Who issues the degree certification, and who signs it?
- What role do consortium partners play that never saw the student in question?
- How are associated partners included in the degree certification?

A mostly internal decision is the question on examination regulations: Do they have to be adapted to cover the integrated program? Is it maybe even necessary to create new guidelines or a whole new set of binding examination regulations?

In addition to these central documents, others might be necessary or simply useful. Depending on the nature of the program, such documents might include scholarship statements or student agreements with individual work plans.

Use the cooperation agreement as the base for a negotiation process on all processes and products connected to the joint program. Include both academic and administrative perspectives, and annex all agreements made between partners and with students. Make sure to integrate financial aspects in the agreement.

JOI.CON teams found out:

The cooperation agreement is the glue of your program. Degree certification is rather a consequence than a dangerous obstacle, but it needs to be considered early in the process.[6] As a start, each partner can submit copies of its regular degrees to the consortium to compare. Yet always keep in mind that your program is unique, and simply copying documents that were designed for another program will get you into trouble. The JOI.CON comparison table once again helps to identify challenges in partners' regulations and potential solutions. The JOIMAN cooperation agreement template is a useful guide for topics.

Challenge 5: Distribute tasks within your consortium and find channels for internal communication.

Individual and institutional commitment is a key prerequisite when setting up a joint program. All partners need to feel their role and responsibility in the consortium to develop a sense of ownership. Some tasks naturally remain with the coordinator, and others need to be negotiated. To reach a common understanding of partners' rules, communication needs to be clear and transparent. Especially in the case of non-European partners, cultural differences might influence that understanding.

Modern networking offers many possibilities, but you need to make sure to select communication tools that all partners are able to use. Besides actual physical meetings, the tools might include anything from group e-mailing to implementing communication channels to share documents or meet virtually for discussion.

JOIMAN recommended:

Assign clear responsibilities and tasks to all consortium partners (macro level) and institutional colleagues (micro level). Involve all potential stakeholders in your institution and beyond as early as possible and include both academic and administrative colleagues. Stakeholders outside your institution might include contacts from the labor market or colleagues creating policies on local, regional, or even national level.

<u>JOI.CON teams found out:</u>

Take your time to get to know your partners before you assign specific roles within the consortium. Most JOI.CON trainees confirmed the importance of a physical kick-off meeting as the foundation for the consortium. Ideally, specific roles are distributed or redesigned at a point when partners know each other quite well already. The initial layout of roles within the consortium often remains stable, yet it is not carved in stone. If partners feel the need for improvement, they need to bring it up and get more involved themselves. That might lead to switching roles or decentralizing activities and sharing tasks differently.

To take responsibilities seriously, regular physical meetings are very important. JOI.CON teams used curriculum elements like summer schools as a platform for annual board meetings that included students. All JOI.CON teams suggested that the number of physical meetings should be increased in further trainings.

Virtual communication channels are necessary and very useful for the program, but they cannot replace getting to know your partner in person. Of course, most parts of communication will realistically have to take place without meeting. A regular rhythm for virtual meetings should be established, for example, a monthly video conference or deadlines for feeding mutual share points. Several trainees confirmed that they were actually looking forward to their regular virtual meetings once they got used to their meeting rhythm and to the faces behind the computer cameras. The coordinator should reserve time for testing new technology and prepare partners to remain patient for initial sessions. JOI.CON trainees reported that the nature of virtual meetings sometimes provoked hasty voting, so agendas should not be overloaded or major decisions reserved for physical meetings. If new technology does not work out for your consortium, traditional communication channels can still get you together. If all partners are dedicated to the program, the channel of communication will not be an obstacle.

While investigating joint programs in JOIMAN and creating fictive ones in JOI.CON, the project partners met many colleagues joining in enthusiastically. Joint programs are not just a strategic vision but have become the reality of HEIs with an international agenda. Once all the processes have been carefully thought through, joint forces achieve unique programs with combined academic strengths. One JOI.CON trainee summarized the greatest challenge and, at the same time, the greatest reward as "getting rid of the idea to develop a blueprint and learning that, if we join our different views and expertise, we will find a way around challenges which seemed far too big at the beginning of our discussions."

NOTES

[1] The JOIMAN report and all other project results are available for free download at www.joiman.eu.

[2] Visit www.joiman.eu to download all detailed results and follow-up events of JOIMAN and JOI.CON.

[3] The comparison table and other JOI.CON results are available at www.joiman.eu.

[4] For categories and descriptions concerning the level of integration consult the JOIMAN report (available at www.joiman.eu), p. 229.

[5] For examples on full cost calculation of the JOI.CON download the final JOI.CON report at www.joiman.eu.

[6] For templates and training examples of cooperation agreements and degree certificates, visit www.joiman.eu.

Chapter Four

Influences on the Sustainability of Joint and Double Degree Programs: Empirical Findings from Programs with German Participation

Mareike Tarazona, German Institute for International Educational Research (DIPF)

In the mid or long run, cooperating universities are mutually obliged in international joint and double degree programs[1] (henceforth referred to as JDD programs). Such an intensive form of cooperation depends on strong cooperative competencies of the participants, and it is highly time-consuming, but it opens up many opportunities of organizational and personal learning. One advantage of JDD programs, as opposed to other types of cooperation or other activities targeting internationalization, is expected to be derived from the *sustainability* of the partnership. This sustainability in the relationship emerges from the strong ties forged by the universities' need to deal with the partnering institutions' curriculum, structures of study, formal procedures, and requirements for study.

In economic scientific research on cooperation, international joint ventures are classified as rather instable because of their hybrid form of organization (e.g., Eberl & Kabst, 2005). Such ventures are embedded in the structures of at least two different autonomous enterprises, and each of these enterprises pursues its own strategies and has established its own organization. Despite the hybrid form of international JDD programs, which need to comply with the organizational and quality requirements of at least two universities, the sustainable organization of programs is feasible, as some long-term programs of more than two decades have demonstrated. The study described here aimed to empirically identify influential factors for sustainable organization. Prior to presenting the findings, the context of research dealing with success factors of international study programs will be discussed.

Surveys of International Study Programs

Various aspects of international education have frequently been studied. These include studies focusing on systems and individual mobility and, more recently, insights into academic courses particularly aimed at providing an international environment. Empirical investigations into factors influencing the success of international cooperation between universities are scarce, though. Existing studies have, for instance, found that the emotional aspects of cooperation seem to be about as important as the more factual aspects (Brandenburg, Höllermann, & Lipp, 2008). Respondents in that study stated that emotional aspects played an important role, particularly regarding initial contact, daily collaboration, conflict resolution, and the success of exchange programs. However, that study suffers drawbacks from the random sample as well as subjective assessment of success. An interesting study of international university consortia was presented by Beerkens (2004, see also Beerkens & van der Wende 2007). This study focused on the interorganizational diversity of universities (i.e., their complementarity with respect to compatibility). Complementarity was shown to bear an influence on the performance of a cooperation. The authors confirmed that higher degrees of similarity do not lead to better performance, but that a minimum degree of compatibility is needed. They concluded that a mixture of complementarity and compatibility, together with appropriate coping strategies, influences the performance of international university consortia.

Methodological Procedure

The study outlined next is theoretically grounded in social capital theory and institutional economics. Based on the theoretical analysis, five content areas were identified for possible influential characteristics and combinations of such characteristics: (1) compatibility, (2) trust, (3) financing, (4) formalization of structures, and (5) organization of networking. To empirically validate which of these factors have a relevant impact on sustainable organization, several assessment and evaluation methods were combined; quantitative as well as qualitative procedures were selected, the focus being placed on quantitative analysis. It was, moreover, necessary to operationalize sustainability. Based on institution economics, operationalization was subjected to a limited number of items:

- The program is established (establishment).

- The existence of the program is not threatened, at least in a mid-term perspective, (operationalized as "future perspective").

- The joint ability to solve problems is high (problem solving).

- Financing is ensured.

Results from the quantitative procedures were based on questionnaires that were sent out to all coordinators of JDD programs with German participation, who could be identified at the beginning of the investigated time period in 2009. A total of 186 persons participated in the survey, corresponding to a response rate of 43.16 percent. The sample was representative of the total population regarding university type and constellation of subjects (for details regarding methodology, see Tarazona, 2012).

Results

Results from the presented study need to be viewed in light of sustainability as defined and operationalized in this particular context. Operationalizations constitute an approach to the construct of sustainability. Beyond that, the questionnaire asked for subjective estimations of the cooperation between the universities, as rated by program coordinators.

First, the question that had to be answered was how sustainable JDD programs actually were. Looking at the ratings given by coordinators of JDD programs regarding the three aspects of establishment, future perspective, and problem solving, a strikingly positive picture emerged. Moreover, financing was secure in about two-thirds of the cases. Programs have been shown to continue even in cases of change of staff, although the workload and engagement mainly rested with the coordinators. Since the success of a program depends on individual commitment, the conclusion can be drawn that the investigated programs as such were sustainable, because the sustainability was grounded in individual commitment.

JDD programs involving similar and thus compatible universities were demonstrated to be particularly sustainable. Other than the findings from Beerkens (2004) and Beerkens and van der Wende (2007), compatibility was not only found to be relevant in terms of a minimal degree of compatibility, but also to remain significant when controlling for other variables. This particularly concerns how easy it was to solve problems with the partner(s). This result led to the conclusion that compatibility plays a more relevant role for JDD programs than in other types of university cooperation. Still, universities can be compatible in terms of several characteristics. Institutional compatibility in particular contributes to sustainability. It is less important whether universities bear similarities in their equipment, reputation, or profile of study courses. Hence, the finding that compatibility leads to sustainability needs to be qualified—particularly the index of "institutional compatibility" is relevant for sustainable organization (consisting of the three characteristics of structures of study courses, organization culture, and formal organization of processes). Similarity regarding reputation turned out to be partially relevant regarding future perspectives—the more similar the programs were, the more optimistically the coordinators regarded the future.

Furthermore, a high degree of trust positively influences sustainability of JDD programs. The effect of trust proved to be relatively high compared with the other assessed variables. In particular, a relationship based on trust makes it easier to find solutions to problems. However, neither is the future perspective influenced by different levels of trust, nor is trust rated particularly high in established programs. These findings can be explained by the fact that trust is generally very high in the types of cooperation investigated. It seems to be a minimal requirement, and it is unlikely that a program without a basis in trust could be launched.

Besides trust, sustainability is positively influenced by an equally balanced commitment of cooperative partners in the program. A similar level of commitment is particularly important for easily finding solutions to problems. There is also evidence that in consortia, commitment was particularly unbalanced, compared to other forms of cooperation. Consortial programs are hence particularly challenged by the task of reaching reciprocity—as is needed for sustainability. Besides, trust remains even in the case of lower levels of reciprocity, which can be explained by trust levels being high when mutual understanding is high, regardless of reciprocity.

From the viewpoint of social capital theory, especially the network perspective, dependence on individual persons (initiators) was expected to be reduced when formalization of structures and the involvement of additional persons grew, as this would lead to a stable foundation. Evidence from the surveyed data regarding this hypothesis is mixed, however. No relationship could be demonstrated between sustainability and the question whether the existence of a program depended on the engagement of particular individuals. However, it turned out to be important whether a designated staff position was appointed or not. Whenever a position was appointed, the amount of time consumed by the program was less of a problem. Beyond this effect, the fact that coordinating posts were appointed did not contribute to sustainability in the study. Solving problems with a partner was even negatively correlated with the appointment of a coordinating post. This may have been a result of the involvement of many persons, thus making the process of solving problems more complex. According to findings from the study, formalization in terms of detailed written coding of cooperation agreements bore no influence on sustainability even if in one interview such a correlation was alleged.

Moreover, it was assumed that the appropriateness of the form of governance and the form of coordination of a JDD program had significant impact. The literature on economics and on international study programs led to the finding of which types of coordination were appropriate. However, coordination forms in the realm of universities turn out to be less differentiated than those described in economics literature for horizontal enterprises. Only in exceptional cases did the cooperating universities appoint a post that was responsible for the general coordination of all partner institutions. Also, the situation has rarely emerged that one university took leadership when the JDD program was not tied to a consortium.

While a differentiation of forms of cooperation turned out to be less effective for JDD programs in terms of concepts from institution economics and network research, another categorization allowed for a more appropriate distinction of JDD programs. Programs showing a high number of graduates and partners, a high degree of mobility among lecturers, and many joint activities in coordination were defined as "cooperation-intensive." These programs were studied separately, because they were characterized by strongly tied study structures, thus representing the hope for stronger harmonization of university systems or organizational learning. Regarding the sustainability of cooperation programs, one characteristic proved to be relevant in the multivariate analyses: Cooperation-intensive programs are more sustainable when the existence of the programs is less dependent on individual commitment. When controlling for all characteristics bearing an influence independent of cooperation intensity, cooperation-intensive programs furthermore proved to be less sustainable than others.

When a program is not financially secured on a long-term basis, this means it is less sustainable: This is part of the definition of sustainability. Moreover, financial security also influences other variables used for measuring sustainability. It is thus surprising that the funding of a university has less often had an impact on the sustainability of a program. Accordingly, whether strategic importance is attached to a program is more important for sustainability. Still, there was no evidence that programs given high strategic relevance were financially more secure. It seems that minimum equipment is required for a program in terms of allocation of tasks to a staff member—in the international office or in the framework of study course coordination, which is often linked with coordination of the JDD programs. Still, contact with the partners is intensive in nearly all of the programs, and additional staff is an important element of relief.

Another aspect of sustainability relates to the question of in how far cooperation gives impetus to innovations at universities and to adaptation or flexibility of existing structures. The interviews as well as the survey rendered clear that some new or harmonizing practices had indeed emerged. Still, JDD programs remain hybrid constructs operating between the university systems into which the cooperating partners are embedded. Hence, new ideas might emerge for how individual aspects might be alternatively organized. Generally, however, deeper-rooted effects on the structures of individual universities cannot be anticipated because practices in teaching and administration are ingrained in the system and in tradition. The potential for individual changes of practices was detected (e.g., regarding the increased flexibility of curricula or bureaucratic structures), but these cases were exceptional. The most frequent changes emerging from cooperation concerned student counseling. Innovations are particularly found in cooperation-intensive programs, programs involving few partners, and programs with high-quality relationships. However, these findings do not give any information about the depth of the impact of changes.

Given that the financial condition of a university or the appointment of a coordinating post bears little relevance for sustainability, it is possible to create JDD programs that are sustainable even without high demands on costs and personnel. That is, programs can be organized by regular staff members (researchers or nonacademic staff members) or some of the tasks can be assigned to other positions (e.g., the international office or teaching staff without portfolio). There is no evidence that the appointment of a coordination post is particularly necessary for the sustainability of cooperation-intensive programs. Still, this statement should be treated with caution: The amount of time needed was viewed as problematic by many of the coordinators who have not been specially appointed. Furthermore, it seems to be beneficial if the coordination of a program is tied to a particular function (e.g., dean or head of study course), thus being partly independent of particular individuals. Dependence on individuals was further found to be problematic regarding the sustainability of cooperation-intensive programs—this did not apply to programs that required less intensive cooperation. Therefore, there is an indication that particularly for cooperation-intensive programs, a stronger degree of formalization bears particular relevance for sustainability, that is, the integration of several persons into the organization and thus the creation of a dense network. Altogether, the programs operate on a rather small scale considering the number of graduates. If the number of graduates is meant to be increased to boost the importance of the program and thus its strategic significance, it is necessary to formalize the program sufficiently and to involve an appropriate number of persons into its organization.

Statements found in the interviews allow for the conclusion that not only are initiators crucial for institutionalizing a study course, but that coordinators, too, render important contributions to the institutionalization of a program (whether they have been appointed to a coordinating post or not). These coordinators continue a program by introducing new practices and contributing to its acceptance within the university. As for institutionalizing a program, intercultural competence and open-mindedness of the responsible staff are as important as university political competencies. However, these findings were deduced from the interviews of a few coordinators only.

Summary

This chapter presents a summary of findings from an empirical study of factors influencing the sustainability of JDD programs. As described, a number of different characteristics can bear an impact on sustainability. In particular, these relate to a high degree of trust, a high level of mutual commitment to the program shown by the cooperating partners, and high institutional compatibility. Findings are less clear-cut for the characteristics of financing and formalization. For instance, beyond a minimum of necessary financing of the program, it seems to be important that the program coordination is formally tied to certain functions (e.g., head of study course). On the other hand, this finding can be qualified for those types of programs that require intensive cooperation. In these cases, a higher degree of formalization regarding active involvement of a larger number of persons seems important.

NOTES

¹ Here, international joint degrees are defined as completion of a course of study that is jointly conducted by at least two universities from two different countries, leading to a single university degree that is officially recognized by each of the countries involved. An international double degree relates to completing a course of study leading up to at least two degrees officially recognized in the different two countries, based on the cooperation of at least two universities from the respective countries.

REFERENCES

Beerkens, E. 2004. *Global opportunities and institutional embeddedness: Higher education consortia in Europe and Southeast Asia.* Univ., Diss.—Twente, 2004. Enschede: Cheps/University of Twente.

Beerkens, E., & van der Wende, M. 2007. The paradox in international cooperation: Internationally embedded universities in a global environment. *Higher Education*, 53: 61–79.

Brandenburg, U., Höllermann, P., & Lipp, D. 2008. The laws of attraction: Erfolgsfaktoren in internationalen Hochschulkooperationen. *Die Hochschule* (01/2008): 4–22.

Eberl, P., & Kabst, R. 2005. Vertrauen, Opportunismus und Kontrolle: Eine empirische Analyse von Joint Venture-Beziehungen vor dem Hintergrund der Transaktionskostentheorie. In B. Schauenberg, G. Schreyögg & J. Sydow (Hrsg.), *Institutionenökonomik als Managementlehre?* 239–274. Wiesbaden: Gabler Verlag.

Tarazona, M. (2012). *Zur Institutionalisierung internationaler Studiengänge. Eine theoretische und empirische Untersuchung zur nachhaltigen Organisation von Joint- und Double-Degree-Programmen.* Berlin: Berliner Wissenschafts-Verlag, Schriften zur öffentlichen Verwaltung und öffentlichen Wirtschaft, Band 224.

| **Chapter 4:** Influences on the Sustainability of Joint and Double Degree Programs

Chapter Five

Cross-Border Graduate Double Degree Program Implementation: Two Case Studies in Japan of Faculty and Administrator Views and Involvement

DIANA YEFANOVA, UNIVERSITY OF MINNESOTA

Study Rationale

This chapter is based on dissertation findings that focused on university efforts in establishing and sustaining cross-border graduate double degree programs (GDDPs).[1] The special effort in this study was to explore how different campus stakeholders understand and view such programs—the rationale, challenges, and benefits—and how their expectations and opinions may influence the program implementation process. Evidence of the increasing connection between higher education institutions around the globe is well documented, but what is less understood is how this connectivity is enacted in specific cases of collaborative cross-border educational delivery. One of these arrangements is analyzed in detail in this study.

The first goal of this study was to examine how stakeholders (staff members, faculty, and administrators) at two selected universities viewed the GDDP implementation process. Another goal was to explore issues around stakeholder access to decision-making processes related to program implementation at those institutions.

Both case study universities were located in Japan. The first case study was an established bilateral dual degree program at a private Japanese university; the other was a more recently established, consortium-based program at a public university. The first case study university partnered with a private U.S. university, and the second with a public Australian university. A total of 23 administrators, faculty, and staff members were interviewed about GDDP goals, benefits, challenges, and success factors in their university context. Study participants either worked with international programs, or with internationalization policies, or were invited to teach in or support the graduate dual degree program.

Universities in Japan, not unlike their counterparts in other countries, have been responding to internal and external pressures to increase international collaboration in higher education, enter new educational markets abroad, and establish strategic partnerships to enhance international visibility. The internationalization of Japanese higher education system is seen by many as a desirable objective in itself, as well as an impetus to broader reforms at the institutional level, while the regulatory framework for cross-border programs has been gradually adjusting to the trend. The political will is also there, as the Japanese Ministry of Education, Culture, Sports, Science and Technology is seeking to provide more funding to bring talented foreign graduate students into the country and send more Japanese students abroad.

The number of GDDPs is still relatively low in Japan, but the proclaimed benefits are significant at individual, institutional, and national levels. In spite of some differences in underlying rationales, many of the main GDDP-related goals and objectives of Japanese universities are similar to those of their counterparts in other countries. Specifically, universities aim to attract high-quality graduate students, increase revenue, and remain competitive in terms of higher education export and knowledge production. Interuniversity partnerships are often viewed as beneficial learning experiences for students, due to combined teaching, curricular, and research expertise from two or more participating institutions (Asaoka & Yano, 2009; Horie, 2002; Ninomiya, Knight, & Watanabe, 2009; Watabe, 2010).

Study Findings

<u>What Stakeholders Agreed On</u>

Interview data analysis revealed a high degree of agreement among stakeholder expectations in both case studies. Administrators shared views on GDDP success factors, such as the program's innovative design and potential benefits for student employment. Program staff and faculty shared views on program rationale and benefits, viewing the program as a beneficial, highly structured international opportunity for student learning and development, in addition to being a part of the university's internationalization strategy. Program staff and faculty also had similar ideas on what constituted major GDDP challenges, pointing out student participation and recruitment, credit articulation, lack of funding, and long-term sustainability.

Faculty in both cases also questioned the ethics of receiving two academic degrees within a same time frame. At a public university, one faculty member was especially concerned about the program's academic quality:

> For administrators it is a new program, of course they try to show that it has a positive influence on university image, but for faculty it is not clear … where is the academic meaning or significance of this … we are not persuaded. And academic meaning is at the heart of a university.

<u>What Stakeholders Disagreed About</u>

The common areas of disagreement among stakeholders within case study institutions indicated (1) lack of faculty and staff motivation to participate in the program, (2) lack of clarity regarding program goals and academic benefits among faculty, and (3) lack of student interest in the program.

At the first case study university, students had consistently participated in the GDDP for a few years by the time they were interviewed. The interviewees talked about faculty awareness of program goals, benefits, and existing resources, and about an agreement among faculty, staff, and administrators on essential program characteristics and potential concerns, including partner institution selection, program costs, ethical concerns, and related domestic student recruitment challenges. These characteristics may have contributed to overall program success and sustainability.

The second case study university achieved less-than-optimal outcomes in its quest to implement that particular GDDP due to inability to provide enough motivation and support for faculty and staff, and to ensure student participation in the end. Currently, the university is working on new strategies for dual and joint degree program implementation in a range of research areas as a member of a multicountry institutional network.

Stakeholder Participation in Decision-Making

The first case study university also had higher overall participation of faculty and staff in the decision-making process at the time the institution established a GDDP, which was framed as an essential part of university internationalization policy. University administrators who created the policies did so in consultation with staff members impacted by these very policies, so the latter were, in turn, able to make some decisions about the resources needed for partnership success.

As GDDPs are not yet demand-driven in Japan, the top-down model of program implementation demonstrated by the second case study may have hindered the establishing of initial staff and faculty buy-in and support. As a result, program staff and faculty saw the program as ineffective, costly, and challenging to integrate into the institutional curriculum. However, the program was still the one that administrators chose to implement. One of the staff members responsible for program coordination mentioned that one of the biggest challenges was not being able to have any double degree program provisions written into university rules or policies, making it extremely difficult for staff to address any related concerns. Staff often did not have enough information, expertise, authority, or control over the program. Therefore they were not able to answer questions by students, faculty, and external players:

> We have different offices in charge of this ... the group leader of the international center has probably the final responsibility but. ...We are not quite sure who has the final responsibility or the ownership of this program.

GDDP Implementation Model

To guide university efforts in engaging campus staff and faculty stakeholders in the GDDP implementation process, a model was developed based on the themes that emerged from cross-case data analysis, including the critical areas of disagreement (and potential internal resistance), among administrators, staff, and faculty members. The model highlights the areas that leadership in bilateral and consortia-based partnerships need to pay specific attention to, such as the pervasive challenges of quality assurance, ethical concerns about the nature of double degrees, and adequate resource utilization, as well as partner communication, in order to build sustainable double degree programs. The ultimate goal is to increase faculty and staff understanding and motivation to implement the program, which may help boost student participation, thus improving the program prospects of survival and sustainability.

This model also presents several areas for policy creation to improve cross-border collaborative program establishment and implementation practices. These measures include developing faculty and staff motivation-building practices, providing information on GDDP goals and benefits more effectively, and engaging all stakeholders in the decision-making process.

FIGURE 5.1: EXPLANATORY MODEL OF STAKEHOLDER ENGAGEMENT

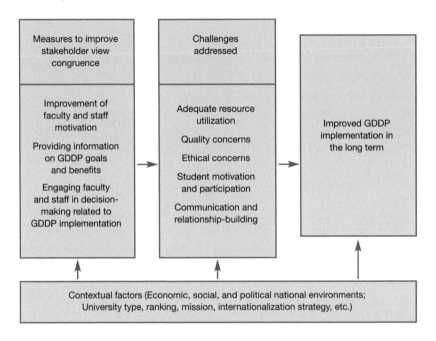

Practical Recommendations—Is There More to GDDP Than a Good Buy?

The relationship between macro-level internationalization policy and micro-level implementation warrants careful examination in varying national regulatory frameworks and cultures. Different groups of stakeholders will have different agendas, levels of power within institutions, and concerns with the introduction of double degree programs. In this study, one of staff member interviewees said he wanted to know what was "the point [of GDDP] beyond the fact that it was a good buy" for students who could "kill two birds with one stone" and gain two diplomas in a relatively short amount of time. For those planning innovative cross-border programs in higher education, these study findings indicate that program implementation should be accompanied by joint decision making among all program stakeholders to address this and other valid questions.

Stakeholder Involvement

Unlike the aforementioned staff member, many interviewed university staff and faculty members in the study fully recognized potential program benefits and university resources that could be applied toward successful GDDP implementation, but felt they had very limited access to decision-making to utilize these resources. Without sufficient joint decision-making within universities in Japan, some GDDPs may be implemented at an ad hoc level given the low levels of subsequent stakeholder commitment and resource utilization. In the Japanese context this possibility is especially relevant because recent university governance reform aimed at autonomy and decentralization may yet take some time to affect rigid university culture, especially at public universities.

Yonezawa, Akiba, and Hirouchi (2009) argued that the value of international exchange, mutual understanding, and respect should be widely shared by the efforts of the entire academic community. In the absence of strong stakeholder commitment to isolated international programs, only a superficial provision might emerge of strategic planning documents for the purposes of acquiring budgetary benefits. Study participants felt that a clear connection between GDDPs and university mission and/or internationalization policy would help future program implementation efforts.

Faculty Motivation and Institutional Support

Faculty incentives were mentioned as one of the success factors in this study. Suggestions included additional support by dedicated staff, English language training, and assistance in motivating domestic students, all focusing on quality assurance, not just the two-for-one aspect of the program. The curriculum internationalization goals Japanese universities espouse should also highlight the importance of empowering and supporting academics in providing international learning opportunities for students, given that such work requires much extra effort for little or no remuneration.

Ways to involve faculty members in this curriculum integration process could include orientations, invitations to relevant meetings for critical review of proposed GDDP implementation, and bringing highly qualified students from abroad to study in graduate courses and conduct research. Offering institutional support for involved faculty may also address the fact that Japanese academics often place more emphasis on the international dimension in their personal research activities (such as international collaboration and publishing) as opposed to directly participating in exchange activities, research, and training with foreign scholars or students (Huang, 2009).

Degree Recognition and Program Quality

It is important to ensure that dual degree awards are respected and recognized by universities and employers. In Japan, GDDP participation may have limited impact on students' careers, in spite of growing employer interest in hiring globally competent employees. Foreign university programs in Japan have traditionally been treated in the legislature as business ventures that function with little relevance to national higher education activity while pursuing commercial interests (Huang, 2009). Credit transfer and administrative issues are among the contentious issues to address in conversation with partner universities, since Japanese law focuses solely on degrees awarded in Japan. Hence, mutual recognition of joint internal quality assurance programs by partners would be helpful, according to Knight (2009), because it is often difficult for institutions to monitor the quality of partner institution's courses and present a realistic picture to staff members and faculty interested in quality assurance.

Furthermore, high quality in a cross-border partnership is often defined based on loyalty and sense of "ownership" by partner institutions, in addition to official quality monitoring and assessment standards. However, GDDP "ownership" has proven hard to achieve: The faculty, staff, and administrators involved aim, in the end, to remain loyal to home institution (Beerkens, 2004). University internationalization strategies are still mostly guided by national regulations and funding frameworks, although individual educators and researchers often work in highly collaborative modes across borders. Additionally, universities are increasingly likely to be operating in a competitive business mode, and the "official story" of cross-border program implementation plans based on institutional aspirations often significantly differ from the on-the-ground collaborative program implementation experience.

Cross-border GDDP upfront costs may be significant, and it is worth investigating whether the investment is justified in the end. Going beyond a "good buy" and addressing the challenges of faculty and staff members' engagement and support could be helpful as Japanese universities intensify strategic efforts to improve their competitive advantage in the global higher education market by encouraging high-quality, interuniversity collaboration.

NOTES

[1] This study used the Institute of International Education (IIE) definition of GDDP (Kuder & Obst, 2009): During a dual or double degree program, students study at (at least) two higher education institutions and receive a separate degree certificate from each one upon completion of the study program. The terms "dual degree" and "double degree" are used interchangeably in this study.

REFERENCES

Asaoka, T., & Yano, J. (2009). The contribution of "study abroad" programs to Japanese internationalization, *Journal of Studies in International Education, 13*(2), 174–188.

Beerkens, H. (2004). Global opportunities and institutional embeddedness: Higher education consortia in Europe and Southeast Asia. Enschede, the Netherlands: CHEPS.

Horie, M. (2002). The internationalization of higher education in Japan in the 1990s. *Higher Education, 43*(1), 65–84.

Huang, F. (2009). The internationalization of the academic profession in Japan: A quantitative perspective, *Journal of Studies in International Education, 13*(2), 143–158.

Knight, J. (2009). Internationalization: Unintended consequences? *International Higher Education, 54,* 8–10.

Kuder, M. & Obst, D. (Eds.). (2009). *Joint and double degree programs: An emerging model for transatlantic exchange.* New York, NY: Institute of International Education.

Ninomiya, A., Knight, J., & Watanabe, A. (2009). The past, present, and future of internationalization in Japan. *Journal of Studies in International Education, 13*(2), 117–124.

Yonezawa, A., Akiba, H., & Hirouchi, D. (2009). Japanese university leaders' perceptions of internationalization: The role of government in review and support. *Journal of Studies in International Education, 13*(2), 125–142.

FURTHER READING

Uroda, A. (2011). Borders bridging degrees: Harbin and Vladivostok's dual-degree programs. Crossing Borders in East Asian Higher Education. *CERC Studies in Comparative Education, 27*(3), 231–261.

Watabe, Y. (2010). *Japanese approaches to organizational internationalization of universities: A case study of three national university corporations.* (Unpublished doctoral dissertation). University of Minnesota, Minneapolis.

Yefanova, D. (2011). *Stakeholder view congruence on cross-border graduate double degree program implementation in Japan, Australia, and the United States.* (Unpublished doctoral dissertation). University of Minnesota, Minneapolis.

Chapter Six

Fostering International Exposure and Cross-Fertilization Through a Platform of Interconnectivity: The Alliance Program and the Metaphor of the Router

Alessia Lefébure, Columbia University

In the past 10 years the international higher education environment has undergone a profound transformation. Among the main markers of the change are the sudden arrival of various international ranking systems, the meltdown of public funding, and the transition to competitive and performance–based resources allocation. The playing field and the rules of the game are no longer the same, and therefore, newcomers have been able to become serious competitors. Domestic reputation alone, based on historical legacy or national networks, does not ensure that global world-class universities will maintain their position forever. Leading research universities are adapting their strategies and their communication to the new context, in order to continue to attract the best and the brightest students and faculties.

In a globalized higher education world, paradoxically, these strategies have rarely been based on international partnerships. Certainly, the global dimension of higher education has been magnified: Each university now speaks to a worldwide audience and defines itself as a global institution. Some of them have tried to establish a global presence through branch campuses abroad and specific infrastructures supporting study-abroad programs.

Yet, in a system of enhanced competition and increased student mobility and volatility, institutional and strategic partnerships receive little attention. None of the major ranking systems seem to value the strength of the international links among higher education institutions. Across different international ranking systems, criteria rarely focus on the international dimension, other than the "international orientation" usually captured by two indicators: the proportion of international staff and the proportion of international students. Even when taken into account, international indicators have little weight and do not necessarily reflect any deep international dimension of the educational experience. Universities can succeed in recruiting their student body worldwide and yet may not be engaged in international partnerships.

Partnerships and networks were one of the pillars of intra-European students' mobility in the late 1980s and 90s. Have these become a concept of the past? Is the current global competition incompatible with the notions of synergy and cooperation?

Four leading universities have proven the contrary. Under the auspices of the Alliance Program, a transatlantic consortium took shape in 2002 with the broad mission of initiating and accompanying new initiatives in the fields of education cooperation, research collaboration, and policy outreach. This chapter analyzes the strategy of the joint venture and underlines the lesson that could be learned from the model.

History and Definition

Created in fall 2002, the Alliance Program emerged as a project from a shared vision among Columbia University and three leading French institutions: the École Polytechnique, Sciences Po, and Sorbonne University (Paris-1). Individually and jointly, the four universities had already implemented global strategies that included creating programs and centers in every region of the globe, developing exchanges with major research and educational institutions throughout the world, and welcoming greater numbers of international students to their campuses. The Alliance represents a common desire of the leadership of the four universities to support the rise of joint educational and academic initiatives, with the concept that they would be stronger and better in collaboration, exchange, and the sharing of ideas and values.

During the first years, the leadership secured the administrative and legal framework, the human resources, and the initial funding. Seed money was used to encourage faculty mobility between New York and Paris, thereby creating the conditions for developing joint initiatives relevant to departments, professors, and students. From the very beginning, the four institutions tried to find a fine balance between a top-down facilitating framework and bottom-up projects and ideas.

Alliance works today as a platform—or as a router—that allows people and organizations to launch pilot programs and experiments in dual-degree programs, multilateral research, executive education, new learning methods, and cross-cultural debates. Successful experiences can be nurtured and eventually generalized, to the benefit of the four academic communities. Thanks to full-time dedicated staff based at Columbia University, Alliance serves as a tool for sharing best practices, communicating within the network, and capitalizing on achievements. Not only can its staff handle the administration and implementation of new projects, but they can also actively promote the vision of the project and help its further development. In each of the French universities, the vice president for international affairs serves in a steering committee and acts as a local relay when needed, and on individual projects, the Alliance staff is in direct communication with the faculty. The different initiatives do not constrain the four universities within the Alliance boundaries. On the contrary, projects often involve external partners, on a case-by-case basis and according to the needs and wishes of the faculty involved.

Because it is not limited to a single institution or to a particular discipline, the Alliance Program endeavors to open a space for discussion among private sector executives, public policymakers, and academics. By doing so, the Alliance builds on the diversity of its partners and their intrinsic plurality to promote durable cooperation across disciplines.

The role and the achievements of the consortium have evolved over time. The early years have been devoted to exploring possible areas for joint research initiatives, encouraging faculty mobility, and allowing departments and schools within the network to identify mutual strengths and complementarities. The traditional student exchange programs have been progressively enriched with dual degrees, in which graduates receive separate national degrees from each institution. Most of the students' mobility within the network is now under a dual-degree scheme, with students sharing their time between an American and a French university and taking full advantage of two faculties, two networks, two academic communities, and two alumni networks.

In 2007 the four universities were able to raise external funds and endow the program, thus transforming it into a long-term, sustainable venture. Since then, the focus has been more on education innovation and pilot projects. In recent years the Alliance has become a laboratory of sorts—an experimental space for initiatives, often on a small scale—and a new way of providing a global education for future generations.

A Mixed-Bag Inventory of Achievements

One of the former directors of the Alliance program wrote in 2006:

> *The Alliance Program is a small, original and somewhat crucial enterprise whose functions could be defined simply. The Alliance program is a flexible engine of academic cooperation based on the idea that our students and our professors would benefit tremendously to be working together. Our mission is to identify the exact disciplines where we could actually create a link and provide the support to launch these initiatives.*

A lot has been achieved since then, but these remarks are still true.

Among the most sustainable outcomes of the Alliance are the dual-degree programs. These programs always start with small numbers: two to five students per year. Universities have to face initial problems related to curriculum coherence, reputation of the degree, coordination in the admission procedure, and harmonization of calendars and procedures. In recent years, the number of students enrolled in all of the Alliance dual-degree or joint programs has increased by 32 percent per year. For example, 200 students were enrolled in 2011–12 compared to 136 students in 2010–11. Today, 22 percent are undergraduate and 78 percent are graduate students.

In addition to dual-degree programs, faculty mobility flourishes and enables several cross-teaching experiences in New York or Paris. A dozen visiting professors teach one semester or one academic year at a partner institution; some of them teach seminars or research workshops during short-term visits. The mobility of the Alliance faculty as a teaching experience is not simply a sabbatical year, because professors create stronger links when they teach. As Alliance's ambassadors, they work for the development of new partnerships between the two institutions. They are asked to teach one full course during one semester and to participate in seminars or workshops. As one of the visiting professors expressed, these teaching experiences are

> *enormously productive. At a personal level, the conversations with colleagues at the University of Paris I and other institutions enriched my work. As a member of the Columbia community, I was able to start building what we hope will be a long and fruitful collaboration between the historians of Latin America in both universities.*

The long-term interaction with scholars on the other side of the Atlantic often lead faculties to start new research projects and the exposure to a different scientific culture can sometimes change their perspectives on basic questions. According to another visiting professor,

> *The lines of French research are often interestingly different from the specific lines of enquiry common in Anglophone universities of the United States and the UK. To go to Paris under the Alliance program was a wonderful opportunity for*

intellectual exploration and research in an academic culture which is very differ-
ent and highly stimulating.

One common effect of the faculty mobility is joint research. When new research projects emerge involving at least two faculty members (each from one side of the Atlantic), the Alliance often supports them through a special seed grant program. Other institutions, such as the Partner University Fund (PUF) of the French Embassy to the United States, continue to sustain the development of the best collaborative research projects started in the past years in the sciences, social sciences, and humanities.

Often, a PhD candidate will want to continue to work under the supervision of the visiting professor at the partner university. Every year, the Alliance awards doctoral mobility grants so that several PhD candidates can spend two or three months at a partner institution under the joint supervision of two professors in their field. Indeed, exciting intellectual journeys are made possible by the Alliance, whether it is a PhD candidate from France discussing her research with professors at Columbia, or an American student using archival materials in Paris to write his art history thesis. So far, these grants have covered the research areas of physics, economics, law, history, political science, public health, African studies, and Middle East studies. Additional resources for student mobility have been obtained through partnerships with banks, companies, foundations, and not-for-profit institutions that were willing to enhance the international dimension of the four universities through scholarships, workshops, and summer schools. Thanks to increased transnational mobility, the Alliance is helping promote a new generation of versatile students and professors able to thrive in various cultural settings.

Besides teaching and research initiatives, the Alliance acts as an international platform for scholars to exchange and debate ideas with policymakers and corporate leaders, through private meetings and specialized workshops on policy issues such as the financial crisis, higher education reforms, energy, and sustainable development. Dozens of joint academic events (lectures, conferences, workshops, and art exhibitions) take place every year in New York or in Paris, connecting scholars, students, civil society, and governmental actors.

Finally, the Alliance serves the concept of internationalization in each of the four universities. Sharing human capital and information has a strong impact on the circulation of knowledge and models across the Atlantic. The mutual trust that was built over the years creates the conditions for confronting and discussing ideas and projects, including relations with third parties and in other regions of the world. Mobility is not limited to the faculty and student body. The entire staff of the four universities, from the human resources (HR) division to the communication office to the student life office to the payroll department, is exposed to different working methods, administrative rules, expectations, and constraints.

This collaborative program is clearly a tool for internationalizing the communities and for quality improvement. Institutions retain their identities and independence but work together in a global context focused on specific and evolving challenges and areas of interest.

"Revolutionary Road"

Under the Alliance program, Columbia University has launched a number of dual degrees in partnership with Sciences Po, the École Polytechnique, and Sorbonne University. Ranging from art history to law to engineering, most of these degree programs are at the graduate level, offering a dual master's degree or a dual PhD. The choice of the discipline and the level is made on a case-by-case basis, according to the needs of the two schools or departments involved in the project.

After several years of experience in joint recruitment, admission, curricula, and graduation, Columbia and Sciences Po decided to launch a dual-degree program at the bachelor's level. Since 2011, students interested in a rigorous and international college experience have had an opportunity to study in both France and the United States while earning two bachelor's degrees through the dual BA program. Students begin their studies by spending two years at one of the Sciences Po campuses—Le Havre, Menton, or Reims—each devoted to a specific cultural and linguistic focus. After two years, students join Columbia University in New York City to complete the interdisciplinary social sciences curriculum. Upon successful completion of the program, students are guaranteed admission to a graduate program at the Sciences Po campus in Paris.

Unlike other dual-degree programs, a joint admissions team visits some of the best high schools in the world, from India and China to Canada, and identifies highly qualified applicants, who can become part of the rich intellectual life of both institutions. By bringing together students from all over the world and having them study full-time for two years at a leading university in Europe before bringing them to a world-class American one, participants are exposed to a wide range of languages, cultures, and experiences. Students discover new educational approaches specific to each country. Differences are stronger in the liberal arts than in business or engineering, the two fields in which dual degrees were first developed. The essay formats are different, as are the classroom discussions and interactions with professors. For students navigating these two systems, it is very stimulating to see that things can be done differently. The result is a cross-fertilization of attitudes and perspectives that makes an immense contribution to the student experience and intellectual conversation in classrooms. Sciences Po and Columbia University place the same emphasis on internationalizing their student body and believe that this is the best way of preparing them to deal with the complex global challenges of the 21st century.

Columbia and Sciences Po therefore share something at the core of higher education: the undergraduate experience, which is creating a community of students who share the two institutions' values. A dual degree in liberal arts at the undergraduate level, with a joint admission procedure, is revolutionary in higher education, but it is one of the only ways of creating a truly global community.

At the graduate level, other joint and dual-degree programs continue to flourish, linking Columbia University professional schools to their counterparts in France. By partnering with the law schools at Sciences Po and Sorbonne University, Columbia faculty members have collaborated to create integrated, English language programs with a distinct focus on international law, global business law, and governance. Students who enroll in these programs complete their JD degree requirements within the standard three-year time frame and widen their professional opportunities thanks to the European Union (EU) exposure.

After completing a dual-degree program at Columbia University schools such as the School of International and Public Affairs (SIPA), the Law School, and the School of Engineering and Applied Science, many students have found that their careers have taken off. In dual-degree classes, the intellectual climate is very different, with new models for student engagement and learning that prepare tomorrow's multilingual, multicultural leaders.

Sustainable Development

Collaborative degree programs and other international ventures can be challenging to put into place and sustain. In the Alliance program, the engine that makes all this work is the endowment that supports the relationship between Columbia and its three French partners. The endowment gives the program a long-term horizon and makes it sustainable and therefore less vulnerable to economic or geopolitical shifts. An endowment is particularly important for a program like the Alliance, which provides a general framework for cooperation and defines specific projects and developments year after year.

Another key element is the involvement of the departments and schools. Only projects that show a positive impact for the departments receive support. The department must endorse individual professors' or students' bottom-up initiatives before the Alliance will support the project. In that way, the success of these projects does not rely upon individuals only, but is progressively rooted into institutions.

The four universities already recruit a high proportion of international students, ranging from 30 percent to 70 percent according to the program, the level, and the field of specialization. American students have represented the largest international community at Sciences Po since the late 1990s, and the number of French students at Columbia University has been traditionally high for decades. The main motivation for establishing dual-degree programs is to attract a more diverse and ambitious pool of talented students, by offering a unique combination of intellectual approaches and a demanding learning environment.

FIGURE 6.1: MAP OF ALLIANCE DUAL DEGREE AND JOINT PROGRAMS (2011 – 2012)

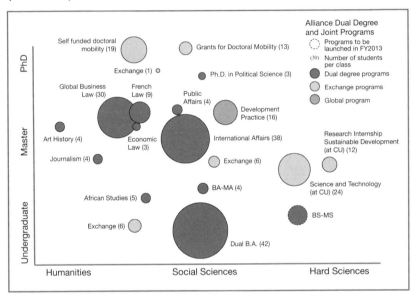

FIGURE 6.2: NUMBER OF STUDENTS ENROLLED IN ALLIANCE PROGRAMS BY YEAR

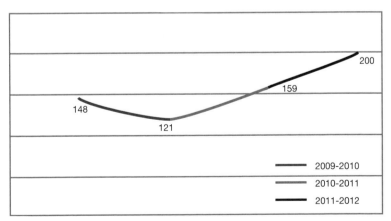

Conclusion

The best metaphor to describe the Alliance would be the router. It creates channels of communication among the four universities by facilitating, translating, explaining, and unfolding in this long-term international partnership. The four universities do not meet on specific, limited projects, but rather open a broad discussion so that specific projects can eventually rise quickly and smoothly.

Each of these institutions builds on the partnership to better prepare its students for the global challenges they will face and to offer their faculty members the best conditions to give an international dimension and exposure to their research. It is a bottom-up approach combined with strong top-down support. Departments and schools are never obliged nor forced into a collaborative project. The Alliance creates incentives and reduces transaction costs. Once departments and schools develop a concept for a project, the most natural way to implement it is through the Alliance network. That is precisely how pilot initiatives emerge and eventually become larger and sustainable.

Finally, a side benefit of the Alliance has been the circulation of knowledge and best practices from one university to another, and sometimes from one department or school to another. The Alliance is often regarded as a laboratory for experiences in higher education international cooperation.

Chapter Seven

Institutional Double Degree Programs Strategy at Technische Universität München

CHRISTOPH STEBER, TECHNISCHE UNIVERSITÄT MÜNCHEN

Technische Universität München (TUM) was founded in 1868 and is today one of Germany's Universities of Excellence. Its 13 faculties count over 32,000 students and feature a portfolio of subjects focusing on natural sciences, engineering sciences, life and food sciences, sports, and medicine. Technology-oriented business management and the TUM School of Education complete these focus areas. TUM is committed to excellence in research and teaching, interdisciplinary education, and the promotion of promising young scientists. The university also forges strong links with companies and scientific institutions across the world.

In the late 1980s, the French Grandes Ecoles approached some Faculties of Technische Universität München to discuss the development of a double degree between these institutions. The first agreements were signed between Ecole Nationale des Ponts et Chaussées and TUM's Faculty of Civil Engineering and Ecole Centrale Paris with TUM's Faculty of Mechanical Engineering.

At the same time, the Ecole Centrale started to organize a network of Europe's most renowned universities in the field of technology with the goal of developing and promoting double degrees. This network is called T.I.M.E., for Top Industrial Managers Europe,[1] and it is mainly because of this initiative that TUM has so far signed a total of 46 double degree agreements in mechanical engineering (23); electrical engineering and information technology (8); civil, geo, and environmental engineering (5); informatics (4); life sciences (3); mathematics (1); physics (1); and economics (1).

The Faculty of Mechanical Engineering became the one that was the most open to such new curricular concepts and degree arrangements, signing umbrella agreements with many of the universities under the T.I.M.E. program. All told, this faculty has signed respective contracts with 23 out of the 53 T.I.M.E. members. The other engineering faculties followed, and 8 out of 13 faculties of TUM now offer the possibility for earning double degrees.

Definition

By a "joint degree" TUM and T.I.M.E. mean an integrated program with one document (diploma) at the end of the program issued by two or more of the institutions involved. Students spend more or less the same amount of time at each university and study in fixed, rigid curricula. Full recognition of the student's transcript is guaranteed.

The term *dual* is mainly used in a similar fashion to *joint* but avoids the legal restrictions that might occur by delivering a single diploma. Usually, there will be no extension of the period of study, and the language of instruction is English. Often dual is used to describe a preset program (e.g., an Erasmus Mundus Master course would be typically a dual). At TUM we don't use dual, to avoid confusion with the German phrase "dual education."

And finally the term *double degree*: We use it for all the programs where a prolongation of the studies is necessary or at least more credits have to be generated. Such courses are not preset. Students follow the normal courses, and after successful completion receive two separate degrees. Students have to experience the different didactic methods of teaching, and usually the language of instruction is the language of the country. To quote Professor Giancarlo Spinelli of the Politecnico di Milano: "Joint programs focus on similarities; the double degree takes advantage of differences."[2]

As TUM decided to follow the T.I.M.E. regulations, most of the agreements are so-called double degrees which implies a longer study time and extra credits (360 instead of 300 ECTS in general for five-year curricula).

TUM's Approach to Double Degrees

But why does TUM support the development of double degrees, and what is the specific interest in creating this tool for student exchange?

Double degrees were at the beginning only designed in the engineering faculties, but the other departments followed more and more frequently. They understand that this is a good opportunity to attract the best students from other universities. As opposed to Erasmus students, these exchange students stay for the full degree, and as they usually belong to the elite in the partner institution, they are also potential candidates for a PhD. The double degree student has to integrate completely; has to learn the respective language, and, in the three or four semesters he or she spends at the partner university, gains a deep insight into the way of life in the chosen country and a truly global mind-set. After this period the student will be familiar with the bureaucracy and other peculiarities in the guest country. He or she will be used to approaching problems from different points of view and adapting to a diverse cultural environment.

Because of these specific skills, the double degree students are also ideal candidates for global companies. These companies know that they can deploy the double degrees graduates not only in the countries they studied in for the double degree, but also throughout the world, because they have become accustomed to adapting to different conditions and circumstances.

Double degrees are a magnet for students interested in an ambitious international education. These programs attract the best from both countries involved. The students coming from abroad are no longer simply exchange students but degree-seeking, full-time students. They contribute significantly to the internationalization of the university.

But it is not only the demand by industry or the chance to gain talented PhD students that makes double degree arrangements attractive for TUM. The development of such courses and agreements leads naturally to a closer cooperation between institutions. Through respective negotiations, the partners learn more about each other and usually the links become closer. Often at the end of such a process the normal partnership has reached another level and can be called—to use a frequently falsely related term—a "strategic partnership." At TUM, we observe that after the successful completion of the discussions about a double degree, the universities, or at least the concerned faculties, stay in close contact and take advantage of this new familiarity for other projects. Often we find the same double degree partner in different projects, be they research proposals to the European Commission or Erasmus Mundus projects for third countries. The advantage after the establishment of a double degree is that both partners will become well acquainted with one another and will learn to trust and rely on each other.

At TUM, double degrees are developed through the respective faculties. It is a bottom-up process—at least in general. The faculties know best the partners that suit them for such a venture. Of course, sometimes the international office or the management of the university will recommend possible partners to a faculty, but it is up to them if they want follow the advice.

In 2010, TUM's board settled on a future policy concerning double degrees and published rules that the faculties have to follow when they design a new double degree. In addition, a document was published in which all the universities were listed with whom a double degree could be signed without problems ("Positivliste").[3] It was recognized that for more than 20 years double degrees with renowned partner institutions have helped to improve TUM's standing outside Germany and play an important role in the international perception and thus the international strategy of TUM.

TUM thus supports the development of new double degrees and encourages the faculties to consider agreements with distinguished institutions. Like its TU9 partners,[4] TUM supports the development of double degree master's programs only, and not on the bachelor's level.

Until now, most of the double degrees were developed with European partners. Only a few agreements have been signed with institutions outside of Europe. But the few are nicely spread over all the continents from Australia to Morocco. Recently, we have observed that more and more universities from all parts of the world that are seeking a partnership agreement want to discuss a double degree straight from the beginning. Interest in double degree agreements has spread, as obtaining qualifications from more than one country is seen as an advantage in the labor market. Here the university acts with caution and advises the same to the faculties. First, there should be no doubt about the quality of the partner institutions. Before a double degree is designed, a firm knowledge of each other in the concerned field is obligatory.

Challenges

When TUM started with the first double degree, it was a new kind of education for a small, elite group of students. The aim was to offer the students a different view of their study fields and to provide a deep cultural experience. The double degrees demand a certain dedication from the student both because of the language requirements and because of the extra amount of credits required. Over the years, more and more programs have been developed that were also called double degrees but without the workload we usually demand. For example, two-year master's level courses where one year was spent at the home and the other at the guest university awarded double degrees at the end. One can ask why every Erasmus exchange is not dignified by granting two degrees. The reason why these programs emerged is manifold: Sometimes it was because of legal constraints and sometimes because of the different attitude toward a master's degree (e.g., in the United States). Also the Erasmus Mundus program devaluated the classical double degrees. With the introduction of Erasmus followed by the Bologna process, Europe moved toward comparability for degree programs. Standardization does not, however, resolve all problems. It facilitates mobility and academic recognition but does not offer any guarantee of high quality of the exchange program. It is the task of the universities to illustrate the added value of their double degrees—particularly if no additional workload or language proficiency is required.

Even at TUM different ways of attaining double degrees could burgeon under the same roof. If the double degrees that follow the regulations mentioned above are to survive, we have to find ways to honor and to distinguish them from the vast number of programs existing in student exchange programs. T.I.M.E. answered this challenge by moving to create a "T.I.M.E. label certificate," which shall be issued with the double degree. But it will be the responsibility of each university to maintain and to promote this particularly sophisticated and excellent exchange opportunity for talented students.

NOTES

[1] https://www.time-association.org/dd/

[2] Spinelli, Giancarlo. (2009). Measuring the success of internationalisation: The case of joint and double degrees. In Hans de Wit (Ed.), *Measuring success in the internationalisation of higher education.* Amsterdam, the Netherlands: EAIE Occasional Paper 22.

[3] This list featured TUM's most important partner universities, partner institutions in TUM's strategic alliances, leading international schools with a similar profile as TUM, and universities with whom a double degree was already in place.

[4] TU9 is the alliance of leading Institutes of Technology in Germany: RWTH Aachen, TU Berlin, TU Braunschweig, TU Darmstadt, TU Dresden, Leibniz Universität Hannover, Karlsruhe Institute of Technology, TU München, and Universität Stuttgart. A total of 51 percent of all engineers with a university degree in Germany come from TU9 universities and 57 percent of all doctorates in engineering are awarded at TU9 universities. Roughly 15 percent of the students at TU9 universities are international students.

Chapter Eight

Increasing Research Capacity and Building and Retaining Skills: Stellenbosch University's Policy for Joint and Double Degree Programs

Dorothy Stevens, Stellenbosch University

Stellenbosch University is one of Africa's top research institutions. It is a medium-size, traditional university that delivers degree programs from bachelor's to doctoral level across a range of disciplines. Located in the heart of the Western Cape wineland region in the picturesque town of Stellenbosch, it offers a pleasant environment conducive to study and research, as well as a temperate climate and beautiful natural surroundings, which make of it a popular tourist destination in addition to being a university town. The main campus (eight faculties) is adjacent to the town center in Stellenbosch, with five additional campuses located in Bellville Park (Graduate School of Business and School of Public Leadership), Tygerberg (Medicine and Health Sciences), Worcester (Ukwanda Centre for Rural Health), and Saldanha (Military Sciences). Stellenbosch is 30 km from Cape Town International Airport and 50 km from Cape Town city center.

In South Africa there is a strong national drive to increase the number of postgraduates to meet the skill and knowledge demands of our economy, with the highest premium placed on the doctorate (Academy of Science for South Africa [ASSAf], 2010).

A seminal report that examined PhD training in South Africa by ASSAf delivered crucial insights into the challenges that South Africa faces in order to increase the number and quality of doctoral graduates that it produces. In its findings and recommendations, the ASSAf report points to the need to look beyond our borders for solutions to increasing the number of doctoral graduates given the systemic challenges in South Africa (ASSAf, 2010).

While the ASSAf report (2010) recommends joint supervision or ensuring international exposure for doctoral candidates through specific initiatives as means to enhance supervisory capacity, joint degrees[1] are not specifically identified as a mode for achieving the desired outcome of an increased number of high-quality PhD graduates. Examining the competitiveness of the PhD in Europe, O'Carroll, Purser, Wislocka, Lucey, & McGuinness (2012) are more specific in identifying collaborative research, cotutelle, and dual and joint degrees as important features to enhance doctoral training (O'Carroll et al., 2012).

While it cannot be expected that joint degrees can provide a mass solution to capacity shortcomings, and it is recognized that only a small number of candidates might follow this path, the concept remains important since it could be included in an institution's strategies to internationalize. Collaborative degree programs undoubtedly offer benefits to all the parties, despite the accompanying challenges that such programs inevitably represent (Bownes, Mather-L'Huillier, & Watson, 2010).

The perspective offered here for South Africa (and Africa) is that joint degrees as a mode of collaborative research have the potential to increase the number of high-quality PhD graduates while building and retaining skills and capacity.[2] Stellenbosch University regards joint and double degrees as vehicles of opportunity. This perspective must, however, be weighed against restraints and opportunities in South Africa. One restraint is the national regulatory framework within which we operate.

Developing an Institutional Policy

During 2007 and 2008, Stellenbosch University developed an institutional position on joint degrees in response to two imperatives. The first was the immigration of one or two highly productive, senior academics. There was a desire to formally continue existing collaboration, and the possibility to award joint degrees meant that Stellenbosch University would gain recognition for its academic input into joint projects while retaining postgraduate students in the process. This was and remains an attractive option, especially to a country where skills are scarce and brain retention is desirable.

The second imperative was the institution's commitment to engage in an agreement with an important industrial partner who set joint PhDs between Stellenbosch University and a foreign institution as a requirement for funding. The aim of the project was to develop capacity among South African graduates by exposing them to the expertise at the foreign institution in a strategically important field.

Of these two imperatives, the second resulted in Stellenbosch University actually developing an institutional policy. Various parties in South Africa and abroad who had experience were consulted, and advice and guidance was sought from the Department of Higher Education and Training (DHET) to ensure that even though South African policy documents did not make specific provision for joint or double degrees, by contemplating these and engaging in partnerships that could result in such awards, Stellenbosch University was not acting outside of the existing regulations.

The policy was formulated by a small group of senior officials with limited input from the broader academic environment. This could be perceived as top-down, but in reality it demonstrated responsiveness. A policy was adopted by the Senate in 2008: the "Stellenbosch University Policy Regarding Joint Doctoral Degrees."

At first the policy limited the scope to joint PhDs. The operational implementation of the policy was delegated to the Postgraduate and International Office (PGIO) at Stellenbosch University. The subsequent policy revisions and requests for entering into joint degree relationships have been egalitarian, and hands-on experiences have taught lessons that have fed directly into policy modification, where necessary. The policy has undergone two revisions (2010 and 2012). The first revision was to also allow for double master's degrees with foreign universities, and the 2012 revision was an effort to clarify our definitions and to incorporate things that we had learned from experience.

The "Stellenbosch University Policy Regarding Joint and Double Degrees at Master's and Doctoral Level with Foreign Universities 2012" defines joint and double degrees in the following manner:

A joint degree results from international academic collaboration between two or more institutions on a jointly defined and entirely shared study programme leading to a joint degree. This means that all partner institutions are responsible for the entire programme and not just their own separate parts.

A double degree results from international academic collaboration between two or more institutions on a jointly defined, but partially shared study programme with some areas being specific to each of the partners while other areas are shared and lead to a double degree. This means that partner institutions are responsible for their own separate parts (the parts are mutually recognized by the partners) but have a shared responsibility in respect of those parts of the programme which are shared.

The policy also offers guidelines for partnerships, including the conditions for entering into relationships that lead to joint and double degrees, and sets the specific factors that must be addressed in an agreement. The PGIO has developed guidelines to assist individuals in navigating the process, and it facilitates the development of individual agreements and ensures that the documentation works with the appropriate committees and follows the necessary channels to gain approval. Signed agreements are deposited with the PGIO, and post-enrollment administration is also managed through this office.

Collaborative Programs at Stellenbosch University

Stellenbosch University has established collaborative programs that involve joint or double degrees with several institutions, at the master's and/or doctoral level and across multiple fields. The majority of the partnerships are with European institutions, because in most cases, they have grown out of longstanding collaborative relationships with these institutions.

TABLE 8.1: STELLENBOSCH UNIVERSITY'S COLLABORATIVE PROGRAMS

Nature of Agreement[3]	Discipline	Partner Institution/s (date of original MOU)	Joint Program Established	Current Enrollments	Awarded
Joint PhD	Chemistry	St. Andrews University, Scotland (24 October 2005)	2010	1	0
Joint PhD	Mechanical Engineering/ Hydrogeology	École Nationale Supérieure des Mines de Saint-Etienne, France (February 19, 2010)	2010	1	0
Joint PhD	Plant Biotechnology	Ghent University, Belgium (July 23, 2008)	2011	1	0
Joint PhD	Mathematics	Vrije Universiteit Brussel (VUB), Belgium (February 13, 2004)	2011	1	0
Joint PhD	Physics	Friedrich Schiller University of Jena (FSU), Germany (March 12, 2008)	2011	0	1
Joint PhD	Social Sciences	University of Leipzig, Germany (May 26, 1999)	2011	1	0
Double Master's	German as a Foreign Language	University of Leipzig, Germany (May 26, 1999)	2011	5	2
Double Master's	Algorithm and Number Theory	ALGANT Consortium4 (April 23, 2009)	2010	4	1
Joint PhD	History, Education, Economics, Health Sciences	Vrije Universiteit (VU), The Netherlands (July 28, 2000)	2011	4	1
Double Masters	Development Economics	Georg-August-Universität Göttingen, Germany (September 28, 2005)	2012	1	0
Double PhD Program	Health Sciences	Karolinska Institutet, Sweden (January 12, 2012)	2012	0	0
Double PhD Program	Health Sciences, Social Sciences	Makerere University, Uganda (April 25, 2006)	2012	0	0
Joint PhD	Health Sciences	Universiteit Antwerpen, Belgium (November 1, 1996)	2012	1	0

Stellenbosch University is not the only South African university that has embarked on joint and double degree arrangements, but the activities in other universities are limited. Beyond South Africa there are pockets of experience in other African countries, but collaborative programs in the form of joint and double degrees remain new territory in a continental sense.[5]

Collaborative Degree Programs as Part of the Internationalization Strategy

Stellenbosch University's strategy with regard to developing collaborative degree programs complements its internationalization strategy in a number of important ways.[6] Stellenbosch University is committed to an outward-oriented role within South Africa, in Africa, and globally (see Stellenbosch University, Vision 2012 statement[7]). In its ongoing process of internationalization, Stellenbosch University seeks to have a diverse student and staff corps, deliver graduates who can integrate into the world as global citizens, and engage in partnerships that will enhance and support its capacity to discover, share, and apply knowledge.

Recognizing the importance of developing researchers at the postgraduate level, and particularly at the level of doctoral education, Stellenbosch University is aligned with international trends that increasingly see the internationalization of doctoral education as intrinsic to an internationalization strategy. It is our view that collaborative degree programs are one of the ultimate expressions of internationalization and address the ambition to deliver global citizens as well as globally competent and competitive researchers.

Stellenbosch University is part of an established, multilayered, international, and academic network that complements the extensive academic networks of individual researchers and research groups in academic departments. Engagement in collaborative degree programs is introducing an international dimension into the experience of being a postgraduate student at Stellenbosch University. This initiative also gives formal recognition to the academic collaboration that takes place in joint projects and greatly increases exposure to new ideas and facilities that may not be available in South Africa. In this manner, Stellenbosch University is retaining and strengthening human capacity while gaining expertise through international exposure.

Requirements for Selecting Partners

When Stellenbosch University decides[8] which foreign universities to partner with for joint or double degrees, the following six requirements as a whole must be met in a substantial manner:

1. The partnership must fit in within the vision and mission of Stellenbosch University and contribute to attaining the institution's goals.

2. Stellenbosch University must benefit from the cooperation with the particular foreign university.

3. The foreign university must have the appropriate expertise in the research area in which the joint or double degree can be awarded.

4. Stellenbosch University and the partner institution(s) must have the appropriate expertise in the research area in which the joint or double degree can be awarded.

5. There must be reasonable prospects of student movement to and from Stellenbosch University and the foreign university.

6. The number of agreements for the awarding of joint and double degrees is limited to agreements that have reasonable prospects of sustainability and active functioning based on a proven track record of collaboration between the institutions.

Stellenbosch University will only award joint or double degrees on the basis of an agreement to be concluded at institutional level, and such an agreement must include or refer to a memorandum of understanding (MOU) for the awarding of joint or double degrees. This MOU must include at least the following items and stipulations:

- Full compliance with all the national and institutional regulations for the awarding of master's or doctoral degrees of both Stellenbosch University and the foreign university.

- Full compliance with the quality assurance requirements and procedures of both Stellenbosch University and the foreign university[9].

- A liaison mechanism for coordinating the master's or doctoral degree between appointed representatives from the different institutions.

- The requirements and procedures for the recruitment, admission, selection, and registration of students.

- Regulations regarding the periods of residency at Stellenbosch University and the foreign university.

- Supervision.

- Examination.
  - The composition and functioning of the joint examination committee.
  - The recommendation of the joint examination committee applies to all institutions (neither Stellenbosch University or the other institution(s) may afterwards award the relevant degree if the joint examination committee did not recommend it).

- Procedures for the handling of student complaints
- Disciplinary measures
- Intellectual property
- Certification and diploma supplement information
- Formalities for the graduation ceremony[10]

Challenges

The main challenge that Stellenbosch University has faced in entering into collaborative degree programs that have joint and double degrees as outcomes has been the absence of specific national regulations addressing the establishment and provision of joint and double degrees. The DHET in South Africa has only as recently as 2012 appointed a task team to develop a national policy and guidelines in respect of joint and double degree programs in tandem with their efforts to draft an internationalization policy.[11] In fact, the establishment of this task team was prompted by interactions between senior Stellenbosch University officials and the DHET. This is a rather unusual order of events, since the expectation would normally be that a national policy should have preceded institutional policy. Nonetheless, if one understands the higher education policy context in South Africa, it is hardly surprising that a policy addressing collaborative degree programs would hardly have received priority attention when considering the myriad other pressing issues that the DHET had to attend to, especially since the advent of democracy in 1994. It was in this spirit that Stellenbosch University acted.

The significant further challenges that Stellenbosch University has encountered have related to definitions, certification of the qualification, differences in the structure of education systems (credit transfer and the level of recognition), and differences in national intellectual property law.

The outcome of joint and double degrees is a single qualification because the partner institutions cannot award the qualifications independently of one another. The fundamental difference from single degrees (awarded by only one institution) therefore lies in the shared nature of the jointly defined study program (known as the "deed") leading to a joint or double degree, and therefore also the depth of the collaboration. Joint degrees lie at one end of a continuum indicating the highest level of collaboration; double degrees, at a further point on the continuum; and toward the other end of the continuum, single degrees (awarded by only one institution). Most of Stellenbosch's joint degree arrangements pertain to research-only degree programs, that is, those without any structured content requiring mutual recognition.

Double degrees are normally more applicable to programs where there are different coursework components offered by the partners (for which there is mutual credit recognition) contributing to the whole, and where the thesis constitutes the shared component through joint thesis supervision and joint examination. For a double master's level degree to be awarded by Stellenbosch University, a candidate must have completed a minimum of 50 percent of the total South African credits for the degree at Stellenbosch University and up to a maximum of 50 percent of the credits at the partner university, leading to the total number of credits required for the degree. Students must at all times be enrolled at Stellenbosch University for the minimum duration required for the master's degree (one year) or doctoral degree (two years).

The manner in which joint and double degrees can be certified (the resultant certificates or diplomas) is generally dictated by the national and legal requirements in each country. Where a country's legislation allows for the award of joint degrees, it is useful to follow the guidelines offered by the Lisbon Convention[12] regarding certification because they allow for flexibility across incompatible national systems, and they protect the national recognition of the candidate's qualification.

Stellenbosch University has a preference for two or more national diplomas[13] (which equal degree certificates) issued officially as the only attestation of the qualification in question with the proviso that each degree certificate must refer to the joint nature of the qualification and have an inscription on each that indicates that the qualification is conferred in conjunction with another institution(s) and together represent the one single deed.

Differences in the structure of various countries' education systems are probably more problematic at the transition from bachelor's to master's degrees than at the doctoral level, but it is acknowledged that candidates are not all equally well-prepared. The appearance of new styles of doctoral training is in part a reaction to this conundrum. It is anticipated that the emergence of such structured doctoral training may impact on the format that is agreed upon in joint arrangements.

In our experience, negotiation and a degree of compromise are required in order to conclude joint and double degree agreements. Our norm is to err on the side of caution in our compromises, so that candidates especially for double degrees tend to have to do slightly more coursework to fulfill the requirements of both partner institutions and, in so doing, ultimately receive the prestigious award which is conferred by the partners. A high degree of integration and mutual recognition of content is the preferred outcome.

Intellectual property law in South Africa favors the institution above the individual researcher with respect to ownership of new innovations or ideas discovered or developed while in the employ or during enrollment at the institution. In some other countries, the intellectual property is vested with the individual researcher. This aspect of incompatibility between different legal systems has had to be carefully negotiated and it must be emphasized that solutions are possible, as are options for mitigation and arbitration in case of possible disputes.

Future Prospects

The future prospects for collaborative degree programs at Stellenbosch University are exceptionally positive. Since making it more generally known within the confines of the Stellenbosch University community, there have been regular requests for more information from staff and students as well as current and prospective partners. It must be emphasized that the uptake is low, but this is entirely predictable. It is a protracted process to conclude all the formalities required to enroll for a joint or double degree. Stellenbosch University has also purposefully decided not to open up the possibility of joint or double degrees with foreign universities on a large scale. The strict requirements have been put in place to ensure quality and to enable the university to keep firm control while institutional learning takes place and experience is gained.

Other challenges that are likely to keep the pool of eligible candidates limited are funding constraints, given that the very nature of collaborative programs involves mobility, which significantly adds to the expense of enrolling for postgraduate studies. With the expansion of Erasmus Mundus funding to African institutions and the fact that Stellenbosch University has been a successful partner in Action 1 and 2 projects as well as INTRA-ACP projects, more opportunities have opened up, and it is entirely feasible that some of these enrollments may develop into joint or double degrees.

Stellenbosch University is gradually building experience in the implementation of collaborative programs and can thus only share initial impressions of what the impact of these have been. They clearly represent an expansion of opportunities for students to formally complete their qualification through a partner, grant access to facilities and complementary expertise available at the partner institution, and represent a prestigious option as well as formalizing the research collaboration between academics who have potentially been collaborating informally. These impacts are thus similar to those reported by other countries in the Institute of International Education's recent report (Obst, Kuder, & Banks, 2011). Currently, we do not have an evaluation plan in place specifically for collaborative programs, but it is anticipated that any existing arrangements will be subject to the same evaluation as all other programs at Stellenbosch University.[14] As time goes by and as more formal thinking crystallizes in the national context, we will also become more experienced in this field and will thus be better placed to comment on the specific impacts of collaborative programs at Stellenbosch University.

NOTES

1. Joint and double degrees in this chapter are seen as particular expressions of collaborative programs. There are also other forms of collaborative programs, such as sandwich programs, twinning programs, etc.

2. This challenges the assumption that exposure to another context through a joint enrollment will necessarily result in the loss of a candidate. Instead it is proposed that joint degree enrollment ensures retention of the young researcher in the local system while he or she gains exposure and experience.

3. Joint degree refers to cotutelle arrangements; double PhD program refers to cases that have a prescribed jointly defined study program.

4. Consisting of Université Bordeaux 1, France; Chennai Mathematical Institute, India; Universiteit Leiden, The Netherlands; Università degli Studi di Milano, Italy; Concordia University/CRM/ISM, Canada; Università degli Studi di Padova, Italy; Université Paris Sud 11, France; and Stellenbosch University/AIMS, South Africa.

5. Examples of collaborative programs, some of which include joint and double degrees: http://www.jamp.org.za/, http://www.bigsas.uni-bayreuth.de/en/partner_universities/index.html, and http://ki.se/ki/jsp/polopoly.jsp?a=68451&d=38524&l=en

6. As Jansen, McLellan, and Greene (2008) explained, even though there is no national policy on the internationalization of higher education, this does not mean that there aren't practices in place and various expressions of internationalization in South Africa. Institutions pursue their internationalization activities with different degrees of institutional policy direction.

7. http://www.sun.ac.za/university/StratPlan/stratdocs.htm

8. Each joint program must be approved by an institutional Academic Planning Committee, which consists of senior staff (deans and or vice deans responsible for teaching and research, as well as other senior academics and administrative officials). This committee contemplates each new arrangement and recommends acceptance to the university Senate or declines and refers cases back to the PGIO. This process is thus institutionally centralized, because the decision to jointly award qualifications requires a high level of cooperation and is regarded as a deep mutual institutional commitment.

9. This takes into account that especially with reference to quality assurance, more policy development at the national and multinational levels is required.

10. Paragraph 10.6 of Stellenbosch University Policy Regarding Joint and Double Degrees at Master's and Doctoral Level with Foreign Universities 2012.

11. http://www.universityworldnews.com/article.php?story=20120908113523552

12. The Lisbon Convention states that:

    "A joint degree may be issued as:

    a) a joint diploma in addition to one or more national diplomas,

    b) a joint diploma issued by the institutions offering the study programme in question without being accompanied by any national diploma,

    c) one or more national diplomas issued officially as the only attestation of joint qualification in question." ("Recommendation on the Recognition of Joint Degrees adopted by the Committee of the Convention on the Recognition of Qualifications concerning Higher Education in the European Region," June 9, 2004, https://wcd.coe.int/wcd/ViewDoc.jsp?id=836481&Site=COE)

13. The term "national diploma" used in this chapter, in accordance with international practice, refers to the paper document or certificate detailing the qualification that has been awarded. It should not be confused with the term "National Diploma," which in the South African context refers to a specific qualification at a particular level in the National Qualification Framework.

[14] Stellenbosch University meets its obligations in terms of the national system of quality assurance (as stipulated by the Higher Education Act, Act 101, of 1997, in particular Chapter 2, and that are required from the university as a public system of higher education) through a well-established and comprehensive institutional quality assurance framework. Within this framework, academic programs are evaluated every six years.

REFERENCES

Academy of Science of South Africa (ASSAf). (2010). *The PhD study: An evidence-based study on how to meet the demands for high-level skills in an emerging economy.* Pretoria, South Africa: Author.

Bownes, M., Mather-L'Huillier, N., & Watson, D. (2010). *A Scottish perspective in an international context— Objectives of joint doctoral programmes and challenges for their development.* Retrieved from https://www.joiman.eu/ProjectResults/PublicDeliverables/Papers/PHD_Scottish_perspective_BOWNES_MAT HER_HUILLIER_WATSON.pdf

Jansen, J., McLellan, C., & Greene, R., (2008). South Africa. In D. Teferra & J. Knight (Eds.), *Higher education in Africa: The international dimension.* Accra/Boston: AAU.

O'Carroll, C., Purser, L., Wislocka, M., Lucey, S., & McGuinness, N. (2012). The PhD in Europe: Developing a system of doctoral training that will increase the internationalisation of universities. In A. Curaj, P. Scott, L. Vlasceanu, & L. Wilson (Eds.), *European higher education at the crossroads between the Bologna process and national reforms.* Dordrecht, Germany: Springer.

Obst, D., Kuder, M., & Banks, C. (2011). Joint and double degree programs in the global context: Report on an international survey (white paper). New York, NY: Institute of International Education. Retrieved from http://www.iie.org/Research-and-Publications/Publications-and-Reports/IIE-Bookstore/ Joint-Degree-Survey-Report-2011

Chapter Nine

Engaging Globally through Joint and Double Degree Programs: National University of Singapore's Internationalization Strategy

BERNARD C. Y. TAN, NATIONAL UNIVERSITY OF SINGAPORE

Overview

Each year, the National University of Singapore (NUS) admits more than 6,500 undergraduate students from Singapore and beyond. Although NUS is consistently ranked among the top 30 in various international university ranking exercises, the competition for high-quality undergraduate students is intense. The trend of globalization suggests that it is very important for universities to offer undergraduate students some level of international exposure. The emergence of knowledge between disciplines suggests that it is very important for universities to provide undergraduate students with interdisciplinary exposure. In the competition to attract high-quality undergraduate students, NUS has attempted to address both issues by offering collaborative programs in the past decade—collaborative programs involving partner universities started in 2004.

There are three major categories of collaborative programs for undergraduate students in NUS:

a. *Concurrent degree programs* combine a bachelor's degree with a master's degree. Sometimes involving two institutions, such programs allow students to pursue both degrees concurrently. The structure of such programs typically allows some of the requirements for the bachelor's degree to also be counted toward the master's degree. Thus, students can save 6 to 12 months when they pursue both degrees concurrently compared to doing both degrees separately. Currently, NUS offers 18 Concurrent Degree Programs (10 of which involve partner universities such as Carnegie Mellon University, New York University, Brown University, Georgia Institute of Technology, Cambridge University, and King's College London),

b. *Double degree programs* combine two bachelor's degrees from two different disciplines. Besides sharing a common set of university level requirements for both degrees, such programs allow some modules to be double counted toward the requirements of both degrees, thus enabling students to save up to two years when completing both degrees together compared to pursuing both degrees separately. Currently, NUS offers 45 double degree programs (five of which involve partner universities such as Waseda University, New York University, and University of Waterloo).

c. *Joint degree programs* combine the strengths of the curricula of two institutions, as well as integrate international experience fully into the course of study. Such programs are jointly taught by two institutions, and the qualification offered upon graduation is validated by both institutions (i.e., one degree certificate carrying the names of both institutions). These distinctive programs confer degrees that are different from the degrees offered in either institution. Currently, NUS offers five joint degree programs with overseas partner universities (such as Australian National University, University of North Carolina at Chapel Hill, and Johns Hopkins University).

The enrolments for collaborative programs have increased steadily over time (as shown in Table 9.1, for the recent three academic years).

TABLE 9.1: RECENT ENROLLMENTS FOR COLLABORATIVE PROGRAMS

Program Type	Academic Year 2010–2011	Academic Year 2011–2012	Academic Year 2012–2013
Concurrent degree program	119	128	133
Double degree program	204	258	317
Joint degree program	151	141	161
Total	474	527	611

Rationale for NUS Internationalization Strategy

The NUS internationalization strategy, which was laid out about a decade ago, has three key foci: (a) building strong global partnerships, (b) attracting top talents from all parts of the world, and (c) promoting student mobility internationally. NUS adopts a two-pronged approach to maintain its position as a leader in global education by bringing the world into NUS and taking our students out to the world. At present, about 1,600 students from our partner universities come to NUS, and about 1,600 NUS students go to our partner universities annually for student exchange (for at least one semester). Student exchange numbers have increased significantly in recent years. Student exchange opportunities allow our students to live and learn independently in a foreign environment away from home. Students often get to take courses not available at NUS. Students who have been through such programs typically develop a global outlook, intercultural understanding, and a network of friends around the world. In some cases, they acquire proficiency in a new foreign language.

Collaborative programs are an important part of the internationalization strategy of NUS. These programs offer our students differentiated learning pathways and help to enrich their campus experience to make this memorable for a lifetime. Designed to attract the best students, these programs have stringent admissions requirements, but provide students with a variety of unique learning opportunities. For a moderately higher workload compared to a single degree, students get to focus on two different disciplines (and in some cases, at two institutions in different parts of the world). Such exposure to multiple cultures and multiple disciplines helps to broaden the minds of students to prepare them for a global marketplace.

Over the years, collaborative programs have (by increasing the options available to students) helped to enhance the attractiveness of NUS as a place of study. Many high-quality students from Singapore and beyond have applied for these programs, because they want a challenging learning environment in which they can grow intellectually and socially. In some instances, collaborative programs have also facilitated research collaboration among faculty members from NUS and our partner institutions.

The rationale for collaborative programs includes producing talents for emerging industries in Singapore. Given that an increasing number of new jobs now sit between disciplines, students who have completed these collaborative programs tend to be in a favorable position to take up new job opportunities and thereby command higher salaries. It would be useful to track the career progression of these students over time.

Approval Process for Collaborative Programs

Collaborative programs are usually initiated by the faculties or schools in consultation with the Office of the Provost. Where partner institutions are involved, the quality of partner institutions (for the relevant disciplines) is a key factor in determining whether the programs will eventually be approved. In addition, the mix of disciplines proposed for the programs is scrutinized for the value this can generate (e.g., good fit with emerging pockets of job opportunities). Thus, the approval of collaborative programs undergoes a rigorous process with established guidelines.

Prior to initiating discussion with partner institutions, the faculties or schools consult the Office of the Provost to seek in-principle approval to allow them to craft the proposals (this is not an indication of final approval). All proposals have to be submitted on a standard template, which includes the rationale for the program, the benefit of the program to prospective students, the structure of the program, the learning outcomes of the program, the quality assurance process of the program, and the fit of the program with the NUS educational philosophy and framework, among others.

In their justification for the program, the faculties or schools have to explain how the program is able to provide NUS students with learning opportunities that would otherwise not be available, how the program can help students develop professional skills in ways that would otherwise not be possible, or how the program can contribute to the international stature of NUS, among others. Established guidelines are available to help the faculties or schools decide on the precise setup of such programs, such as the management structure (e.g., a joint steering committee), admissions requirements (which are sufficiently stringent given the demands of such programs), residency requirements, curricula requirements, period of candidature, transfer of credits, continuation and termination of candidature, and grading and graduation requirements.

Upon submission, thorough scrutiny of these proposals is carried out by the University Committee on Educational Policy, which reviews the policy aspects of the proposal. Following this, the Board of Graduate Studies and/or the Board of Undergraduate Studies examines the operational and technical aspects of the proposal to make sure the programs (if approved) can be run smoothly. The final approval comes from the NUS Senate.

During the operation of collaborative programs, specific attention is put on critical issues such as coordination among partnering faculties or schools (including partner institutions, where applicable), selection and advising of students (to help them negotiate the complexities of such programs), and monitoring of student progress (to make sure they can cope with the rigors of such programs). Quality assurance of such programs is carried out regularly through examining employment indicators, examining enrolment indicators, consulting industry leaders, and conducting joint reviews of program details periodically, among others.

The University Committee on Educational Policy has oversight of all collaborative programs and has the authority to scrutinize the ongoing feasibility of such programs. In the process of quality assurance, when indicators and feedback for specific collaborative programs reveal that the value propositions of these programs no longer exist, then these programs will be discontinued.

Challenges

While collaborative programs are a part of the NUS international strategy and an effective means for NUS to compete for and attract strong students in Singapore and beyond, there are significant challenges involved in the establishment of such programs.

First, the negotiation process among institutions is complex. Although collaborative programs that involve NUS and other top institutions are attractive to strong students (because of the global dimension of learning), much time and effort is always needed to negotiate the approval process of both institutions. Cultural and philosophical differences among institutions can sometimes be major hurdles. Furthermore, partner institutions may be governed by their national laws and policies regarding collaborative programs, and these laws and policies must be adhered to strictly.

Second, finding good complementarities among disciplines is not a straightforward task. While it is common knowledge that new job opportunities tend to emerge between disciplines, there are numerous possibilities for combining disciplines to create collaborative programs. It is never easy to predict which combinations of disciplines will yield optimal outcomes in the future. Such uncertainties are mitigated through examining the practices of leading universities globally and consulting with industry leaders.

Third, the faculties or schools tend to be more eager to propose new collaborative programs than to review (and possibly discontinue) existing collaborative programs. This is not surprising given the desire of the faculties or schools to be competitive internationally. The more options they have that can help them attract strong students, the better. Nevertheless, the administration of collaborative programs can be costly in terms of overhead, and the proportion of students enrolled in these programs is relatively small compared to the overall student population in NUS (less than 10 percent of NUS students are enrolled in collaborative programs; less 5 percent of NUS students are enrolled in collaborative programs involving partner universities). Hence, the faculties or schools have to make the necessary trade-offs when managing their portfolio of collaborative programs.

In spite of these challenges, it is clear that collaborative programs have helped NUS attract some of the best students from Singapore and beyond in the past decade. Indeed, a growing number of students enrolled in NUS have affirmed that collaborative programs are their reason for coming to NUS. This is also likely to be the case for other leading universities in the world. Given that the global competition for talented students is likely to continue (perhaps at an even more intense pace in the future), collaborative programs are likely to remain a key feature in the educational offerings of NUS in the years to come.

Chapter Ten

The MSc Integrated Water Resources Management: A German-Jordanian Master Program

Lars Ribbe, Cologne University of Applied Sciences, Manar Fayyad, Jordan University, and Joern Trappe, Cologne University of Applied Sciences

Introduction

The Institute for Technology and Resource Management in the Tropics and Subtropics (ITT) at Cologne University of Applied Sciences (CUAS) and the Water, Energy and Environment Center (WEEC) at Jordan University run a collaborative master's degree program called Integrated Water Resources Management (IWRM). Funded by the German Federal Ministry for Economic Cooperation and Development (BMZ), this cooperative endeavor started in June 2006, and in September 2007 the first intake of students started their studies.

The objective of the MSc IWRM is to educate students to ultimately become experts who are well trained in the field of water resources management. Beyond the technical and managerial knowledge related to water resources, these experts should be familiar with the practices of project funding and international cooperation and be able to work in international, interdisciplinary environments. Furthermore, the MSc IWRM program aims at promoting the concept of IWRM within the context of European–Arab cooperation. Target groups of the program are recently graduated professionals with working experience in public or private institutions, authorities, and enterprises of the water sector. The participants should be active in or dealing with water or natural resources management, and have an interest in learning and working in an intercultural and multidisciplinary environment.

Status Quo and Achievements

The master's program is offered as a double degree. Participants receive two degrees, one from each university. The study course is designed for a small number of qualified students (up to 20 participants). The first semester takes place in Jordan, and the second semester is in Germany. During the third semester, students are preparing a master's thesis with relevance to water-related concerns in the Arab world. The language of instruction is English, and students are offered extracurricular Arabic and German language courses. As of January 2013, five intakes have finished the program with a total of 69 graduates.

The program participants are selected out of a total of approximately 60 applicants each year and shortlisted on the basis of their (a) previous studies and grades, (b) curriculum vitae, (c) letters of motivation, (d) suggested project proposals, and (e) English proficiency. The number of applicants is growing, with additional requests coming from Asia, Sub-Saharan Africa, Latin America, Europe, Canada, Australia, and the United States.

The course of study aims at a composition of students from different scientific backgrounds, in order to promote an interdisciplinary learning environment and exchange of multiple methods and viewpoints related to water resources management.

To date, most students were either re-employed or found an adequate job with another employer in the field of IWRM in the Arab region or at funding agencies in Germany. Almost all graduates improved their working conditions and status after graduation. The following presents a glimpse on the placement of alumni in the market (public and private entities working in the water sector):

- Water utilities
- Ministries and water authorities (water resources, irrigation, agriculture, and environment in different Arab countries)
- Water resources research institutes
- Consultancy companies and offices in Arab countries and Germany
- Non-governmental organizations

- International organizations (UN-ESCWA, BGR, UNDP, Global Water Partnership)
- German Association for International Cooperation (GIZ) (e.g., GIZ Jordan, Palestine, Syria, Morocco, BGR)
- KfW Development Bank, Germany
- Universities and international research projects
- Universities (PhD)

Cooperation and Network

Beyond education, the MSc IWRM has succeeded in providing a platform of dialogue and cooperation for researchers in both universities and associated organizations. In 2011 the Amman-Cologne Symposium was established to support the scientific dialogue in the field of IWRM. Under the patronage of HRH Prince Hassan bin Talal and HRH Princess Sumaya bin el Hassan, two public symposia were conducted in 2012: "Water and Energy Nexus" and "Water for Green Economy in the MENA Region." Both aimed at identifying best-practice approaches, cooperative strategies, and future fields for research and application in water and energy resources. To promote green economic growth, they brought together academia, governmental institutions, and the private sector in the region and from Germany.

In 2013 the MSc IWRM program was a co-organizer of the second Arab Water Week, together with the Arab Countries Water Utilities Association (ACUWA). Alumni activities are actively incorporated into the continuously growing network of IWRM. A first IWRM alumni meeting was organized in January 2011 parallel to the graduation process of the third intake and the public symposium.

Establishment of the Program and Institutional Strategies

The MSc IWRM program was initiated as a response for the call of proposals initiated by BMZ to establish bicultural master programs between German universities and universities in Arab countries. A delegation of ITT visited several universities in Jordan (2006), and finally a partnership was established where the highest level of mutual interest was visible. The selection considered aspects such as research interests, similar content of existing MSc programs, and experience in offering postgraduate courses. A proposal submitted to the German Academic Exchange Service (DAAD) was ultimately selected to conduct the MSc IWRM program.

At the time Jordan University did not have a clear goal of becoming an international university. By now, that goal has solidified, and one of the main objectives is to continue international cooperation by the establishment of more international double and joint programs. Jordan University regards the MSc IWRM program and its achievements as highly effective and valuable. It is considered an example of successful cooperation between universities from different countries.

CUAS and especially ITT have a long history of international cooperation projects and maintain a vast network of university partnerships mainly with higher education institutions from Latin America, Africa, and Asia and—to a lesser extent—with partners in Europe and North America.

The ITT offers various master programs related to natural resources management with special emphasis on tropical and subtropical regions. All postgraduate programs stress a holistic interdisciplinary approach covering environmental, ecological, agronomic, and socioeconomic aspects of the management of natural resources.

Some of the master's programs are offered together with partners abroad to provide students with the chance to study in different settings and gain insights into other cultural, environmental, and social realities. Together with the Autonomous University of San Luis Potosi, a four-semester double degree program called Environment and Resources Management (ENREM),[1] has been offered since 2008. In Vietnam ITT offers a master course together with the Vietnam Academy for Water Resources (TERMA VN).[2] It is an exported version of the same degree program offered in at CUAS in Cologne, with a focus on water resources management.

Both WEEC and ITT have advanced significantly through the establishment of the MSc IWRM. Both institutions aim to achieve excellence in research and education on sustainable resources management. Under the framework of the common master program, both partners benefitted from the specific expertise in relation to the niche market of IWRM in the Middle East and North Africa (MENA) region. The Jordanian partners, in particular, could bring local knowledge and experience, while in Germany experts— including Germans and other partners of ITT around the globe—could offer knowledge from their industrial experience. The joint master program offers its common students an education with excellent job opportunities, which an education at only one of the two study sites alone would not be able to offer. Good market prospects for the graduates mean direct benefits regarding reputation and a productive alumni network—benefits that the two partners will ideally be able to harness in the years to come.

To summarize, the motivation for both parties to enter into the cooperation were manifold:

- It strengthens partnerships and deepens relationships toward successful proposals beyond teaching (bilateral or multilateral research and training partnerships).

- It offers students the opportunity to have part of their education abroad.

- Providing a systematic recognition of modules at partner universities means no waste of time for individual exchange processes with arbitrarily chosen universities and provides for efficient exchange modalities.

- The curricula are enriched with expertise from the partner countries, for example, jointly elaborated teaching modules (content + case studies from multiple countries).

- In the future the collaboration is expected to deepen and focus on increasing the scope and quality of the products offered together, in particular to increase the attractiveness of the master course to people from the Gulf countries as well as other parts of the world.

- Looking at the lessons learned, the following criteria could be formulated as recommendations for establishing new joint programs:

- Resources: Capacities and commitment from within each university need to be guaranteed along with the option to obtain external funding.

- Quality: Will the quality of the resultant program be at minimum as high as the current quality at both sides? A compromise leading to lower quality, even for a transitional period, is unlikely to be successful. Quality assurance in a bilateral program requires much more effort than in a single degree program.

- Mutual interest: Will both parties gain? How can you quantify the win-win situation?

- Caretaker: Will there be a staff member at each university with responsibility for the program? Institutional linkages alone are not sufficient.

Quality Assurance

The master's program is accredited at both universities. Jordan University has an internal accreditation process with reporting obligations to the Ministry of Higher Education. The accreditation took place in 2008 and the re-accreditation in 2012. At CUAS an external accreditation company conducted the accreditation in 2008, with re-accreditation scheduled for 2013.

To fulfill all the requirements of each university, the curriculum was developed together in several workshops. Lecturers and staff from both institutions discussed and arranged the structure and the content of each module with the aim of providing a competence-oriented master's program. The program was revised and refined in the first three years, making use of several instruments of quality assurance.

A course coordination committee consisting of course coordinators, professors, and staff of both involved institutions meet regularly to organize the strategic and operational management of the course. At least once a year university leadership participates in the meetings.

Regular evaluation of all modules and lecturers provides the ability to adjust modules and identify demand for capacity development of the lecturers. A program evaluation through a commission established by Deutsche Gesellschaft für Internationale Zusammenarbeit (GIZ) and DAAD took place in 2011. Alumni surveys and close contacts to the alumni community permit feedback to be obtained from graduates regarding the relevance of the study content and overall satisfaction with the study program.

Lecturer seminars, which take place at least once a year, are an additional pillar of quality assurance. During these seminars, the optimization potential of the program is discussed, with lectures and support regarding didactical and pedagogical competencies provided to the lecturers.

From the beginning, an advisory board consisting of German, Jordanian, and international experts from administration, research, international cooperation institutions, and the private sector was established. The board provides guidance on course content, relationships with the job market, funding, and cooperation potential. The board consist of members from the following institutions:

- GIZ (Deutsche Gesellschaft für Internationale Zusammenarbeit)
- KfW Development Bank
- BGR (Federal Institute for Geosciences and Natural Resources)
- DWA (German Association for Water, Wastewater and Waste)
- Dorsch International Consultants
- UN-ESCWA (United Nations Economic and Social Commission for Western Asia)
- RSS (Royal Scientific Society)
- CEDARE (Center for Environment and Development for the Arab Region and Europe)
- ACWUA (Arab Countries Water Utilities Association)
- DAAD (German Academic Exchange Service)

Experiences and Challenges

Running a collaborative program successfully requires a tremendous effort: communication, mobility, and motivation of all involved individuals—especially in the establishment phase! This effort goes far beyond running a home-grown master's course; thus the expected benefits should be clearly formulated and, if possible, quantified to ensure that the extra effort is worthwhile.

WEEC and ITT faced multiple challenges during development and implementation, such as:

- Different learning and teaching cultures.

- Different legislation and administrative processes and cultures.

- Financial difficulties arose in the later phase but significant resources were required at both universities at any time. Without the appropriate initial funding provided by BMZ, the MSc IWRM would not have been established.

In addition, the lack of administrative experience and legislation regarding international programs at Jordan University pose continuous challenges for the program sustainability.

In 2014 the core funding of the project provided through BMZ will come to an end. This confronts the two organizing institutions with a huge challenge. In Germany no study fees can be levied. Both universities have undertaken efforts to meet this challenge by defining and evaluating cost-reducing measures, such as introducing special tuition or excursion fees, verifying external funding options, or reducing personnel and travel expenses.

A further concrete measure toward the sustainability of the MSc IWRM program is the national accreditation of the course in Jordan with the aim to run it as a national program, which would allow it to register students not going to Germany in the second semester. In Cologne options of joining modules of the MSc IWRM with other master programs are currently being scrutinized. The transformation of the MSc IWRM program into a financially independent institution, however, cannot yet be achieved under the current dimension of the program. Strong efforts from both sides are being undertaken to sustain the program after funding is over.

Perspectives

Both universities have reiterated their commitment to continuing the collaborative master program IWRM. The master's program is considered as a successful example of a collaborative effort of the two universities toward one common goal. As the funding from

BMZ will phase out, new forms of funding need to be explored. Recently, several students were supported by funding institutions other than DAAD (e.g., the Arab Fund). Further potential donors are now being addressed. Self-paying students may play a bigger role in the future, even though the willingness to pay for such a program is considered as rather low, as so far most employers typically belong to the public domain with rather unattractive salaries.

Both universities are currently enhancing their capacities regarding web-based communication and e-learning. This will open up opportunities to intensify communication within the coordination team without increasing travel costs. For teaching, e-learning modules are already employed and will be developed further in order to take part in web-based trainings and webinars, while reducing travel costs of teachers and students alike.

Conclusion

The impacts of the collaborative master programs have been very positive for the two participating institutions, WEEC and ITT. The program supported the strategic goals of internationalization. The example from the MSc IWRM served as a basis to establish further programs, and it is considered a key point of departure for the future internationalization strategy as they provide a systematic and long-lasting institutional framework for international educational collaboration and research cooperation.

Even though the efforts have been very intense during the establishment phase, we conclude that the benefits outweigh the costs. Thus we consider our endeavors toward cooperation at the postgraduate level as successful and intend to intensify the efforts in this direction for the benefit of students, staff, and the institutions as a whole.

Promoting scientific excellence, providing support to societal development and—just as important—building bridges between cultures, the IWRM MSc Program provides an excellent opportunity to function as role model for international university cooperation.

NOTES

[1] MSc ENREM, supported by BMZ, BMBF, and CONACYT; for further information, see www.enrem-master.info

[2] MSc TERMA-VN, supported by DAAD; for further information, see www.termavn-master.info

Chapter Eleven

Double Degree Programs at a Brazilian Research University: The Case of Unicamp

Leandro R. Tessler and José Pissolato Filho, Universidade Estadual de Campinas (Unicamp)

Overview

Until very recently, Brazilian higher education was practically isolated from the rest of the world (Tessler, 2012). The whole system was self-referenced, with local practices and idiosyncrasies. The drive for internationalization started just a few years ago. However, already in the late 1990s, the engineering schools of six Brazilian universities (PUC-Rio, UFC, UFRGS, UFRJ, Unicamp, and USP) were actively engaged in establishing double degree programs. At Universidade Estadual de Campinas (Unicamp) we define double degrees as the programs in which the student is awarded two degrees and certificates, one from Unicamp and one from the partner institution.

The concept of double degree was introduced in Brazil by French partners and is the result of long-term cooperation with French institutions with the support of the Brazilian agency CAPES. During the 1990s the European context was very favorable for academic mobility. The Bologna process established the drive to have students do part of their studies in a different country. In Brazil, a group of engineering professors who had been partly educated in France convinced CAPES that it could be interesting to sponsor a pilot program of international mobility for the top engineering students. Thus, the first "sandwich" programs were established. As the name implies, the students would study during the first and last years in Brazil and spend the middle years abroad. The excellent academic performance of the first students sent to France motivated the Ecoles Centrales to propose double degree programs. Establishing such programs was a challenge: The Ecoles Centrales are known for providing a very broad engineering education, in contrast to the Brazilian tradition of focused professional training. Brazilians count credits as the number of weekly hours in the classroom; Europeans use ECTS. Moreover, the dephasing between the northern and southern hemispheres imposed an extra year for students who participate in the project who would graduate in six rather than five years.

Institutional Policy

At Unicamp the establishment of double degrees has to follow a series of institutional safeguards and approvals (as is the case with any degree program). For undergraduate degrees, the main forum for discussions is the Central Undergraduate Committee, headed by the Dean of Undergraduate Studies, where each program director has a vote. In the beginning, double degree programs faced fierce opposition from nationalistic sectors in Brazil, who perceived double degrees as part of a hidden agenda to recruit top engineers or to allow French engineers to work in Brazil. After a discussion process that took a few years, the first programs were approved and established in 2002. Top students stay at Unicamp for five semesters, then four in France, and the last three at Unicamp. This means that the engineering undergraduate degree will take six years to complete, in contrast with the usual five years that an engineering degree takes in Brazil. Actually, the number of years required to graduate in engineering in Brazil enable a combination of a bachelor's (three years) plus master's (two years) Bologna degree. Since the double degree with the Ecoles Centrales began 10 years ago, 107 Unicamp students have participated in the program, studying in Paris, Lyon, Nantes, Lille, and Marseille. Although there was no explicit policy toward establishing new programs, another double degree was established in 2005 with Paristech, the cluster of 12 prestigious institutions in the Paris area. This program has a wider scope, including not only engineering students but also students of physics, mathematics, and chemistry. Through this framework Unicamp has sent 125 students to France. Similar programs exist now with the French engineering networks INSA and Télécom, and with Supéléc. In 2007 Unicamp signed double degree program agreements in engineering with the Politecnico di Milano and Politecnico di Torino, the first non-French institutions. Currently, there are negotiations going on with German institutions.

From the institutional point of view, the double degree programs became an extra factor of attraction to the already prestigious undergraduate programs. There are no special double degree programs. Outstanding students already enrolled in regular undergraduate programs are eligible to apply for the double degrees. Because selection to participate depends on the academic records, students wishing to take part in the programs are strongly advised to obtain high grades in the courses from their first day at Unicamp.

Providing financial support for students undertaking double degree programs has been a priority for Unicamp. Some 67 students who went to France could benefit from Eiffel Scholarships provided by the French government. There are also CAPES scholarships, and more recently, private companies have sponsored some students.

Besides the double degree programs, Unicamp has had over the years numerous PhD theses in cotutelles, in which the student has a second advisor in a partner institution. Until 2009, cotutelle projects were restricted to French institutions and were concentrated in engineering, then were made available to any country. In this context, a new form of double degree programs was started at the PhD level. The double PhD in history was established with specific rules with Rice University in 2012 after successful cotutelles (Lee, 2013). Unlike cotutelles, where the principle of "one thesis, one degree" is applied, in the double degree each institution grants a PhD after a thesis is presented once to a jury involving the advisors from both institutions. The thesis can be written in either English or Portuguese, but must have the abstract in the other language. The defense takes place in one of the institutions. This new form of double degree will certainly be the basis for other agreements. It is clearly understood by the institution that the student will not have completed two PhD programs, but that the degree undertaken under the supervision and standards of both universities is recognized and certified by each university.

Although Unicamp does not have a specific strategy for double degrees, it has been supportive of new initiatives over the years. Double degrees are a very efficient tool for internationalization and, since their beginning, have had effects beyond just the education of undergraduate students. The contact between French and Brazilian faculty members of engineering has resulted in cotutelles of PhD thesis and cooperative research. Many articles that resulted from this cooperation have been published in the last few years.

Because of the differences between the Brazilian *mestrado* and both the North American MSc and European master's degrees, so far Unicamp has not engaged in a double degree at the *mestrado* level. In Brazil, *mestrado* is a research-intensive degree that typically takes two years (or more) to complete. Equivalence among *mestrado*, MSc, and master's is a controversial issue even at the government level.

The success of the double degree programs had a very curious effect in the current times of accelerated internationalization. Very often foreign universities approach Unicamp with double degree proposals. Our attitude is always very careful. We never start cooperation by establishing a double degree. Rather, double degrees are a result of cooperation. We like to compare the establishment of double degrees to a wedding: We start dating, establish a relationship, then get to know and especially to trust each other. As a consequence of this trust, which takes some time to build, we can be in a position to sign the wedding contract (or double degree agreement) and then send our students to spend two years with our partner and fully accredit all the education they receive.

Unicamp is extremely careful about new programs, and it takes years of good academic relations with partner institutions before a new double degree program can be envisaged. We do not want to risk the high standards of undergraduate or graduate programs that took decades to be established. The main reason for the success of double degree programs has been the guarantee of a high-quality education the students receive in both institutions.

Challenges and Future Development

There are some specific issues concerning double degrees that still need attention. One obvious difficulty is the large size of the programs. When only a handful of students were involved, it was much easier to find financial support. Nowadays, new resources are necessary. One French transnational private company realized that students involved in a double degree have the potential to become good engineers with a knowledge of French culture. It is fully supporting some students in France, conditioned on having them as interns in France and in Brazil. It is a win-win situation: The students have financial assistance for their double degree education and the opportunity of an internship in a top company. The company has access to some of the best future engineers.

At the undergraduate level there is still much to be done in relation of curriculum compatibility. As with most Brazilian institutions, Unicamp curricula are still not flexible enough, but after 10 years of double degrees, the idea of full accreditation of activities in the partner institution is coming through. In this sense, double degrees are creating the indirect benefit of bringing modern curriculum design to Brazil. Nevertheless, the engineering profession is regulated by an extremely conservative professional council in Brazil, which still does not fully grasp the value of international education.

There is also concern regarding the asymmetry in the numbers of students in each direction. Unicamp has already sent more than 230 students to double degree programs and has hosted fewer than 30. This specifically concerns the engineering undergraduate programs. Most European students still regard Brazil as an exotic place to be rather than a place where they will get a top-quality engineering education. Moreover, the exclusive use of Portuguese as the instruction language poses an obvious barrier, although Unicamp provides a specific intensive Portuguese course to all its foreign students. To make Unicamp more attractive to foreign students, some core curriculum engineering courses will be taught in English starting in August 2013. There is a general feeling that this should break a barrier to many students. Learning Portuguese will still be a fundamental part of the double degree education at Unicamp. There is a consensus in the sense that immersion in the local culture must be part of the double degree at any level, and learning the local language is clearly part of this.

Double degree programs have been the most effective tools for internationalization at Unicamp, even before internationalization was part of the institutional agenda. The internal discussions triggered by the first double degree projects and the success of the programs have contributed to create a positive agenda regarding internationalization. Although, in the beginning, the concept of double degrees was restricted to undergraduate engineering programs having French institutions as partners, recent developments have expanded them to science and humanities, to different countries, and to the graduate level. There is no explicit institutional agenda to increase the number of double degree programs, but the stimulus provided by the success of the early ones is very relevant. However, it should be strongly emphasized that Unicamp's establishment of a new double degree program is not the reason for cooperation but rather a consequence of cooperation. In short, double degrees have made Unicamp a better institution, and Unicamp is open to establishing new programs with selected partners over the world.

REFERENCES

Lee, R. C. (2013, January 27). Rice becomes more global with dual-degree program. *Houston Chronicle: Houston.* Retrieved from http://www.houstonchronicle.com/news/houston-texas/houston/article/Rice-becomes-more-global-with-dual-degree-program-4226172.php#ixzz2JIXOhzji

Tessler, L. R. (2012). The internationalisation of higher education in Brazil. In M. Stiasny & T. Gore, (Eds.), *Going global: The landscape for policy makers and practitioners in tertiary education* (pp. 189–198). Bingley, UK: Emerald Group.

PUC-Rio = Pontifical Catholic University of Rio de Janeiro, UFC = Federal University of Ceará, UFRGS = Federal University of Rio Grande do Sul, UFRJ = Federal University of Rio de Janeiro, Unicamp = University of Campinas, USP = University of São Paulo.

Chapter Twelve

Joint Degrees: A Top Priority of the European Union's Mobility and Cooperation Program

XAVIER PRATS MONNÉ AND CLAIRE MOREL, EUROPEAN COMMISSION[1]

Higher education institutions are increasingly seeking to establish with their international counterparts deeper partnerships than those offered by traditional study-abroad programs. Joint degrees are one of the most promising forms of academic cooperation, as a vehicle not only for student mobility but also to deepen transnational cooperation in curriculum development, quality assurance, and mutual recognition of qualifications. This area, where the European Union has already gained valuable experience, will be a top priority of the European Union's future mobility and cooperation program for the 2014–2020 period; this new program will mark a step-change in institutional cooperation, through enhanced support for education and training institutions working together to find joint solutions to shared challenges.

The Erasmus Program Has Shaped Europe's Higher Education Landscape …

International cooperation between higher education institutions (HEIs) within the European Union (EU) started with the exchange of students on the basis of bilateral agreements. Since 1987, the Erasmus program has played a key role in stimulating mobility: almost three million students have participated in the program, as well as over 300,000 higher education teachers and other staff. Erasmus has changed their lives and has also transformed the way HEIs relate to and cooperate with each other; it has proven to be an important catalyst in the reform of higher education systems. By funding transnational projects, Erasmus has enabled European HEIs to improve teaching and strengthen their institutional leadership and management. The widespread use of learning outcomes as well as EU-wide transparency and recognition tools (in particular, the European Credit Transfer and Accumulation System [ECTS] and the diploma supplement) have contributed to better understanding and trust among institutions across Europe. The program has helped to shape a new European higher education landscape, leading to the launch of the "Bologna process" aiming to create a European Higher Education Area and many of its distinctive features, including comparable and compatible study programs.

… and Erasmus Mundus Has Promoted International Cooperation through Joint Degrees

While from its early days the Erasmus program has been largely associated to individual mobility, it has also supported numerous multilateral cooperation activities between European universities, in particular the development of joint courses, teaching modules or complete joint study programs. These initiatives that focus on increased curricular integration among European universities were strengthened and expanded in the conclusions of the 2001 Bologna Ministerial Conference in Prague, which called for more modules, courses, and curricula offered in partnership with HEIs from other countries.

Nowadays, joint and double degrees have a prominent role in the internationalization strategy of European universities. They represent a successful aspect of EU's international cooperation, and the emergence of a new and deeper partnership model through which HEIs seek to firmly embed their international experience within their curricula and deepen the international experience of students and faculty at home and abroad. Furthermore, in a context of financial pressure and increased competition to attract international students, for many European universities the joint development and implementation of international study programs by HEIs from different countries is an efficient way to increase their worldwide visibility and attractiveness.

European universities have accumulated a unique experience in this field through their participation in Erasmus Mundus. Through this program, university consortia (composed of a minimum of three universities located in different Member States or European Economic Area [EEA] countries) develop highly integrated joint curricula at an excellent level, with joint student applications and joint selection, admission, and examination criteria. HEIs must offer students a recognized and mandatory mobility period in at least two HEIs and guarantee the delivery of a joint, double, or multiple degree to all successful students. Since the start of the program in 2004, the EU has funded 138 Erasmus Mundus joint master's courses and 43 joint doctoral programs, involving over 16,000 students, doctoral candidates, and academic staff from all over the world. Joint programs, selected exclusively on the basis of excellence criteria and through a bottom-up approach, cover a wide range of subjects as varied as "Scale Modelling of Physical, Chemical and Bio-molecular Systems"; "Coastal and Marine Engineering and Management"; "Public Health in Disasters"; "Social Work with Families and Children"; and "International Vintage, Vine, Wine and Terroir Management."[2] The most represented disciplines for joint master's degrees are science, mathematics, and computing (28 percent), followed by social sciences, business, and law (25 percent); for joint doctorates, the share of these disciplines is 42 percent and 23 percent. We should, however, keep in mind that most joint degrees are multidisciplinary.

Practically all EU countries are represented in Erasmus Mundus courses. Some of them (such as France, Germany, Italy, or the Netherlands) are particularly well represented, while others are much less involved. The European Commission has always considered that the excellence of the joint degrees (their absolute quality) had to prevail on any other selection criteria, such as thematic or geographic representativeness. This is why these factors are not taken into account during the selection phase. However, the commission has funded projects aimed at raising awareness and supporting the participation of universities from European countries less represented in joint degrees. These contact seminars involving potential applicants from the countries concerned (mainly new EU Members States) have contributed to the increase of the number and quality of joint degrees from these countries.

They can be delivered in any official language of the EU (although most are offered in English) but must offer the possibility to learn the national language of the hosting HEIs. So far, Erasmus Mundus master's courses have been funded for five consecutive intakes of students, and the best ones from the first phase of the program have been renewed for another five intakes.

During these consecutive intakes, the number of scholarships offered has regularly decreased (from 17 to around 7 by intake), leading the consortia to increase their self-funding and sustainability efforts. Under Erasmus+, the intention is to award scholarships for three consecutive intakes with the possibility of a continuation subject to a performance quality review at the end of this period. This continuation will be driven by the same objectives of self-funding and sustainability as in the current program. On average, each Erasmus Mundus master intake enrolls 30 students.

Joint degrees bring to life the principles promoted through the Bologna process, namely, increased mobility, comparable degree, and quality assurance procedures. Among the three levels of higher education (BA, MA, PhD), the MA was certainly the most appropriate for launching the Erasmus Mundus laboratory of curricular integration in line with Bologna's convergence process, but for different reasons: The master's level is still fully under the educational umbrella as opposed to doctoral programs, which are on the frontier between education and research. Master's programs are less developed, structured, and regulated than bachelor's (a few years ago the MA level was almost inexistent in some countries that had long BAs immediately followed by PhDs): focusing on master's was believed to provide a competitive advantage to attract the best international students to European universities. Because the program aims at competing with other high-level scholarships schemes, it had to address a similar audience, that is, master's level students (and more recently PhD candidates).

However, the possibility to develop and implement joint BA programs is offered under Atlantis and under the curriculum development strand of the internal Erasmus program. Under the Atlantis program the EU has cofunded 44 joint- or double-degree projects with its partners in industrialized countries,[3] mostly with the United States. The program has supported consortia of HEIs in developing integrated joint study programs, with students from both sides spending a substantial period of study abroad and receiving either a joint or a double degree. An evaluation report from 2011[4] found the Atlantis actions to be broad-ranging and flexible, enabling governments to pursue a variety of political and economic goals added to opportunities offered to HEIs, and especially "new players" to enter the international education arena. Furthermore, the report shows that in addition to the normal impact from this kind of cooperation of students and professionals, there are important effects on institutions, such as their capacity to participate in international activities, the creation of new academic networks, and the expansion of existing ones, as well as improving curriculum quality. As of 2014, the Atlantis program will be integrated into Erasmus+. The program will continue to offer scholarships to students interested in attending high-quality joint programs.

After almost 10 years of experience, Erasmus Mundus has brought numerous benefits to higher education systems, institutions, and students. Despite this positive assessment, there will be a number of challenges to tackle as the new generation of joint degrees is implemented once the Erasmus+ program and Marie Skłodowska-Curie Actions are launched in 2014.

Joint Degrees Have Had an Impact on Higher Education Systems …

Cooperation through Erasmus Mundus has modified the attitude and disposition toward the Bologna process of those participating in joint degrees, in particular the application of the credit system, mutual recognition, promotion of mobility, and, most importantly, European cooperation in quality assurance. In some countries, it has contributed to the adaptation of national legislation, particularly in the area of the recognition of joint degrees. It has also had a positive effect on the appreciation of the Bologna process beyond the EU, for example, by contributing significantly to the adoption of a common credit and mobility recognition system and joint quality assurance mechanisms, notably in the European Neighborhood countries. In this region, the combined effect of Erasmus Mundus and Tempus, a program for the modernization of higher education, has been particularly successful.

… on Institutions …

Having two or more institutions joining forces to offer a joint degree results in higher academic standards than what the institutions would achieve separately. Offering joint programs raises an institution's international profile, allows the development of international "niches," stimulates international collaboration on teaching, and enhances an institution's ability to adapt swiftly to emerging needs.

The Erasmus Mundus joint programs are open to non-EU universities, which increases their potential for innovation and internationalization. This inevitably poses additional practical, financial, and structural challenges to universities that are more difficult to overcome than those arising from cooperation within the European context. But such challenges constitute further stimulus to find appropriate solutions that often trigger creative approaches. Academics involved in the program still find the effort worthwhile and consider that joint- and double-degree programs are powerful tools for quality assurance (as academic staff are incited to review, adapt, and improve the content of their curricula and teaching practices) and to attract talent from all over the world. Indeed, universities involved in the program do not need to spend much effort in promoting their courses, as the Erasmus Mundus brand easily attracts the best students worldwide. In the last three years, more than 30,000 student applications have been received every year by 120 to 130 Erasmus Mundus master consortia, representing an average of 250 applications per course, for an average of 10 scholarships awarded.

… on Students …

Independent evaluations[5] have concluded that Erasmus Mundus joint degrees have had a positive impact on the graduates' employability. When asked about the most important factor for having been hired by their current employer, graduates agree that the experience they gained during their Erasmus Mundus course played a crucial role, in particular their new intercultural competences and exposure to study or research in different countries.

HEIs participating in Erasmus Mundus offer their students excellent courses with embedded, structured mobility, which allow participants to develop new types of transversal skills that are particularly appreciated by employers. Furthermore, most of the Erasmus Mundus joint programs have adapted their study programs to include practice-oriented teaching and learning methods, such as project-based learning, placements, and internships. In addition, many joint programs involve noneducational organizations (enterprises, NGOs, private and public research centers, public organizations, etc.) among their associated partners to ensure, on the one hand, a better match between the skills and competences taught in the joint program and those required in the professional fields concerned and, on the other hand, to provide concrete employment prospects to their graduates.

A survey[6] conducted in 2010–2011 among 2,800 former Erasmus Mundus students showed that 3 percent were still unemployed when the survey was conducted; 50 percent of the graduates had found a permanent employment; 25 percent pursued a PhD degree; and 22 percent held a determined contract or were self-employed. Of the employed graduates, 72 percent stated that they were satisfied with their current job situation.

However, more needs to be done to tap into the full potential of joint or double degrees regarding employability, including by making them better known to employers. This is one of the tasks of the alumni association of Erasmus Mundus (EMA), with the support of the European Commission. EMA organizes regular initiatives to promote the program among employers. For example, by inviting employers to its development conferences, where they share their experience with students and graduates. This was recently the case during the Geomundus symposium that covered different geoscience disciplines such as earth and environmental studies, geographic information science and geoinformatics, and agriculture. EMA also works on concrete projects in close cooperation with enterprises.

… and on Academic Staff

Through Erasmus Mundus, the European Commission has put special emphasis on the development of student-centered cooperation with joint teaching and supervision. This brings together academics and results in complementary activities and opportunities for participants to create networks and upgrade skills and knowledge. Joint research carried out by academics in this closely knitted context of cooperation between peers can result in better quality research outputs.

The Development of Joint Degrees Still Faces Some Challenges

Notwithstanding the encouraging achievements described above, there are still a number of challenges linked to the development of joint degrees. Institutional regulations (e.g., grading systems, examination regulations, enrolment procedures, and tuition fees policy) and national legislation (particularly related to the delivery of joint degrees) make the undertaking of joint programs difficult for the involved HEIs, both from the academic and administrative sides. Mutual trust between institutions is key to overcoming these barriers. This type of cooperation works particularly well when the HEIs involved have clear international strategies. Such strategies usually acknowledge the important role that joint programs can play for the institution and therefore build in flexibility in program management, allowing for a smoother implementation of joint programs. The development of these strategies has led to a steady increase in the number of countries and institutions participating in joint programs, including those outside the EU, as the latest Bologna implementation report shows.[7]

Through the program and the international dialogue on higher education policies that the EU has with a number of non-EU partners, the issue of joint degrees and related national regulations is often raised, to see how legal barriers to the development of joint degrees could be removed. Through Erasmus Mundus, national regulations in some EU countries have evolved to authorize and facilitate the development of joint degrees.

Joint programs demand a lot of the institutions and individuals involved, including resources. The EU financial investment on joint degrees is in relative terms much higher than for credit mobility: With the same amount of funding, a much larger number of individual beneficiaries could be reached, if the same funds were used for credit mobility. However, the investment in joint programs for individuals, institutions, and the visibility of European universities in the world is worthwhile.

Finally, if the attractiveness of the European Higher Education Area depends largely on the universities themselves and on the support given to international cooperation strategies, it depends as well on the conditions imposed on the entrance and mobility of non-European students in the EU. With the aim of making these rules better adapted to the situation of non-EU students and researchers, the European Commission will soon be proposing a revision of the directive on the conditions of entry of third-country nationals for the purposes of research or studies, which should alleviate the current immigration procedures applied to these target groups and, as a result, further increase the worldwide attractiveness of European universities.

The Future: From Erasmus Mundus to Erasmus+ (2014–2020)

One of the most understated consequences of the shift toward a globalized knowledge economy is that talent attracts capital more effectively than capital attracts talent. Countries with high proportions of graduates and effective education systems also tend to have high levels of foreign direct investment and innovation. And education pays also for the individual: Be it in times of growth or recession, European graduates are far less likely to be unemployed than nongraduates. The 27 heads of government of the EU have acknowledged this reality by identifying higher education as one of the top priorities of the "Europe 2020" strategy, the EU policy framework to promote growth, innovation, and jobs. A key priority of this strategy is to increase attainment levels: the EU has a headline target for 40 percent of 30- to 34-year-olds to hold a higher education or equivalent-level qualification by 2020. But raising attainment levels is not enough: The quality and relevance of education and research programs and the capacity of HEIs to innovate are just as crucial for the contribution of higher education to growth and jobs. Discipline-specific knowledge must be underpinned by transferable skills, especially in information and communication technologies (ICT), creativity, and entrepreneurship.

The governments of the 27 EU countries and the European Parliament are currently discussing the European Commission's proposals for the 2014–2020 EU budget, including a new single program for mobility and cooperation in education and training (covering also youth and sports), tentatively entitled Erasmus+, to extend the benefits of the Erasmus brand name to other education programs (e.g., Leonardo for vocational education and training). Similarly, the renewed Marie Skłodowska-Curie Actions for researchers propose new features such as "industrial doctorates," a scheme that aims to reinforce cooperation among universities, research centers, and businesses, and to increase the mobility flows among these sectors. The European Institute of Innovation and Technology (EIT), established five years ago, will enhance the links among education, research, and innovation; the EIT and its Knowledge and Innovation Communities (KICs) are already producing joint academic degrees and patents, generating startup companies, internships at the partner companies, and management mentoring programs in innovative majors.

The Erasmus+ program will focus its financial resources on supporting the Europe 2020 strategy: to equip people with the skills and transferable competences they need to find a good job and build a successful career, such as adaptability, problem solving, teamwork, and entrepreneurship. It aims to enhance the systemic impacts of mobility, in particular by supporting one million teachers, trainers, and education staff to acquire new skills abroad. Erasmus+ will also mainstream the current programs and offer non-EU countries, their HEIs, and their academic staff and students' greater levels of support under the same delivery mechanisms as their counterparts in the EU.

Increasing international student and staff mobility, including to nontraditional study destinations, will be a key objective of Erasmus+: While the precise budget for the 2014–2020 period will only be determined in the second half of 2013, it is safe to say that significantly higher funding will be allocated to both incoming and outgoing mobility of students and staff, to and from non-EU countries. The European Commission proposal foresees a budget of 19.5 billion euros over seven years (approximately US$26 billion), which is a 70 percent increase compared to the current EU education programs and the biggest increase of all EU budget chapters. In headline terms, the Erasmus+ proposal aims to provide grants to five million people to study, train, or volunteer abroad, twice as many as currently benefit. Between 2014 and 2020, up to 135,000 students and staff would be able to benefit from this international mobility. Under the Marie Skłodowska-Curie Actions, the international dimension will continue to be emphasized, and approximately 20 percent of all Marie Curie Fellows will be recruited from outside Europe. In addition, HEIs will continue to be able to foster research-based links with partners around the world, implemented through mobility periods.

Joint- and double-degree programs represent a particularly successful aspect of the EU's international cooperation activities: Given their potential for systemic impact, and the added value of EU funding in this area, these joint programs will be a core element of the new EU education and training programs for 2014–2020. Joint doctorates will be funded under Marie Skłodowska-Curie Actions, ensuring closer synergies between their educational and research components; joint master's programs will be supported under the Erasmus+ program.

The joint programs will continue to be run by consortia consisting of HEIs from at least three European countries. Participation of non-European institutions in joint degrees will be encouraged, as peer learning, cooperation, and comparison with other higher education providers worldwide facilitates the circulation of knowledge and skills and enhances the overall quality of the education provided. The need for more global cooperation and strategic partnerships involving non-European HEIs is crucial in order to tackle global challenges such as climate change, sustainable energy, and food safety and security.

High-level scholarships will continue to be offered to the best students worldwide. If the European Commission's priorities and budget are endorsed, around 34,000 students will benefit from these scholarships, compared to 16,000 during the previous seven-year budget. Similarly, up to 300 HEI consortia would be supported during the program's life span.

A stronger involvement of enterprises will also be encouraged to increase the relevance of joint degrees for the labor market. New measures are envisaged to ensure the high quality of the offered courses, such as rolling quality reviews, a more systematic use of the self-assessment tool developed under the Erasmus Mundus Quality Assurance project,[8] and measures to support the long-term sustainability of excellent programs via a more systematic use of cofunding mechanisms, in particular with enterprises.

NOTES

1 xavier.prats-monne@ec.europa.eu; claire.morel@ec.europa.eu. For more information: http://ec.europa.eu/education/lifelong-learning-policy/higher_en.htm

2 Full compendium on: http://eacea.ec.europa.eu/erasmus_mundus/results_compendia/selected_projects_action_1_master_courses_en.php

3 More information is available at http://ec.europa.eu/education/external-relation-programmes/industrialised_en.htm

4 The interim Evaluation of EU-US and EU-Canada agreements can be found at http://eacea.ec.europa.eu/bilateral_cooperation/publications/joint_publications_en.php

5 http://ec.europa.eu/dgs/education_culture/evalreports/index_en.htm

6 Survey results are accessible at: http://www.em-a.eu/en/erasmus-mundus/graduate-impact-survey.html

7 http://www.ehea.info/Uploads/(1)/Bologna%20Process%20Implementation%20Report.pdf

8 http://www.emqa.eu

Chapter Thirteen

Joint and Double Degree Programs in Germany

CHRISTIAN THIMME, GERMAN ACADEMIC EXCHANGE SERVICE (DAAD)

In view of the Bologna process and the changes it has brought to Germany's university system, the German Academic Exchange Service (DAAD) has strengthened its support of structured and integrated mobility in internationally oriented degree programs. The DAAD encourages universities to form partnerships that allow students to complete part of their studies at the other university with the certainty of having their coursework recognized. The core elements of the partnerships include the integration of "windows of mobility" in the degree programs, extensive curricular agreements and learning agreements with students to ensure that the periods of study abroad optimally fit into the courses of study, and that all completed coursework is fully recognized. With funding provided by the Federal Ministry of Education and Research (BMBF), the DAAD has not only allocated structural funding to create and cultivate such university partnerships, but has also set aside a major share for student scholarships. The programs have different focuses. For example, some fund basic partnerships that allow smaller groups of foreign and German students to spend one semester or an entire academic year at the partner university,[1] others finance a fourth year abroad in undergraduate programs that provide additional academic and intercultural value,[2] and others help to establish study programs that offer double or joint degrees.

The Added Value of Joint and Double Degrees

"In order to further strengthen the important European dimensions of higher education and graduate employability," Germany's university political agenda calls for study programs that "lead to a recognized joint degree."[3] For universities, joint and double degrees are central to internationalizing study and instruction. Such degree programs can result in a larger variety of available courses—especially if a university chooses a partner with a different area of specialization. Outstanding graduates can be recruited as young researchers for master's degree programs and doctoral study. At the same time, these partnerships encourage the exchange of university instructors and employees. From the point of view of the DAAD, international degree programs have the potential to strongly enhance the prestige and reputation of a university.

The students also benefit from courses of study with joint or double degrees. These courses of study allow students to study abroad in a calculable, efficient manner without prolonging their education, as all of their completed coursework is recognized. Almost all such degree programs offer personal and academic counseling and ensure that the guest students are well integrated into the student body at the partner university. The result is an increase in intercultural value; thus, earning a dual qualification is undoubtedly attractive for students. According to a graduate survey conducted by the Franco-German University, almost 60 percent of those surveyed indicated that their double or joint degrees proved to be an advantage when applying for jobs.[4] The findings of the survey correspond with those of an older DAAD survey of human resource personnel on the same topic.[5] Again, almost 60 percent of companies with an international orientation claimed that applicants with double degrees have "definitely better" (18.7 percent) or "somewhat better" (40.9 percent) chances of getting hired than candidates with single degrees. When asked what they considered especially attractive about joint and double degree programs, they listed foreign language knowledge, intercultural knowledge, foreign academic knowledge, and foreign internships.

Joint and Double Degree Programs in Germany

The latest study by the Institute of International Education (IIE) on double degrees ranked Germany near the top with respect to its number of international degree programs with double degrees (Obst, Kuder, & Banks, 2011). The "Hochschulkompass," an online database operated by the German Rectors' Conference (HRK; see www.hrk.de), currently contains 469 international degree programs (234 undergraduate and 235 graduate programs) with joint and double degrees. This figure, however, is not based on a systematic statistical study, but on information provided voluntarily by the universities themselves. Therefore, we can assume that the true figure far exceeds 500 programs today.

Just in 2011–12 alone, a total of 127 degree programs received funding through the DAAD program called the Integrated International Degree Programmes with Double Degrees. Another DAAD program, International Doctoral Study in Germany (IPID), currently funds 20 bilateral doctoral degree programs. The Erasmus Mundus program provides funding to 70 multilateral master's degree and 21 PhD programs with double degrees in Germany. The DAAD also supports double or joint degree programs with other funding instruments that are more specific in scope, for example, the German-Language Degree Programs in Central and Eastern Europe and CIS States (10), the Brazilian UNI-BRAL program (4) and the German University Foreign Study Programs (46). There is an especially strong focus on German–French cooperation; a total of 140 binational integrated degree programs are funded through the Franco-German University alone (Hellmann, 2012).

DAAD Integrated International Degree Programs with Double Degrees

Established in 1999 as a bilateral program with Great Britain, the DAAD Double Degree Funding Program gradually expanded its scope in the following years to include other European countries. In 2005 the program began offering funding to joint and double degree programs with countries worldwide (with the exception of France, for which the Franco-German University is responsible). The program provides financial support to courses of study, which are divided between both partner universities to a relatively equal extent and conclude with two national degrees (double degrees) or a jointly issued degree from both universities (joint degrees). The projects are eligible for up to eight years of funding through this DAAD program. These generally consist of a one-year preparation phase, a four-year trial phase, and a three-year implementation phase, each of which must meet specific minimum requirements. The preparation phase is used to develop the degree programs, for which university administrators can apply for up to 10,000 euros to cover travel, materials, and personnel costs. In addition to a concept for the new degree program, the funding application must also include a cooperation agreement signed by the respective university or a statement of intent, in which both parties agree to offer a joint or a double degree program and waive at least 50% of their tuition fees.

During the trial phase, at least five German and five foreign students must be enrolled in the new degree program. The conditions for funding include the following:

- A joint cooperation agreement signed by the administrations of both universities that provides a description of the binational curriculum of the joint or double degree program (complementary academic and intercultural education), indicates the credit points awarded for each module (or individual course), provides a course and examination schedule, and indicates the respective national or binational degrees.

- A curriculum for the joint or double degree program (or if applicable, in two variants for German and international participants), to which both universities agree, describing the qualification profile of the national degrees.

- An agreement outlining student admission procedures to the joint or double degree program, credit transfer modalities (e.g., European Credit Transfer and Accumulation System (ECTS) for Erasmus countries) for awarding credit for courses completed abroad and joint procedures for administering the final examination.

- Conferral of degrees separately issued (double degrees) or jointly issued (joint degree) by the partner universities at the successful conclusion of the integrated degree program.

- A description of the degree(s) in the form of a Diploma Supplement.

The DAAD also expects the partner universities to engage in the exchange each year, establish an equivalent duration of study for their programs with jointly enrolled classes, offer preparatory (subject-specific) foreign language courses, provide both academic and nonacademic student advising services, and require above-average achievement from students who receive scholarships. Binational degree programs are eligible for a maximum of 50,000 euros in funding, of which up to 20,000 euros may be allocated for structural purposes (staff and materials expenses). The remainder is to be used for scholarships. The program is designed to provide full scholarships to German students, and foreign students are eligible for partial scholarships. Partnerships between several universities may apply for another 25,000 euros for each additional university.

The funding requirements for the implementation phase are more demanding. In addition to meeting the terms described above, the partner universities must now acquire accreditation for the joint or double degree program and issue joint examination and study regulations. The partners must also provide proof that at least five students from each university have participated in the exchange each year. During the implementation phase, the structural costs decrease in favor of scholarship funding. The DAAD understands that the administrative costs—especially in the preparation and trial phases—are particularly high, and therefore, provides support as startup financing. However, the DAAD expects the universities to contribute an increasing amount of their own resources to maintain the degree program as time goes on. This funding requires that the universities meet high-quality standards. The program accepts and reviews funding proposals every year. Furthermore, the projects are selected by an independent review board of university professors. In 2011–12, the DAAD awarded funding to 127 projects. Most of the partnerships were created with universities in Europe (71 degree programs), followed by Asia (28), and North/South America (24).

FIGURE 13.1: INTEGRATED INTERNATIONAL DEGREE PROGRAMS WITH DOUBLE DEGREES, NUMBER OF PROJECTS PER CONTINENT (2011 - 2012)

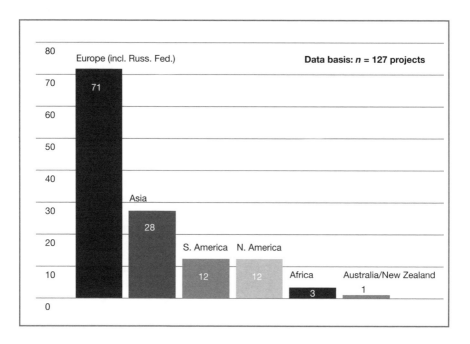

The most popular partner countries were the Russian Federation (18); China (11); Spain (9); the United States (9); and Poland, Italy and the Netherlands, each with 8 degree programs.

In our experience, joint or double degrees are especially well-suited for master's degree programs. Of all the programs supported by the DAAD, 85 conclude with master's degrees and 42 with bachelor's degrees. The vast majority of university partnerships (106) have chosen to confer double degrees, presumably because joint degrees require a much greater effort to establish. Interestingly enough, the largest number of joint degrees are issued to graduates in language and cultural studies programs—one-third of all joint degree programs combined.

In terms of their subjects, 45 percent of the degree programs are in law, economics, and social sciences, far outnumbering those in engineering (27 percent) and language and cultural studies (17 percent).

FIGURE 13.2: INTEGRATED INTERNATIONAL DEGREE PROGRAMS WITH DOUBLE DEGREES, SUBJECT GROUPS (2011–2012)

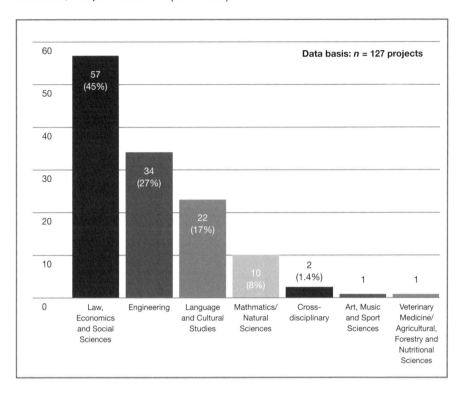

An impressive number of projects (82 percent) succeeded in negotiating a full waiver of tuition fees with their partners, which illustrates the importance that the universities attach to these cooperation programs.

Once the preparation phase has successfully concluded, only a very low percentage of the projects are denied further funding through the DAAD (well below 10 percent). The main reason why the DAAD would cancel funding or the university partners terminate their cooperation is that the project failed to meet the formal requirements mentioned above. In a brief survey of projects funded during the last funding period, the most common problem involved difficulties between the partners, though the reasons were extremely varied (cost-cutting measures, important contact partners leaving their jobs, problems with the recognition of the degrees). Several also mentioned the high administrative costs connected to establishing double and joint degree programs. Some respondents complained about a lack of reciprocity with regard to their student exchange or a general lack of interest on the part of the students.

With regard to promoting structured mobility, one of the top funding priorities of the DAAD and BMBF is to continue expanding degree programs with joint or double degrees. The budget of this DAAD funding program has steadily increased in recent years and totaled approximately 3.6 million euros in 2012. It is clear to everyone that these projects place high demands on the participating universities. Not surprisingly, an array of new challenges, problems, and hurdles arose quite early on as universities, funding organizations, and university research departments began developing and implementing integrated international degree programs with joint and double degrees. To support the universities in these efforts, a variety of guidelines, recommendations, information flyers, and best-practices examples have been published by various sources (European University Association, 2004; HRK, 2005; Nickel, Zdebel, & Westerheijden, 2009).[6] An attachment to the study released by Ulrich Schüle contains a useful checklist for developing joint and double degree programs (Schüle, 2006).

The DAAD holds conferences for the project directors of the degree programs at regular intervals (most recently in November 2012) and provides info sheets on its website (e.g., about examination regulations and cooperation agreements; see www.daad.de/doppelabschluss. The publications listed above systematically describe the various stages of introducing and implementing joint and double degree programs. They include detailed instructions and advice on all important matters, starting with the very first planning session (choosing partners, resource assessment, and academic fundamentals); the development and implementation phase (agreements, financial and administrative aspects, university and state-specific rules and regulations, language issues, curriculum development, mobility for students and university instructors, admission requirements and examination regulations, student advising services, etc.); and finally management, marketing, long-term financial and staff sustainability, quality assurance, and evaluation of the double degree programs.[7]

The DAAD's structural funding programs help German universities put their internationalization strategies into place. As the largest funding organization of such degree programs in Germany, the DAAD focuses on those aspects that are especially significant in terms of internationalization. During the application process, the DAAD is interested in proposals for new degree programs that the university administration is willing to support and cofinance. After all, while international degree programs can strongly enhance the attractiveness and reputation of a university, their failure or termination can result in a damaging loss in reputation. According to a transnational survey by the IIE, almost 30 percent of university partnerships had terminated their degree program, whereby Germany and France had the lowest cancellation rates (Obst, Kuder et al., 2011, pp. 26-39). For this reason, it is sensible and ultimately essential to integrate such programs into an institutional strategy in order to maintain the degree programs in the long term. In the IIE survey, the universities were asked about the greatest challenges in establishing double degree programs (Obst, Kuder, & Banks, 2011, pp. 32-39). Among the 10 most mentioned aspects, three were related to the integration of the program into the university's institutional strategy. Topping the list was the problem of guaranteeing the sustainability of the program; at second place, financing the program; and finally, securing the necessary institutional support. Even though joint degree programs are most often initiated by university professors and are largely motivated by the academic interests of their respective departments, such programs require the support of the university on the whole to provide financing, academic and administrative resources, and marketing measures for the degree programs.

From the perspective of the DAAD, this funding program has proven extremely successful. In the near future, the DAAD will have the program evaluated by an external assessor in order to learn more about its effectiveness, as well as the problems and difficulties of establishing joint and double degree programs in hopes of improving and further developing the funding program.

NOTES

[1] International Study and Education Partnerships (ISAP), http://www.daad.de/isap

[2] Bachelor Plus, http://www.daad.de/bachelorplus

[3] On the Path to a European Higher Education Area. Communiqué of the Meeting of European Ministers of Higher Education in Prague, 19 May 2001. http://www.bologna-bergen2005.no/Docs/00-Main_doc/ 010519PRAGUE_COMMUNIQUE.PDF http://www.ond.vlaanderen.be/hogeronderwijs/bologna/links/ language/2001_Prague_Communique_German.pdf

[4] Franco-German University (FGU), Graduate Survey 2011. http://www.dfh-ufa.org/fr/hilfe/downloads/ aktuell/enquete-double-diplomes-internationaux/

[5] Survey of HR personnel on the subject of international double degrees "Dual Diplomas," conducted by IW Consult on behalf of the DAAD, Cologne 2003, p. 10. https://www.daad.de/imperia/md/content/hochschulen/ doppeldiplom-programm/infoservice/endbericht_daad_umfrageiwconsult.pdf

[6] The most comprehensive and up-to-date guidelines are those published by the EU project JOIMAN (www.joiman.eu), specifically: Guide to Developing and Running Joint Programmes at Bachelor and Master's Level, and: How to Manage Joint Study Programmes, Guidelines and Good Practices from the JOIMAN Network.

[7] Also see the chapter in this book by Mager, Poller, and Girotti.

REFERENCES

European University Association. (2004). 10 Golden rules for new joint master programmes. http://www.jointdegree.eu/uploads/media/10_Golden_Rules.doc

Hellmann, J. (2012). Binational integrated degree programmes: The academic added value of bilingualism and biculturalism as demonstrated by the degree programmes of the Franco-German University. *Fremdsprachen Lehren und Lernen*, 2:84ff.

HRK. (2005, February). Recommendations for developing double diplomas and joint degrees.

Nickel, S., Zdebel, T., & Westerheijden, D. F. (2009). *Joint degrees in the European Higher Education Area, obstacles and opportunities of transnational degree programme partnerships illustrated by EUREGIO Germany-Netherlands.* Centre for Higher Education Development and Center for Higher Education Policy Studies, Gronau/Enschede, 2009. http://www.che.de/downloads/JointDegrees_english_final.pdf

Kuder, M., Obst, D., & Banks, C. (2011). Joint and double degree programs in the global context: Report on an international survey (white paper). New York, NY: Institute of International Education. Retrieved from http://www.iie.org/Research-and-Publications/Publications-and-Reports/IIE-Bookstore/Joint-Degree-Survey-Report-2011

Schüle, U. (2006). *Joint and double degrees within the European Higher Education Area,* (CIDD papers on international business education), Consortium of International Double Degrees, Paris 2006.

Chapter Fourteen

Collaborative Degree Programs in the Chinese Context

LIU JINGHUI, CHINA SCHOLARSHIP COUNCIL

Collaborative degree programs are collaboratively offered by Chinese higher education institutions and their overseas partners at the undergraduate level or above that confer degrees. Despite the short history of collaborative degree programs in China, they have witnessed significant growth due to government support and public demand.

Related Policies and Rules

In recent years, the Chinese government has launched a series of policies and rules to encourage, regulate, and guide Chinese-foreign cooperation in running schools,[1] including those that offer collaborative degree programs.

Regulations of the People's Republic of China on Chinese-Foreign Cooperation in Running Schools

In March 2003, the State Council launched *the Regulations of the People's Republic of China on Chinese-Foreign Cooperation in Running Schools*. It is stipulated that "for Chinese-foreign cooperation in running schools (institutions and projects), the State adopts the policies of opening wider to the outside world, standardization of running schools, exercising administration by law and promoting its development."[2] This regulation, at the state level, provides a clear definition and provides a guarantee of cooperation in running schools and collaborative degree programs. After that, a good number of cooperatively run institutions and educational projects appeared.

Implementation Rules for the Regulations of the People's Republic of China on Chinese-Foreign Cooperation in Running Schools

In June, 2004, the *Implementation Rules for the Regulations of the People's Republic of China on Chinese-Foreign Cooperation in Running Schools* was published by the Chinese Ministry of Education. It is a regulation at the operational level that "encourages Chinese education institutions to cooperate on running schools with their overseas partners whose academic reputation and teaching quality are worldly recognized; encourages cooperation in fields and disciplines that are newly emerging and urgently needed by the country." It "encourages Chinese and foreign institutions to cooperate on running schools in the West and the less-developed areas of China."[3]

China's National Outline for Medium and Long-Term Education Reform and Development (2010–2020)

In July, 2010, *China's National Outline for Medium and Long-Term Education Reform and Development (2010–2020)* was launched. It encourages Chinese institutions "to introduce and work with the world leading universities, educational and research institutions and enterprises to jointly set up teaching, training and research institutions and cooperative projects in China," "to support faculties and students exchange, credit accreditation, and collaboratively confer of academic degrees." It shows a clear direction for development of Chinese-foreign cooperation in running schools and collaborative degree programs.

Collaborative Degree Programs

By April 2013, the numbers of educational projects and institutions for Chinese-foreign cooperation in running schools certified by Chinese Ministry of Education were 799 and 45, respectively,[4] which represented a 41 percent and 36 percent increase compared with 2011. In addition, there are several collaborative degree programs that are done directly through university exchange programs. The three countries with the biggest number of partner universities are the United Kingdom, the United States, and Australia. Business and management, information technology, and engineering are the most popular academic disciplines at the current stage.

Different Models of Collaborative Degree Programs

Collaborative degree programs are offered mainly through two channels in China: Chinese-foreign cooperatively run educational institutions and Chinese-foreign cooperatively run educational projects.

Collaborative Degree Programs in Chinese-Foreign Cooperatively Run Educational Institutions

According to *the Regulations of the People's Republic of China on Chinese-Foreign Cooperation in Running Schools*, the Chinese-foreign cooperatively run educational institutions are defined as "the cooperation between foreign educational institutions and Chinese educational institutions in establishing educational institutions within the territory of China to provide education service mainly to Chinese citizens."[5] Those institutions "offering education for academic qualifications shall grant academic qualifications certificates or other education certificates in accordance with the relevant provisions of the state."[6] If the joint educational institutions grant the certificates of academic qualifications or certificates of academic degrees of a foreign educational institution, the certificates "shall be identical with the certificates of academic qualifications or certificates of academic degrees issued by the foreign educational institution in its own country and shall be recognized by that country."[7]

Up-to-date, collaborative degree programs offered through cooperatively run educational institutions mainly include following models:

Cooperatively run institutions within Chinese universities that grant students Chinese academic degrees. The partner universities jointly design the curriculum; faculties from the foreign institutions come to teach; credits earned from the foreign institution are accredited by the Chinese side; and students are conferred Chinese academic degrees upon graduation. An example is the Sino-German College of Tongji University cooperatively run by Tongji University and the German Academic Exchange Service (DAAD), which jointly educate the postgraduate students in such areas as Electronic and Computer Engineering and Mechanical and Vehicle Engineering and grant Chinese academic degrees.

Cooperatively run institutions within Chinese universities that confer foreign degrees. The cooperatively run institutions and educational projects introduce the curriculum of the foreign institution and integrate it with part of the Chinese courses; the foreign institutions recognize all the credits and grant students their academic degrees. An example is the Lambton College of Jilin University, cooperatively run by Jilin University and several foreign universities, such as Northwood University in the United States, which grant the corresponding certificates from those foreign universities.

Cooperatively run institutions within Chinese universities that grant the academic certificates from both institutions. Two institutions jointly determine the teaching goals and plans, and integrate both curriculum design and teaching modes effectively. Faculties teach on both sides, and credits are recognized and students granted academic degrees from both sides separately. An example is the China-EU Institute for Clean and Renewable Energy at Huazhong University of Science & Technology (HUST), cooperatively run by HUST and the Paris Institute of Technology, France. On completion, students receive degree certificates issued separately by each of the universities involved.

Recently, six high-standard, cooperatively run schools have been approved: the Sino-French Institute of Renmin University of China, Southeast University-Monash University Joint Graduate School (Suzhou), China-EU Institute for Clean and Renewable Energy at HUST, Beijing-Dublin International College at the Beijing University of Technology (BJUT), Sun Yat-sen University-Carnegie Mellon University Joint Institute of Engineering at Sun Yat-sen University, and SJTU-Paris Tech Elite Institute of Technology at Shanghai Jiaotong University.

In 2012 the Chinese Ministry of Education approved the establishment of several cooperatively run universities, including Shanghai New York University, Wenzhou-Kean University, and Duke Kunshan University.

Collaborative Degree Programs in Chinese-Foreign Cooperatively Run Educational Projects

"Chinese-foreign cooperatively-run educational projects refer to that the Chinese educational institutions and foreign institutions, without establishing educational institutions, provide the educational teaching activities based on cooperation of discipline, major, course etc., mainly to Chinese citizens."[8]

Programs Conferring Chinese Academic Degrees

In this case, Chinese and foreign institutions cooperate on selected disciplines. Students study, conduct research, and earn credits from foreign institutions, and then receive Chinese academic degrees upon graduation. Although this type of academic degree does not highlight the involvement of the foreign institution, the latter is involved in both the educational plan and process. For example, the joint PhD program funded by the China Scholarship Council (CSC) is designed to support doctoral students from Chinese institutions for up to 24 months' overseas study and research. Students will be conferred Chinese academic degrees upon successful defense of a thesis.

A good example is the cooperatively run Program for Training Physician Scientist of Tsinghua University and University of Pittsburgh. Students will finish their eight-year study in three phases: three years' study at Tsinghua for basic biochemical courses, two years' training at Pittsburgh for research skills (sponsored by CSC), and another three years at Tsinghua for clinical medicine learning. Students will be granted a Doctor of Medicine degree by Tsinghua University on completion.

Double Degree Programs

Study programs collaboratively offered by a Chinese institution and its overseas partner are commonly known as sandwich programs such as "2+2," "3+1," or "1+2+1." Two institutions agree on a joint development curriculum and a credit recognition system, and students study in each institution for two years and are conferred academic degrees separately issued by both institutions involved.

For example, Beijing Forestry University (BFU) cooperates with Michigan State University (MSU) in the United States in the double degree projects of Turfgrass Management, in which the teaching plans are developed by the two universities and credits are mutually recognized. In the first two academic years, classes are given by teachers of BFU, and in the next two, classes are organized by MSU. The graduates will be granted a Bachelor of Agronomy degree by BFU and a Bachelor of Science degree in Turfgrass Management by MSU.

Joint Degree Programs

Chinese and foreign institutions cooperate on selected disciplines and design curriculum and teaching modes together. Students register in both institutions and are supervised by professors from both sides. Credits earned from both institutions are accredited by each other; a single certificate of academic degree issued and signed by both institutions is conferred on completion.

The Joint Degree Program of Peking University (PKU) and the Georgia Institute of Technology, sponsored by CSC, is a case to point. The PKU and Georgia Tech students are registered with both institutions and supervised by professors from both sides. Students must go to the other institution to study under their foreign supervisor for two years. Credits earned from both institutions are accredited by each other. Students will receive one single certificate of doctoral degree with seals of both PKU and the Georgia Institute of Technology.

Positive Impact, Challenges and Future Developments

Positive Impact

Collaborative degree programs increase the level for Chinese-foreign cooperation in running schools, broaden educational offerings, and meet the diverse public demands of higher education and student's demands for receiving a world-level education and earning foreign degrees without going abroad or with going abroad for a shorter amount of time.

These programs increase channels for international exchange and cooperation; introduce world-level educational resources; advance internationalization of Chinese higher education; attach more importance to the international standards for running schools; and help to imbue students with global vision, international experiences, and the skills needed to succeed in today's global economy. These programs also contribute to higher education reform by reforming school-running mechanisms, promoting discipline and personnel training, and increasing campus vitality. They deepen collaboration between faculties and increase collaborative research projects.

It is a win-win model of mutual benefits, which help to strengthen academic research collaborations, raise foreign universities' visibility and reputation in China, and increase their international student enrollments.

Challenges

Collaborative degree programs are still in the initial stage where achievements and challenges coexist.

- The quality of educational resources and collaborative degree programs needs to be further improved.

- A comprehensive and internationalized evaluation and authentication systems should be established.

- Distribution of collaborative degree programs lacks of geographical balance. Collaborative degree programs are mainly conducted in relatively developed regions, like Beijing, Shanghai, Zhejiang, and Jiangsu, rather than economically less-developed regions.

- Repetition of academic disciplines is common. Disciplines such as business and economics management take a large proportion, with a scarcity of emerging and interdisciplinary fields of studies.

Future Developments

As stipulated in the *National Outline for Medium and Long-Term Education Reform and Development (2010–2020)*, China will "set up several exemplary and leading Chinese-foreign collaboratively-run institutions and programs"[9] and improve collaborative degree programs from the following aspects:

- Enforce the quality assurance mechanism for Chinese-foreign collaboration in running schools by setting up organizations or agencies to conduct accrediting activities regarding the teaching quality of the collaboratively run institutions and educational projects.

- Improve administration of collaborative degree programs. Both founders of the collaboratively run universities in China and abroad must be at leading level; the collaboratively run educational institutions must be set on their strongest disciplines and academic uniqueness must be stressed; collaboratively run educational projects must be focused on their disciplinary advantages and innovative curriculum design.

- Support and promote successful practices of Chinese-foreign cooperatively run institutions and educational projects.

- Implement the "going abroad" strategy, and encourage educational institutions to set up collaborative degree program overseas.

- CSC has been sponsoring study abroad programs for students at different levels, from undergraduate to PhD degrees. These initiatives have greatly encouraged and promoted cooperative degree programs, and brought innovations to the teaching and training modes in Chinese universities. In the future, CSC plans to launch more initiatives to expand the scale for sponsorship and support institutions in China and abroad to collaborate on academic disciplines with mutual interests.

NOTES

[1] Chinese-foreign cooperation in running schools is a general definition for Chinese-foreign cooperation on both educational institutions and projects.

[2] The State Council, P. R. China, *Regulations of the People's Republic of China on Chinese-Foreign Cooperation in Running Schools*, http://www.crs.jsj.edu.cn/index.php/default/news/index/3

[3] Ministry of Education, *Implementation Rules for the Regulations of the People's Republic of China on Chinese-Foreign Cooperation in Running Schools,* http://www.crs.jsj.edu.cn/index.php/default/news/index/6

[4] *List for Chinese-Foreign Cooperative Running Institutions and Projects,* http://www.crs.jsj.edu.cn/index.php/default/approval/orglists/1

List for Chinese-Foreign Cooperative Running Institutions and Projects, http://www.crs.jsj.edu.cn/index.php/default/approval/orglists/2

[5] The State Council, *Regulations of the People's Republic of China on Chinese-Foreign Cooperation in Running Schools,* http://www.crs.jsj.edu.cn/index.php/default/news/index/3

[6] The State Council, *Regulations of the People's Republic of China on Chinese-Foreign Cooperation in Running Schools,* http://www.crs.jsj.edu.cn/index.php/default/news/index/3

[7] The State Council, *Regulations of the People's Republic of China on Chinese-Foreign Cooperation in Running Schools,* http://www.crs.jsj.edu.cn/index.php/default/news/index/3

[8] The State Council, P. R. China, *Regulations of the People's Republic of China on Chinese-Foreign Cooperation in Running Schools*, http://www.crs.jsj.edu.cn/index.php/default/news/index/3

[9] Ministry of Education, P. R. China, *China's National Outline for Medium and Long-Term Education Reform and Development (2010–2020),* http://www.moe.gov.cn/publicfiles/business/htmlfiles/moe/A01_zcwj/201008/xxgk_93785.html

REFERENCES

The State Council, P. R. China. *Regulations of the People's Republic of China on Chinese-Foreign Cooperation in Running Schools.*

Ministry of Education, P. R. China. *China's National Outline for Medium and Long-Term Education Reform and Development (2010–2020).*

Ministry of Education, P. R. China. *Implementation Rules for the Regulations of the People's Republic of China on Chinese-Foreign Cooperation in Running Schools.*

List for Chinese-foreign cooperative running institutions.
http://www.crs.jsj.edu.cn/index.php/default/approval/orglists/1,

List for Chinese-foreign cooperative running projects.
http://www.crs.jsj.edu.cn/index.php/default/approval/orglists/2

Chapter Fifteen

A Third Wave of International Education: International Collaborative Programs in Australia

STEPHEN CONNELLY AND JAMES GARTON, RMIT UNIVERSITY

Introduction

A "third wave" of international education is developing in Australia, which gives more emphasis to broader collaboration between Australian higher education institutions (HEIs) and the rest of the world. This third wave builds on the first wave of aid education, commencing in the 1950s and 60s, and a second wave of "mass commercial education" from the late 1980s, largely in the Asian region. According to Universities Australia (2012), the peak organization representing Australian higher education:

> *This third wave approach emphasises a broader and deeper conception of international education integration extending to faculty and research links, doctoral studies, wider disciplinary representation and Australian student study abroad. The goals here are educational richness and not simple revenue payoff.*

A key element of the third wave is "international collaborative programs," defined by Knight (2008, p. 4) to include joint, double, and multiple degree programs resulting from academic cooperation among HEIs in different countries. This type of collaboration is fundamental to internationalization in universities, as discussed further below. In this chapter, we use the generic term *collaborative degree* to encompass different types of program collaborations between among institutions. The term *double degree* describes the arrangements whereby two institutions collaborate to devise a combined program structure that will result in the awarding of a degree from each participating institution; that is, students qualify for two degrees. The term *joint degree* refers to the arrangements whereby students participating in a multi-institution program qualify for one degree that is jointly awarded by the participating institutions.

In terms of Australian government policy, engagement with Asia remains a key focus. This has been made particularly pertinent by the release of the recent white paper, *Australia in the Asian Century* (Department of Prime Minister and Cabinet, Australian Government, 2012), which places education at the forefront of Australia's engagement with Asia and recognizes China, India, and Indonesia, among others, as critical players in the 21st century. According to this white paper, "Australia will have stronger and more comprehensive relationships with countries across the region, especially with key regional nations—China, India, Indonesia, Japan and South Korea" (p. 25).

Nonetheless, Australian international education in universities is broadening in a third wave of global engagement, as shown in the case studies in this chapter featuring international collaborative programs with Europe, the United States, and Asia.

A Comprehensive Approach

The success of international collaborative programs such as those described by Knight (2008) relies closely on the links between these collaborative initiatives and broader institutional objectives, in the style of comprehensive internationalization (CI), as advocated by Hudzik (2011). CI requires an institution-wide approach across the whole gamut of internationalization activity, supported and promoted at all levels of the institution.

Increasingly in Australia, HEI internationalization strategies are comprehensive in the manner Hudzik (2011) advocates, and these strategies include objectives related to broad areas of international activity, such as the policy and culture of internationalization, internationalization of curriculum and research, staff and student exchange, student recruitment, development of offshore partnerships and presences (including transnational delivery), and professional development of staff to support internationalization. Cooperation between institutions in different countries to provide collaborative degree study opportunities for their students, in one country or the other or both, can be a vehicle for implementation of all of these elements of a CI agenda. To elaborate, at the strategic level of policy and culture of internationalization, institutional planning and academic policy should allow for collaborative degree programs to be implemented and operate success-fully, including a credit transfer policy and the granting of, or qualification for, awards.

In terms of internationalization of curriculum, good practice in collaborative degree arrangements means both institutions working together not only on program matching and credit arrangements, but also on the development of customized content for the stu-dents in the particular degree program, in part to bring cohorts of students from each institution together either physically or virtually in classrooms.

Collaborative degree arrangements have as their base collaboration in teaching, but in order to ensure longevity of the relationship there should be opportunities for research collaboration that are identified early in the discussions, aligned with the teaching col-laboration. Collaborative degree arrangements provide the opportunity for staff exchange between institutions, at the different stages of the collaboration for the purposes of coteaching and coassessment, as well as visiting fellowships.

Whether they involve students crossing borders or not, collaborative degree programs are a different form of cooperation, and institutions need to encourage the development of academic and professional staff to support this type of activity. Ideally, students at both institutions should be able to access the collaborative degree opportunity. It is often the case that the collaborative degree option is more appealing to one student cohort than the other (e.g., European or Asian students are more mobile internationally than Aus-tralian students), but each institution should endeavor to use strategies such as student exchange to achieve a mix of students at each stage of the program.

Collaborative degrees are an opportunity for institutions to attract students they oth-erwise would not, thereby enhancing student recruitment activity. Such arrangements are also an opportunity for either or both participating institutions to establish a presence at the partner institution, to not only support teaching cooperation, but also coordinate other cooperative activities.

Measures of success for collaborative degrees should be established at the outset of discussions, to enable participating institutions to gauge progress toward agreed objec-tives and make decisions about continuing the collaboration at appropriate junctures. Critical to success is collaboration between academics and international office staff from the beginning of discussions. International offices have a crucial role in encouraging and facilitating synergies across the academic and nonacademic functions of the university, in particular to protect the university from financial and reputational risk, and to coordi-nate new elements that may develop in the partnership as it grows (Connelly, Garton, & Olsen, 2006, p. 15).

Some measures of success include the following:

- Approval processes are streamlined, and internal and external approvals are granted in a timely manner.

- Student enrolment is growing, with participating institutions attracting new cohorts of students and competing more effectively in their home environments.

- Students are academically successful in the programs.

- Financial objectives are achieved.

The institutional relationship grows beyond the collaborative degree collaboration to encompass research cooperation, staff exchange, student exchange, and curriculum development.

Case Studies

Australia–China

Engagement with China is very often a key plank of Australian universities' internationalization activities. See the recent white paper, *Australia in the Asian Century* (Department of Prime Minister and Cabinet, Australian Government, 2012), as mentioned earlier in this chapter.

Transnational education has become a difficult endeavor in China as the regulatory framework has shifted. Double-degree collaborations such as those developed by Swinburne, Griffith, and the Royal Melbourne Institute of Technology (RMIT) Universities at undergraduate level over the past eight years enable development of teaching collaborations as an initial relationship-building exercise, while avoiding the pitfalls of transnational delivery. Close to one thousand students have enrolled in the programs thus far. The model is relatively straightforward:

- Each university identifies a degree for "pairing" with the partner university (e.g., food technology and applied science), and via program and course matching and a system of cross credits, an academic program is created leading to the award of one undergraduate degree from each university to students completing the combined program.

- Each award is approved by the Academic Board at the relevant home institution. Generally, the internal approval process takes already established, and approved programs at each institution and simply approves the program matching and granting of credits required to enable students to qualify for both degrees.

- The double-degree arrangement is described in an overarching agreement signed by both parties.

- The agreement, along with relevant paperwork, is lodged with the Ministry of Education (MoE) in China.

- The MoE approves the double-degree arrangement and assigns a quota enabling the Chinese university to recruit "in score" students for the program. This is critical for recognition of the foreign degree when Chinese students return home.

- Students generally complete an initial period of study in China followed by further studies in Australia (total duration depends on the field of study). They then submit their Chinese thesis for marking at their home institution from Australia, and upon successful completion, they qualify for a degree from each institution.

The benefits of the model include the following:

Teaching is collaborative, including guest lectures in each direction, development of customized course content and courseware, and cosupervision of final year projects.

- Avoidance of transnational delivery in China.

- Quality regimes applying to teaching programs are internal and based in the home country for each institution, since each teaches its own content (or approved codeveloped content) in its own location.

- A pipeline of students intending to complete programs at the Australian university is established, enabling better forward planning of recruitment and admissions.

- Students progressing to the Australian award become a known quantity as the institutional relationship grows and can be targeted for preparatory programs (e.g., English) while enrolled in the Chinese component of the program.

- International student recruitment for the Australian university moves from a retail recruitment model via agents to a cohort recruitment model, enabling efficiencies and targeting of known student cohorts.

- Chinese students are able to access foreign studies and qualifications but spend less time (and money) abroad.

- Institutional relationships are established based on teaching collaboration, which can grow to research interactions and staff and student exchange over time.

The Chinese authorities are currently approving these types of programs in areas other than business, management, and information technology in order to encourage collaboration and internationalization in priority academic areas.

The challenges of this model of cooperation in double degrees include the following:

- Identification of a suitable partner institution is always the critical success factor in any proposed collaboration. In this case suitability includes identifying a partner institution that understands the MoE approval process.

- MoE approval is by no means guaranteed, and it is currently almost impossible to obtain in the business, management, or information technology disciplines.

- Agreements and paperwork submitted to the MoE need to clearly identify the proposed responsibilities of the foreign institution.

- Students generally flow in one direction, from China to Australia.

- Preparation of students in the Chinese component of the program for transfer to the Australian component needs to be carefully managed and implemented to ensure their smooth transition to life and studies in Australia.

- Transferring cohorts need to be integrated in the Australian degree program with local students to deliver the in-country experience they expect.

Australia–United States

The Swinburne University of Technology (SUT) in Melbourne, Australia, has developed a successful collaboration with Northeastern University (NU) in Boston to deliver a postgraduate double-degree program for Australian and international students in Melbourne. The structure of the program enables students to complete two years of study and obtain a Master of Commerce (International Business) degree from SUT and a Master of Science in Leadership degree from NU. Students complete 8 units of study from each institution, and via a system of cross credits (subject to academic and graduation requirements), they qualify for a degree from each institution.

Benefits of the model include the following:

- A Northeastern Study Center established at SUT coordinates the program. It also identifies and helps to implement other opportunities for collaboration between the two institutions.

- Australian students and international students studying in Australia have access to an international degree otherwise unavailable to them.

- The program has been highly popular with international students in particular, enhancing both institutions' offerings to that cohort.

- NU has been able to access students in Australia it otherwise would not have.

- The NU components are taught by NU staff in Melbourne, providing access for students to professors from both institutions.

- NU visiting professors generally stay for a period of about six weeks, enabling close collaboration with SUT academics on the double-degree program, as well as other areas of cooperation.

- The programs are melded together so that academic content from each institution is interwoven throughout the two-year program.

- Students have the opportunity to undertake units of study at NU in Boston during midyear intensives.

Challenges include the following:

- Face-to-face teaching by NU professors is resource intensive.

- Moving to alternate delivery modes for NU content diminishes the value proposition for potential students of face-to-face access to NU professors.

- The program has not been as popular with Australian students as international students.

- Students in the program have minimal access to or interaction with NU students in Boston.

Australia–Europe

The Erasmus Mundus program (2009–2013) has encouraged the development of joint programs at the master's and doctoral level. At master's level, joint programs are offered by a consortium of European universities from at least three different countries (which may also include countries from other parts of the world). This form of program mobility does not sit easily with the norms of Australian postgraduate student study habits or mobility, and hence participation by institutions and students will always be low. If the forms of degree cooperation between Australian and European universities are to be successful in the long term, collaborative programs will need to follow one of two possible models:

The first is to replicate the SUT-NU collaboration described in the preceding section, whereby European program offerings are brought to Australia. The SUT experience, presaged in pre-implementation market research and borne out by enrolment patterns, has been that Australian students need some convincing of the value of enrolling in a foreign degree program, whereas international students either already in Australia or intending to study there see enormous value in pairing an Australian degree with a foreign degree such as one from the United States or Europe. That perception of value among Australian students is likely to change over time, but to what extent and how quickly are uncertain.

The second model is to offer Australian degree programs in Europe in conjunction with local partner institutions, aimed principally at European students and with options for Australian students to participate in program segments. Some of these options could be single units of study taught in block mode, entire semesters on exchange, or completion of the Australian component at home and the European component abroad.

Institutions in Europe and Australia have been developing expertise for some time in various forms of program collaboration. The willingness or capability to collaborate on either side is not in question. Two impediments to successful degree collaboration between Australian and European universities are, however, obvious. The first is tuition, since the overwhelming majority of Australian postgraduate students pay tuition—some paying fairly substantial amounts—and the expectation will be that European and Australian students will need to pay fees for collaborative degree programs in the absence of funding options such as EU programs. The second impediment relates to the involvement of Australian students in the programs. Students in Europe and (predominantly) Asia see value in collaborative degree programs offered cooperatively by institutions from different countries and will travel to participate in such programs. Australian students will need convincing before they participate in numbers that will make collaborative programs viable.

Future Trends

Familiar challenges will remain as institutions seek to advance international collaboration, including collaborative degree arrangements. Internal issues, such as academic policy, capability and capacity of institutions to participate, and the place of internationalization in institutional strategic planning, will impact on the success of these programs. Externally, domestic and foreign regulatory environments will continue to affect the ways in which institutions are able to collaborate across borders. Additionally, in order to achieve broad internationalization objectives, universities seeking foreign partners deemed appropriate for collaborations such as joint or double degrees will also need to evaluate proposed partnerships for potential for research collaboration, helping to further deepen the ties that are generated by teaching collaborations. This latter issue is an important consideration for Australian universities as they seek to implement sustainable internationalization programs, as much as it is a factor in decision making for universities around the world.

The arrival of foreign corporations and educational institutions (e.g., Indian, American, and European) into Australia will bring new forms of competition to the Australian domestic education environment, but also opportunities for collaboration in ways that Australia is familiar with in other parts of the world. International student flows are already changing, with traditional source countries now competing effectively as destination countries. Institutions need to consider ways in which education can be brought to the student, rather than relying on the student to come to them. Global economic conditions are forcing students to reevaluate the type of education experience they are seeking, and the manner and location of that educational experience, which in turn forces institutions to reevaluate delivery modes and locations.

Conclusion

The continuing development of a third wave in Australian international education is fundamentally a shift from the transactional approach to partnerships typical of the second wave or phase of trade, along a continuum of collaboration to a more transformational approach, as noted by Sutton and Obst (2011, p. xiv): "Transformational partnerships combine resources and view linkages as sources of institutional growth and collaborative learning." This is the overall direction of the collaborative initiatives described in the preceding case studies: They are generative rather than static. They provide building blocks for greater engagement, necessitating innovation in academic policy, for example, the credit transfer policies, internationalization of the curriculum, and research opportunities that are built into double-degree arrangements.

Externally, HEIs in Australia will need to ensure that international collaborative programs continue to play a strategic role in building on the strong base provided in the trade phase with Asia, to develop global engagement that also involves Europe, the United States, and Latin America. Internally, within the institutions, a comprehensive approach to all aspects of internationalization will require best practice leadership and management in strategic planning, financial and human resource management and other facets of administration, and teaching and research, with appropriate support and opportunities for staff and students.

Innovative ways to cooperate internally within HEIs and externally with international partners will be key to a successful role for collaborative degrees in the third wave of Australian international education.

REFERENCES

Connelly, S., Garton, J. & Olsen, A. (2006, September). *Models and types: Guidelines for good practice in transnational education* (Report for the Observatory on Borderless Higher Education). Retrieved from http://www.obhe.ac.uk/documents/view_details?id=31

Department of Prime Minister and Cabinet, Australian Government. (2012). *Australia in the Asian century* (white paper). Retrieved from www.asiancentury.dpmc.gov.au

Hudzik, J. (2011). *Comprehensive internationalization: From concept to action* Washington DC: NAFSA. Retrieved from http://www.nafsa.org/Resource_Library_Assets/Publications_Library/ Comprehensive_Internationalization__From_Concept_to_Action/

Knight, J. (2008, September). *Joint and double degree programmes: Vexing questions and issues* (Report for the Observatory on Borderless Higher Education). Retrieved from http://www.obhe.ac.uk/documents/view_details?id=631

Sutton, S., and Obst, D. (2011). Introduction: The changing landscape of international partnerships. In S. Sutton and D. Obst (Eds.), *Developing strategic international partnerships: Models for sustaining innovative institutional linkages.* New York, NY: Institute of International Education. Retrieved from http://www.iie.org/en/Research-and-Publications/Publications-and-Reports/IIE-Bookstore/Developing-Strategic-International-Partnerships

Universities Australia. (2012). Policy and advocacy [tab on Universities of Australia website]. Retrieved from http://www.universitiesaustralia.edu.au/page/policy—-advocacy/international/

Chapter Sixteen

Russian-European Double Degree Programs: Key Factors of Success

ELENA A. KARPUKHINA, ACADEMY OF NATIONAL ECONOMY AND PUBLIC ADMINISTRATION

This chapter focuses on one of the most complex varieties of academic partnerships, double degree programs (DDPs) between Russian and European universities that usually lead to two degrees (or certificates) issued by each of the partner universities. Joint degree programs are not of special interest in this chapter, as under current Russian law the graduates should receive National Diplomas. At the same time, the phenomenon is developing in Russia within international consortia of universities, and the challenges and problems faced by the participants of joint and double degree programs are very much the same.

The chapter has two aims. The first is to present the results of the study of DDPs between universities in Russia and European Union Member States funded by the EU Delegation to Russia, carried out in 2010–2011, in which the author of the chapter was one of experts.[1] The second is to explore the factors that determine the success or failure of alliances in higher education in a Russian-European context.[2]

History of Academic Partnerships in Russia

The modern history of Russian-European academic partnerships goes back to the early 1990s when, on the one hand, demand arose for professionals able to work in an emerging market economy and civil society, and on the other hand, Russia opened up to the international community as a new promising marketplace.

The dynamic development of educational partnerships between European and Russian universities, starting in the early 1990s (Stage 1: 1990–2000) was affected by the following factors:

- The market economy and the emergence of new market segments.

- Increasing activity of foreign capital in the Russian economy.

- Growing demand for new generation specialists, with market economy knowledge and skills.

- Interest from employers (primarily in joint and foreign companies) in Western degrees as a guarantee of quality and relevance of knowledge and skills.

- Young people aspiring to receive a Western education (without necessarily going abroad).

For Russian universities the 1990s were a time of hope and disappointment. When the new Law on Education (2003) was passed, Russian universities gained permission and opportunities to establish ties with foreign universities and to take part in international programs. This led to intensive development of international contacts, revision of educational content, and the introduction of new methods in education and university management.

At the same time, substantial cuts in public funding for education brought a rapid expansion in applied programs, a reduction in demand for theoretical programs, and a fall in academic quality. In an attempt to capture their own niche on the market, many institutions reduced their portfolio of subjects to the ones that immediately met market demand, such as law, economics, and management, and offered only a limited number of academically challenging courses in sciences and mathematics. Needless to say, the graduates in the latter fields either looked for retraining, sought employment in the West, or found themselves among the unemployed.

The more progressive higher education institutions (HEIs) set themselves the goals of achieving high academic standards, on the one hand, and the practical aspects of their programs, on the other, in order to gain competitive edge for their graduates. It was extremely hard for Russian universities to maintain academic quality, both because of the sharp reduction in state funding and the tremendous difficulties of retaining and developing their academic and research potentials.

Another reason was the sudden change in the graduation profile of students in Russian institutions. In the past, the dominant demand was for engineering and the natural sciences, but in the 1990s this was replaced by a jump in the demand for socioeconomic, legal, and humanities expertise. In many of these areas the Russian education system had no teacher training schools that were comparable to what was available in Western Europe, and the schools that were established could not yet provide a high academic standard. The supply of Russian natural science and engineering schools was, on the contrary, substantially higher than the demand.

The main drivers of launching DDPs in the first stage were the following:

- Initiatives of Russian and European universities and business schools to establish DDPs in areas of demand in the expanding Russian market (management, business administration, foreign languages).

- Projects by international charitable foundations, aimed at establishing nongovernmental teaching institutions. It was during this period that some nongovernmental universities were founded that subsequently had a substantial impact on Russian education.

- International cooperation. There is no doubt that the EU-funded TEMPUS program played a crucial role in this as it gave students and teaching staff the opportunity to take part in international mobility projects, but also required inter-institutional cooperation in organizing and supporting collaboration, unlike the majority of grants (especially in the early stages) from other foreign foundations for overseas travel. This approach was actually predetermined by the involvement of Russian HEIs in TEMPUS. The program resulted in genuine financial support for Russian institutions, students, and teaching staff during the most difficult financial period. It was largely thanks to this program that Russian institutions acquired the necessary skills to fill in applications for international grants, fundraising, partnerships, and so forth.

In 2000 we witnessed the beginning of the next stage in the development of DDPs, which was characterized by the emergence of such programs across the whole of Russia, not just Moscow and St. Petersburg. At the same time, the new subject areas had been covered. It should be noted at this point that there was a diversification and specialization opportunities were provided in the framework of the DDPs. In the first stage, the most popular joint programs were management, economics, law, and language training; during the second stage, areas such as engineering, medicine, biotechnology, information technology, public sector management, tourism, and hospitality also became popular.

The critical role in this stage was played by international organizations, offering different forms to support the promotion of European programs in Russia and Russian universities, interested in developing international cooperation. In July 2003, the UK Secretary of State for Education and Skills and the Russian Minister for Education signed a Statement of Intent, "Russian–UK Partnerships in Higher Education" (the BRIDGE program). The project started in 2004 and ran until 2008. A total of 44 DDPs and 14 joint research programs were launched in Russian universities together with British universities.

A joint Russian-Finnish project, Cross Border University, started in 2004 for joint master's programs (double degrees). Four Russian universities (including three from St. Petersburg) and five universities in Finland were involved. Certain subjects were identified in this project as priorities: international relations, information technology, business, economics, law, public health, history, forestry, and bio-energy production.

For the first time, in 2005, the Russian Ministry of Education and Science announced a tender, operated by the National Training Foundation, to set up a multilateral project to monitor and support the establishment and implementation of double degree study programs. There were small grants to strengthen partnerships of Russian and European universities, which were very important to demonstrate the fact that DDPs were no longer the periphery of Russian educational system.

The third stage of DDP development (2010–2020) is linked to the completion of substantial structural changes in the higher education system. On the one hand, the stage of setting up leading universities has been completed: Moscow State and St. Petersburg State Universities, which received special status entitling them to work to their own standards and issue their own degrees; Federal and Research Universities; and 57 innovation HEIs.

The end of 2010 saw the final stage in the transition of Russian higher education to a two-cycle system. Serious changes were introduced, and in 2011 the adoption of the two-cycle system (bachelor's–master's) was completed. The third generation of educational standards to fit the two-cycle system was adopted, which gives more freedom and at the same time more responsibility to Russian universities. One of the tasks of the Russian universities is to increase the level of internationalization, increasing academic mobility and creating joint programs. Expert forecasts suggest that the establishment of double master's degree programs will enter a new level of development.

Double Degree Programs between Universities in Russia and European Union Member States: Major Trends and Specific Features

The research study on double degree programs between Russian and European universities, funded by the EU Delegation to Russia, was carried out by a group of experts from January to November 2010. The research elicited considerable feedback from Russian universities, EU embassies, international education agencies, the Russian Ministry of Education and Science, and the Federal Education and Science Supervision Agency (*Rosobrnadzor*), which demonstrated the urgency and relevance of the topic for Russian HEIs.

The project priority goal was to analyze the current state and scale of DDPs between Russian and EU HEIs, and determine what place they occupy in the context of Russian higher education and whether they are effective tools in achieving compatibility of higher education programs.

In carrying out the research, the expert group used a variety of methods, including:

- Questionnaires sent to Russian HEIs.

- Interviews with HEIs vice-chancellors, directors of DDPs, representatives of international departments of Russian universities and employers.

- Interviews with representatives of embassies and missions of EU Member States.

- Meetings with Russian and foreign experts and representatives of the Russian Ministry of Education and Science.

- Surveys and interviews of DDP students in Russian universities.

- Content analysis and comparative analysis of DDP-related documents.

- Internet search of Russian and European university websites.

The questionnaires sent to 345 universities[3] under the jurisdiction of the Russian Ministry of Education and Science (medical academies report to another ministry) were completed by 226 (65 percent) HEIs, 74 of which confirmed they were running DDPs (239 in absolute figures) with universities from EU Member States.

A large proportion of DDPs are run at the master's level (65 percent), with significantly fewer at bachelor's level (20 percent). There are some double degrees running for the five-year specialized degree (9 percent). The most complex DDPs to implement are PhDs: Doctoral programs make up only for 6 percent of the total number of DDPs.

In terms of number of contracts signed to set up DDPs with Russian universities, the undisputed leaders are the French institutions. Their share is approximately 37 percent (89 programs), followed by Germany with 22 percent (53 programs) and the UK with 17 percent (40 DDPs). Finnish HEIs are also actively engaged in inter-institutional cooperation with Russia: they are currently implementing approximately 22 (9 percent) DDPs (mostly with institutions in Russia's North-Western Federal District). Other countries should be mentioned, such as the Netherlands and Italy, with seven programs each; Spain, with five programs; Sweden and Cyprus, with three programs each. HEIs in Austria, Belgium, Bulgaria, Luxemburg, Poland, Czech Republic, and Estonia each have one DDP with Russian universities.

The geographical spread of DDPs in Russia, although impressive, still shows that the majority of international partnerships are located in Moscow and St. Petersburg. In general, the largest number of institutions running DDPs with European partners is concentrated in the Central (33 percent, or 24 institutions) and North-Western (22 percent, or 16 institutions) Federal Districts of Russia. The Volga and Siberian districts both rank third, with each of them running double degrees in 12 (16 percent) institutions. Altogether, the other Federal Districts account for just 13 percent of the total: The Urals District has four institutions with double degrees; the Southern Federal District has three HEIs; and the Far-Eastern and North-Caucasian have two and one, respectively.

If analyzed according to specialization area, the findings from the questionnaires to Russian HEIs indicated that management and economics (as well as engineering specialties and courses) constitute a major part of all the proposed subject areas. These two subject groups represent 45 percent and 35 percent, respectively, of the 239 programs identified. The management and economics heading includes management, economics, and international management; engineering includes computer science and a few highly specialized programs (such as chemical engineering and biotechnology). Humanities make up 14 percent, with primarily history, law, modern languages, and international relations. Natural sciences (physics, mathematics, chemistry, etc.) account for approximately 6 percent of all the proposed subject areas.

The study demonstrated that the practical experience built up in the Russian education community has generally led to widespread existence of DDPs being jointly developed and implemented within the framework of integrated curricula. This is a significant achievement for Russian universities that aim to break the usual stereotypes of rigid state standards and adopt a flexible approach to resolving issues of restructuring program development and delivery of disciplines and courses. They also have the goal of creating fundamentally new mechanisms for quality assurance and control. However, the European concept of DDPs presupposes that students take part in the courses at one of the partner universities, while the time spent by students of the inter-institutional partnership is of equivalent duration. In many Russian universities, studying for part of the program at a partner institution is widespread. In the majority of the cases, the cost to travel to and study in the partner country must be borne by the student and his or her family, which essentially prevents the physical mobility of the Russian students from being an essential and integral element of the program.

Distance learning is being developed as an alternative to academic mobility, and many Russian students follow courses and modules taught by overseas staff through distance learning. One specific distinguishing feature of DDPs between Russian and European universities is the asymmetry in student mobility numbers at the partner universities. The same goes for mobility among teaching staff. Obviously, this situation raises questions about specific features of DDPs in Russia.

On the basis of the research findings, the conclusion is that, despite growing interest from Russian universities toward DDPs, the number of participants remains limited. Approaches and practices for the establishment of such programs overlap to a great extent with European practices, while in many other aspects, they provide their own particular examples and models.

The different models and types of programs point to the variety of approaches adopted by Russian universities in the concept, design, and implementation of DDPs. This is partly because the partnerships are at different stages of development and have varying levels of institutional and financial resources. At the same time, DDPs are not an end as such; participating parties are united in their efforts to solve important issues that are on the Russian educational agenda, the first being to raise competiveness of Russian education and its graduates internationally.

It is difficult to ascribe the complex and multidimensional DDPs to one single scheme with one common denominator. Therefore, any attempt to categorize them will depend on the criteria system, for example:

- Presence of a Western partner: from "strong" to "weak" presence (especially in the validation model).

- Language of instruction: from "exclusively in the foreign language" to "exclusively in Russian."

- Level of curriculum integration: from "full" to "minimum required" for the award of the qualification from the Western or Russian institution.

- Exclusively on-site tuition to full distance learning, with intermediate variations to incorporate both approaches.

There is no doubt that this is an acutely topical subject and would make a suitable theme for an in-depth study.

Motivation Patterns, Difficulties, and Risks

Regarding the motivation behind DDP arrangements, Russian universities, aware of the gap between them and European HEIs in terms of concepts and several key processes and procedures, saw the possibility of awarding DDP qualifications recognized in the West as well as opportunities to build teaching staff capacities. This, among other things, definitely implied raising student and staff competitiveness. Increasing student admissions and academic reputation were also seen as salient factors.

The above mentioned study showed that DDPs are the logical results of previous collaboration between universities. In most cases, there is joint work within international projects or successful professional connections between researchers and academics from both universities. It is interesting that 43 percent of universities attribute the leading role for establishing DDPs to the senior administration of the Russian university. At the same time, the role of European universities is also measurable—in 35 percent of cases the initiative came from the foreign partner. Neither the Russian Ministry of Education and

Science nor the local authorities demonstrated any interest in establishing partnerships between Russian and European universities.

In reply to the question about how Russian universities have benefited from DDPs, Russian educational establishments pointed out that an exposure to European education was extremely helpful as it prepared staff and students to work in a multicultural environment and, ultimately, in the global market. The universities also reported that collaborative programs led to a change in the organizational culture and quality assurance philosophies in their institutions and helped strengthen their links with employers and industries. Interviewed students mentioned major changes in student–tutor relationships, education becoming more student-centered, and confidence in their abilities and potentials being strengthened.

Problems and risks, where ranked, were that poor knowledge of European languages by Russian students and staff as well as lack of experience in implementing joint projects were major impediments, even more serious than the legal and financial issues that had to be sorted out to enable the partners to launch DDPs. From the point of view of existing Russian legislation, the implementation of DDPs is the most unregulated program, which results in many difficulties for universities in Russia and abroad. It is only fair to point out, however, that DDPs are usually established not because of a well-thought-through Russia-wide policy, but rather because of grassroots initiatives from the HEIs themselves. The absence of any regulatory framework for DDPs might appear to give Russian universities more leeway to act. Actually, it greatly hampers their development because it leaves unresolved issues such as recognition of periods of study, parity of degrees or qualifications, and so forth.

Despite the major transformation of Russian education regarding modernization of the content and methods of teaching, new approaches to the concept of quality in the learning process are very unevenly distributed in Russian universities and are far from being complete. In the most general terms, the existing difficulties lead to the following, according to respondents:

- The Russian structure of degree levels or cycles, while close to the European model (bachelor's–master's), is structured on a 4+2 model (or five years for specialist qualification). The three-year bachelor's degree that is widely taught across Europe is not recognized in Russia, which makes recognition of a graduate's degree from a European university virtually impossible. Therefore, it is very difficult to attain a master's degree in Russia for someone who received a bachelor's in Europe. At the same time, no consideration is given to the fact that primary and secondary education in European countries lasts for 12–13 years, compared to 11 in Russia. The problem is being discussed widely in Russia now, but is still unresolved.

- The tuition for Russian students is high; there are more classroom hours; and independent work is poorly developed.

- There are different approaches to university education in Europe and Russia: a student-oriented approach in European countries (the tradition and obligation of a European HEI is professional interest toward each individual learner) and the teacher-oriented approach in Russia (a still popular idea, according to which the teacher covers the entire content of the course).

- The relations between students and teaching staff at European universities are more democratic than in Russia.

- There are different learning assessment systems: Russian oral exams versus European essays and exams, team work, group projects, and presentations in the form of reporting, and so forth.

- A system of assessment criteria for knowledge and skills in Russian HEIs, especially in the humanities, is absent or insufficient developed.

- There are different systems to ensure education quality.

Almost all respondents noted the difference between the education systems in the approach to quality standards in education, the role of the teacher, the proportion of classroom hours and independent work by students and learners, and the evaluation of learning outcomes. The third-generation standards adopted by the Russian Ministry of Education and Science in 2010 substantially extend the autonomy of Russian universities. There is an opportunity to level off the differences, but this will definitely require time and concerted effort.

What Makes a Double Degree Program Successful?

The complexity of managing academic programs is increased significantly in the context of international programs. For such a challenging partnership as a DDP to run effectively, each party needs to be confident in the abilities and desires of the partner to collaborate. Therefore, bear in mind that cooperation between different players is always, in essence, a kind of compromise: All the stakeholders are primarily governed by their own interests, but it is necessary not to be too intransigent if the program is to be a success.

In the agreement that is signed by the institutions, there must be clear and comprehensible rules and procedures for joint work and quality control requirements. The formulation of a single operational framework inside joint programs is not possible without first structuring the relations between the partners, where the "soft issues" play a tremendous role. Experience shows that the cultural (norms and values), technical (teaching methods and evaluation procedures), and social (ways of thinking, working, and interacting with each other) differences between partners do not play a crucial role in the success of the collaboration, even if solving these problems is complex.

The problem is not a cultural clash, but a lack of mutual understanding, flexibility, or the wish to understand and overcome cultural differences that can stop the partners from gaining collaborative learning as a valuable benefit from the process. Differences are inevitable, but they should not frighten partners; they should be viewed as something that needs to be managed in terms of cultural compatibility, trust, and commitment toward a common goal, all of which lie at the heart of every DDP. The program should create its own shared culture (a set of intellectual values and behavior rules) that takes into account the cultural specificity of each partner and matches their shared, agreed interests.

The list of stakeholders and the diversity of viewpoints raise several issues that must be addressed—from simple questions about achieving communication between stakeholders to the complicated tasks of agreeing to mutually acceptable approaches to quality assurance management of programs. The drive toward greater cooperation and harmonization in the European educational space envisaged under the Bologna process has accelerated moves toward achieving shared and workable understandings of quality assurance mechanisms and, more broadly, shared visions of educational practice that can facilitate the level of integration and mobility called for in Europe. In Russia we are still some way from attaining full consensus as to what constitutes the *qualitative* aspects of education, rather than the more straightforward, if still difficult, task of quantitative measurements for the purposes of credit.

In conclusion, establishing and developing DDPs require management techniques to solve the many problems and challenges faced by HEIs and to address a multifaceted and complex organizational process. The process itself requires management, organizational and intellectual efforts, and training of all parties.

The hardest part of managing partner relations is that those relations are virtually imperceptible: they cannot be touched, taken apart, or analyzed through formal procedures, and there is no one correct way to manage them. Such relations have to be built in a long and painstaking process requiring attention to detail and complete honesty. A prior history of trust and cooperation between individuals taking part in designing a joint study program helps build up trust between the partners and is thus conducive to the program's success.

NOTES

[1] The European Union's ENPI Program for Russia. Analysis of DDPs between EU and Russian HEIs. Prepared by Karpukhina Elena, Sinytkin Igor, and Mishin Alexander. March 2011.

[2] This part is based on practical experience of the author, who participated in the organization and launch of different joint programs with European universities and business schools and participated as an expert in different international studies on the issue.

[3] At that time the number of state universities was 665, which means that more than 50 percent of State Russian Universities received the questionnaires. http://www.gks.ru/free_doc/new_site/population/obraz/vp-obr1.htm

Chapter Seventeen

Collaborative Degree Programs in East Asia: Findings from a Survey

Takako Yuki, Japan International Cooperation Agency (JICA) Research Institute

Overview of Cross-Border Double or Joint Degree Programs

In East Asia, demand for higher education has surged and has been developing significantly. Cross-border higher education has played an important role in this development. Not only has such mobility of students become common in East Asian countries, but the programs have also evolved toward twinning and joint or double degree programs, enabling students to obtain foreign degrees or diplomas in less time and at a lower cost than staying abroad for the entire period.

For example, the number of Japanese universities establishing double degree programs with foreign institutions has been growing steadily over the years (Ministry of Education, Culture, Sports, Science and Technology [MEXT], 2009, p. 180). As of 2008, 260 double degree programs at 85 universities were active in Japan. Macaranas (2010) compared the availability of twinning and double/joint programs in 14 Asian countries[1] and indicated that half of the countries, including Malaysia, Japan, and Australia, provided both twinning and double/joint programs as of 2006. In Malaysia, the success of twinning programs that have been facilitated by the appropriate legal and regulatory changes since the mid-1990s led the way for double/joint degree arrangements (Knight & Sirat, 2011).

Furthermore, a survey conducted in leading universities in the Association of Southeast Asian Nations (ASEAN)[2] plus three countries (China, Korea, and Japan) indicates that senior officers of these leading universities perceived that cross-border collaborative degree programs (including double/joint degree programs) would become more common in the future (Kuroda, Yuki, & Kang 2010). Recent policy trends in this region also support the enhancement of cross-border collaboration in higher education. For example, in 2005 the first East Asia Summit recognized higher education as an important sector for regional cooperation.[3] At the second Japan-China-Korea Trilateral Summit, held in Beijing in October 2009, the leaders of the three countries agreed to promote an Asian version of the European Union's Erasmus Mundus program, called Campus Asia (Korean Educational Development Institute [KEDI], 2009; MEXT, 2010). Double degree programs are part of the Campus Asia program.

Double degree programs appear to be more feasible than joint degree programs because of regulations, and they are more commonly implemented according to a study of Japan and six East Asian countries, namely, the Philippines, Thailand, Malaysia, Singapore, Vietnam, and Indonesia (Japan International Cooperation Agency [JICA] & Asia SEED, 2012). Double degree programs can be implemented if they meet the criteria for a degree in each of the partners' higher education institution, whose quality is assured in their own country. On the other hand, a joint degree program, where a single degree certificate is provided jointly by both institutions after ensuring that the degree meets the criteria of both countries, is not yet legally allowed in Japan. However, such a possibility is being discussed. Indonesia has similar regulatory constraints, as it does not allow organizing a single program jointly with a partner country. In Thailand, the granting of a joint degree is allowed based on "the guidelines for academic cooperation between Thai Higher Education Institution and Foreign Higher Education Institution" B.E.2550 (2007) drafted by the Ministry of Education. Yet, as of 2011, the number of joint degree programs was much lower than that of double degree programs. In Malaysia, the number of joint degree programs also seems to be limited, and most of such programs are implemented by top public universities.

Expectations and Challenges

To examine the expectations and challenges of cross-border collaborative degree programs in East Asia, this section focuses on the results of a survey of leading universities' cross-border collaborative degree programs in Southeast Asia and in the four other countries (China, Japan, Korea, and Australia). This survey was conducted by the JICA

Research Institute in 2009–2010. The 300 leading universities were systematically selected on the basis of (1) the number of times that a university was ranked in three international university-ranking sources or (2) its membership in eight international university associations.[4] After selecting the 300 leading universities, their cross-border collaborative degree programs were identified through the following three steps. The first step was to search for the relevant national information from the ministries of education or from key publications.[5] The second step was to conduct website searches for each of the 300 leading universities with relevant keywords, such as twinning and double/joint degrees, and to look through the home pages of the offices of international affairs or the equivalent, which often list partnering universities according to the different types of memorandums of understanding. Last, the document and website search results were compiled into one list totaling 1,048 identified collaborative degree programs with the corresponding information, including the name and country of the partner university, the source of the search results, the contact address of the office in charge (e.g., international affairs) or an alternative contact, and when possible, the level of degree (e.g., bachelor's), field of study, and type of program.

The survey design identified the cross-border collaborative degree programs, and a draft questionnaire was reviewed and discussed with participants from the target countries at a workshop jointly organized by the JICA Research Institute and the Southeast Asian Ministers of Education Regional Centre for Higher Education and Development (SEAMEO RIHED) in Bangkok on June 30, 2009. Thereafter, the questionnaire was distributed to officers in the office of international affairs or other relevant office responsible for the degree program that was identified. The questionnaire asked about the degree program's features, expected outcomes, and challenges. Of the 1,048 identified degree programs (full sample) of leading universities, 254 responses (subset sample) were received.

Although the response rate of the program survey may not appear high, the basic features do not seem to be substantially different with regard to the respondents compared with a complete sample of identified programs. For example, the sample of cross-border collaborative programs at leading East Asian universities is more likely to be at the postgraduate level than at the undergraduate level. Master's degrees appear to be the most popular in both the full sample programs and the subset of sample programs that responded to the survey. At both the postgraduate and bachelor levels, the most popular academic fields are the social sciences, business, and law. Engineering appears to be the second most popular academic field. On the regions of the partner universities, around 30 percent of the programs are partnered with Western Europe, followed by Northeast Asia, North America, and Oceania Pacific, either in the complete or subset of sample programs.

For the degree of collaboration between higher education institutions across borders, the responses of the subset sample programs provide information on the following four items: (1) teaching staff, (2) study location, (3) curriculum provider, and (4) degree provider. Table 17.1 summarizes the distribution of the sample collaborative degree programs that responded to our survey by item and degree of collaboration. According to the degree providers, approximately 60 percent of collaborative degree programs are grouped into "bilateral programs," which require high collaboration between partner institutions in two or more countries, that is, double/joint degree programs. The rest includes twining programs, where degrees are issued by either one of the partner institutions.

TABLE 17.1: NUMBER OF COLLABORATIVE DEGREE PROGRAMS THAT RESPONDED TO THE SURVEY BY ITEM AND LEVEL OF COLLABORATION

Item of collaboration	One-side led programs		Bilateral programs		N.A. or Missing		Total	
Teaching staff provider	33	(13%)	190	(76%)	26	(10%)	249	(100%)
Location of study	46	(18%)	187	(75%)	16	(6%)	249	(100%)
Curriculum provider	43	(17%)	176	(71%)	30	(12%)	249	(100%)
Degree provider	92	(37%)	145	(58%)	12	(5%)	249	(100%)

Source: JICA Survey.

Expectations

Regarding program-level perceptions, respondents were asked to identify the significance of a given item on the expected outcomes of cross-border activity, using a 5-point Likert scale: 4 = *highly significant*, 3 *fairly significant*, 2 = *moderately significant*, 1 = *slightly significant*, and 0 = *not significant*. Table 17.2 compares the expected outcomes of the cross-border collaborative programs between two groups separated by the degree of collaboration according to degree providers. The double and joint degree programs show that the expectation "to achieve research excellence" is more significant than for other collaborative programs. The expectation "to improve the quality of education" tends to be viewed in both types of programs as fairly important.

Regarding the perceptions of the political dimension of the expected outcomes, the pattern seems to be similar to that found for the academic dimension. For most elements of the political dimension, the mean scores of the perceived significance for bilateral programs are higher than those for one-side led programs. However, on average, this difference is not statistically significant.

Overall, the key expected outcomes for cross-border collaborative programs pertain more to academic and political dimensions than to economic dimensions. The economic dimension shows a pattern opposite to those of the academic and political dimensions. Namely, the expectations "to meet the demands of the Asian regional economy" and "to generate revenues for your own institution" are perceived as less significant by double or joint degree programs than by other collaborative programs.

The perceptions of the economic dimension as an "expected outcome" may be more affected by the level of economic development in the respective countries than by other dimensions. To address this potential economic effect, the sample collaborative degree programs were first separated into two categories: (1) programs conducted between institutions in low-income and high-income countries and (2) programs conducted between institutions in middle-income and high-income countries. For each category, any differences in the expected outcomes were compared between one-side led programs and bilateral programs. The differences are statistically significant for the second category (i.e., programs between institutions in middle-income and high-income countries). In addition, the academic, political, and economic dimensions of the expected outcomes are perceived as being more important by bilateral programs (i.e., double/joint degree programs) than by one-side led programs. One exception is generating revenues, which is perceived in one-side led programs as being more important than in bilateral programs.

TABLE 17.2: SIGNIFICANCE OF "EXPECTED OUTCOMES" OF COLLABORATIVE DEGREE PROGRAMS IN EAST ASIA BY ITEM AND LEVEL OF COLLABORATION

| Expected outcome | Mean by degree provider | | | |
	One-side led programs	Bilateral programs	Difference	
Academic				
To improve quality of education	2.98	3.09	-.11	
To achieve research excellence	2.56	2.83	-.27	*
To promote intercultural/ international awareness and understanding	2.89	3.09	-.21	
Political				
To promote global citizenship	2.66	2.72	-.05	
To promote regional collaboration and identity of Asia	2.71	2.71	.00	
To promote national culture and values	2.67	2.60	.07	
To improve international visibility and reputation of your university	3.05	3.07	-.03	
Economic				
To meet the demand of global economy	2.80	2.62	.18	
To meet the demand of Asian regional economy	2.93	2.50	.43	***
To meet the demand of your national economy	2.91	2.83	.08	
To generate revenue for your own institution	2.83	1.64	1.19	***
Academic	2.81	3.00	-.20	
Political	2.77	2.78	.00	
Economic	2.87	2.40	.47	***

Note: 4 = "Highly significant"; 3 = "fairly significant"; 2 = "moderately significant"; 1 = "slightly significant"; 0 = "not significant". *p.<1, **p.<.05 , ***p.<.01 in T-test of differences in means between "one-side led programs"and"bilateral programs."

Source: JICA Survey.

Challenges

If compared to the expected outcomes, most of the sample collaborative degree programs tend to perceive challenges as not significant or only slightly or moderately significant. Among the various challenges, those perceived as being most significant appear to be difficulty of recruiting students and difficulty of resolving language issues, although the degree of significance is not high. Other aspects worth considering include insufficient financial resources and difficulty of ensuring quality. These programs are less likely to perceive risks with regard to social aspects, such as a brain drain or a loss of cultural or national identity.

As Table 17.3 indicates, for differences according to the degree of collaboration by degree provider, the challenges or risks tend to be perceived as more significant in one-side led programs than in bilateral programs (i.e., double/joint degree programs). When the challenges are categorized into the three dimensions (social, academic, and administrative), this trend is very evident, particularly for the social dimension of challenges, as shown in the last three rows of Table 17.3. Brain drain and overuse of English as a medium are considered more significant in one-side led programs than in bilateral programs as well as inequity of access and loss of cultural or national identity.

Similarly, the academic dimension of challenges is also perceived as more significant in one-side led programs than in bilateral programs. For each element of the academic dimension, the means of one-side led programs were higher than those of bilateral programs, although most were not statistically significant. However, one element with a statistically significant difference was the difficulty of ensuring quality. Kuriyama, Saito, Mayekawa, and Muta (2008) conducted a survey of universities in Japan with graduate schools to examine the characteristics of cross-border collaborative degree programs at the graduate level. According to responses from the 12 currently active programs, the main difficulties encountered by Japanese graduate programs also appeared to be administrative, such as lack of accreditation and regulations for credit transfer.

For the administrative dimension of challenges, the means of each element for "one-side led programs" were overall higher than those of "bilateral programs." Among the several elements of the administrative dimension, "insufficient administrative capacities" and "difficulty of credit transfer recognition" are perceived as more significant in one-side led programs than in bilateral programs. "Miscommunication with partner universities" is also considered as a more significant challenge than in bilateral programs.

TABLE 17.3: SIGNIFICANCE OF "CHALLENGES" OF COLLABORATIVE DEGREE PROGRAMS IN EAST ASIA BY ITEM AND LEVEL OF COLLABORATION

Challenges	Mean by degree provider			
	One-side led programs	Bilateral programs	Difference	
Social				
Inequity of access	1.58	1.27	.31	*
Brain drain	1.66	1.27	.38	**
Overuse of English as medium	1.48	1.09	.40	**
Loss of cultural or national identity	1.51	1.13	.38	**
Academic				
Difficulty of assuring quality	2.06	1.62	.44	**
Irrelevance of education content	1.69	1.53	.16	
Difficulty of employment prospect	1.73	1.51	.22	
Lack of accreditation	1.57	1.44	.13	
Administrative				
Insufficient financial resource	1.94	1.70	.25	
Insufficient administrative capacities	1.94	1.51	.43	**
Miscommunication with partner university	1.71	1.38	.33	*
Difficulty of credit transfer recognition	1.69	1.35	.34	*
Differences in academic calendars	1.86	1.71	.15	
Difficulty of recruiting students	2.10	2.19	-.09	
Difficulty of resolving language issues	1.87	2.13	-.26	
Social	1.56	1.19	.37	**
Academic	1.76	1.53	.24	
Administrative	1.87	1.71	.16	

Note: 4 = "Highly significant"; 3 = "fairly significant"; 2 = "moderately significant"; 1 = "slightly significant"; 0 = "not significant". *$p < 1$, **$p < .05$, ***$p < .01$ in T-test of differences in means between "one-side led programs" and "bilateral programs."

Source: JICA Survey.

Conclusions

According to the program-level survey of leading universities in several countries in East Asia discussed above, the expectations for cross-border collaborative degree programs, including double/joint programs, appear more often in the academic and political dimensions than in the economic dimension. Although the institutions see few risks or challenges in cross-border collaboration as a whole, they perceive more risks in the administrative and academic dimensions (e.g., insufficient administrative capacities and difficulty of ensuring quality) than in the social dimension. When the collaborative degree programs are divided into two groups, either double/joint degree programs or other forms, the challenges tend to be perceived as less significant in the former than in the latter. This tendency is particularly notable for the social dimension of challenges, such as the brain drain and inequity.

Policies can address the perceptions of higher education institutions regarding the expected outcomes and risks in engaging in collaborative degree programs, such as those identified above and may further promote and facilitate collaboration among institutions. As this study has found, program providers perceived the quality of education to be a significant expected outcome of their cross-border collaborative degree programs, but they simultaneously see ensuring quality as a challenge. Given current policy directions in establishing a new Asian framework for quality assurance in cross-border higher education and credit transfers by the Southeast Asian Ministers of Education Organization (SEAMEO) and the Asia-Pacific Quality Network (APQN), regulatory and procedural frameworks should be improved to encourage higher education institutions to deepen their commitment to cross-border collaborative degree programs in the region.

Because this survey is, to the author's knowledge, the first such attempt in this region, its limitations may be addressed by increasing the scope of the target higher education institutions and their degree programs and by improving the response rate. This survey only focused on leading universities in the East Asia region, and the responses are not representative of the 14 countries. Because the sample distribution across the countries was unbalanced, therefore, this chapter does not claim that the analysis is representative of all existing cross-border collaborative degree programs in the entire East Asia region. Even among the respondents, the valid responses provided had limited factual information, such as the number of students and their countries of origin. With support from local stakeholders with an increasing interest in this area, the information could be made more comprehensive.

NOTES

[1] They are Cambodia, Malaysia, Laos, Philippines, Indonesia, Singapore, Thailand, Vietnam, Australia, South Korea, Taiwan, China, Japan, and Hong Kong.

[2] The ASEAN countries surveyed are Cambodia, Indonesia, Malaysia, Myanmar, Philippines, Singapore, Thailand, and Vietnam.

[3] See the ASEAN website: http://www.aseansec.org/21002.htm (accessed July 21, 2011).

[4] See Kuroda et al. (2010) for details of the selection criteria for the 300 universities.

[5] Chinese data were found online (http://www.crs.jsj.edu.cn/check_info.php?sortid=2 accessed June 24, 2009), and Korean and Vietnamese data were sent directly from the Korean Educational Development Institute (November 30, 2008) and the Ministry of Education and Training of Vietnam (April 1, 2009). Key publications used included *Education Guide Malaysia (2007)* by the Ministry of Higher Education Malaysia (for Malaysia); *Collaborative Degree Programmes between Thai and Foreign Higher Education Institutions (2006)* by the Commission on Higher Education (for Thailand); and *Godeung Gyoyuk Jipyo Mit Jisu Gyebal Yeon Gu*

[Indicators and Indices for Development of the Internationalization of Higher Education] *(2006)* by the Ministry of Education, Culture, Sports, Science and Technology (MEXT) and the Korean Educational Development Institute (KEDI) (for Korea).

REFERENCES

Japan International Cooperation Agency (JICA) & Asia SEED. (2012). *Tounanajia niokeru kokkyouwokoeru koutoukyouikuno genjyou to kadainikakaru monbukagakusyou JICA goudoucyousa saisyuuhoukokusyo* [Final report of a MEXT-JICA joint research on the status and issues of cross-border higher education in Southeast Asia]. Tokyo, Japan: JICA.

Knight, J. & Sirat, M. (2011). The complexities and challenges of regional education hubs: Focus on Malaysia. *Higher Education, 62,*593–606 .

Korean Educational Development Institute (KEDI). (2009). *Asiapan Erasmus program "Campus Asia" Ui chu jin jeon ryak gwa jun mang* [Driving strategies and prospects of Asian version of Erasmus program "Campus Asia"]. Seoul, Korea: Author.

Kuriyama, N., Saito, T., Mayekawa, S., & Muta, H. (2008). Research on the current situation of joint degree programs in Japanese graduate schools. *Journal of NIAD-UE (Research on Academic Degrees and University Evaluation), 8,* 1–20.

Kuroda, K., Yuki, T., & Kang, K. (2010). *Cross-border higher education for regional integration: Analysis of the JICA-RI survey on leading universities in East Asia* (JICA-RI Working Paper 26). Tokyo, Japan: Japan International Cooperation Agency Research Institute.

Macaranas, F. M. (2010). Business models in Asia-Pacific transnational higher education. In C. Findlay, & W. G. Tierney, (Eds.), *Business models in Asia-Pacific transnational higher education: The changing nature of a dynamic market* (121–62). Singapore: World Scientific.

Ministry of Education, Culture, Sports, Science and Technology (MEXT). (2009). *FY2009 white paper on education, culture, sports, science and technology*. Tokyo, Japan: Author.

MEXT. (2010). *Nitchukan ni okeru daigaku kan koryu no sokusin* [Promotion of universities collaboration in Japan, China and Korea]. Retrieved from http://www.mext.go.jp/component/b_menu/shingi/giji/__icsFiles/afieldfile/2010/01/20/1289240_1.pdf

World Bank. (2008). *World development report 2009: Reshaping economic geography*. Washington, DC: World Bank.

ACKNOWLEDGMENTS

This chapter was prepared based on the JICA Research Institute project, Cross-Border Higher Education for Regional Integration and the Labor Market in East Asia. This research project is co-led by Kazuo Kuroda. I appreciated the advice and comments from Supachai Yavaprabhas, Jane Knight, and other experts on this research. I also received valuable information from various JICA members, although the views expressed here do not represent the official positions of JICA.

Chapter Eighteen

International Joint and Double Degrees in Latin America: Current Trends

JOCELYNE GACEL-ÁVILA, UNIVERSIDAD DE GUADALAJARA

Introduction

According to the 3rd Global Survey of the International Association of Universities (IAU), international joint and double degree programs (JDDs) have become a strategic activity of the highest priority among higher education institutions' (HEIs') internationalization programs, along with student mobility, research collaboration, and international students. In the global context, Latin America is lagging behind with the least number of JDDs, behind Africa and slightly below the Middle East (IAU, 2010). Therefore, the aim of this chapter is to describe the findings of the most recent survey on JDDs, the *Survey on International Joint and Double Degree Programmes 2012* (carried out at the end of 2012), in order to look for new regional trends and compare them globally. Although the 2012 HEI sample is smaller than the 2009 one, it provides relevant insight into the regional trends of JDDs, given that the respondents were chosen from a selected group of HEIs actively engaged in an internationalization process and enjoying regional visibility in this regard.

Background: Main Global Trends

Recent studies have described JDDs' main characteristics (Knight, 2008a; 2008b; Obst, Kuder, & Banks, 2011; Knight & Lee, 2012) and identified the following global trends: Most JDDs were established between 2001 and 2009, with double degrees (DDs) by far more popular than joint degrees (JDs); most of them have been implemented at the master's level, and a large number of participating institutions indicated that they plan to develop more at this level; the most frequently cited academic disciplines for current and future JDDs are business and management, along with engineering; the most dynamic regions and countries in this topic are Europe (France, Germany, Italy), Australia, the United Kingdom, and the United States; the most desirable partner countries for future collaboration at the master's level are China, the United States, France, India, and Germany; the main motivations are broadening educational offerings, strengthening research collaboration, advancing internationalization and raising international visibility/prestige; the most frequently mentioned challenges for developing JDDs are securing adequate funding and ensuring sustainability. It is worth mentioning is that while 95 percent of HEIs reported JDDs to be part of their internationalization plan, only 55 percent had a clear institutional policy on program development, and barely 45 percent had implemented particular strategies for their marketing (Obst, Kuder, & Banks, 2011).

Major Findings from a 2009 Survey

The principal source of information on JDD trends in Latin America is the 2009 survey published by the Observatory on Borderless Higher Education (OBHE) (Gacel-Ávila, 2009), which presented the following major findings: Although international DDs were by far the most popular programs, JDs were predominantly national and most of them were established between 2000 and 2008. While the private sector has been the leader in JDDs, which indicates a marked trend to increase fee-paying students' enrolment through the prestige of these programs, the public sector's main focus is to widen access and equity. France, Spain, the United States, and Germany were the top country partners. In tune with the global trend, most JDDs were in professionally oriented fields like business and management, followed by engineering, at the postgraduate level (32 percent and 15 percent in master's and PhD programs, respectively). Specific to the Latin American context, sharp differences in trends emerged between the private and public sectors: While private institutions offered the most JDDs at the bachelor's level, the public sector did so in postgraduate programs, especially in the life sciences, social sciences, and humanities. The most frequently quoted rationales for JDDs were to (1) foster the internationalization of the curriculum, (2) offer new and innovative programs, (3) attract foreign students, (4) increase institutional prestige, and (5) increase graduates' employability. A few obstacles mentioned in Latin America and not reported in other regions were the absence of national regulations, the lack of administrative support, and the lack of students' foreign language skills.

The 2012 JDD Survey for Latin America

<u>Methodology</u>

The 2012 survey was built around a case study made of 51 HEIs from seven Latin American countries and applied through an online questionnaire, with a 55 percent response rate. The criteria to select participants were to (1) be a relevant institution in its respective national system, (2) have a proportional distribution between the public and private sector, and (3) be an HEI enjoying regional visibility for its internationalization process. Although the sample does not pretend to be representative of the whole higher education sector, as the participating HEIs are both relevant in their national system and enjoy a high profile in internationalization, the survey provides a valuable insight into regional trends and thus enables a comparative analysis with the 2009 findings and global trends. Of the valid answers, 64 percent were from the public sector and 36 percent from the private sector, which is consistent with both sectors' participation of 51 percent and 49 percent, respectively (Calderón, 2012; CINDA, 2011). The respondents were distributed among institutions from Mexico (46 percent), Colombia (18 percent), Argentina (14 percent), Chile (11 percent), Brazil (7 percent), and Ecuador (4 percent).

<u>Terminology</u>

The following concept definitions of the different types of programs were provided to respondents in order to establish a common understanding. JDDs belong to a generic category designated as *collaborative degree programs,* which can either be international or domestic. The term *collaborative* implies close cooperation among partner institutions in curriculum development, design, organization, and delivery of the program, including joint research and, most importantly, in the requirements for the degree award (Knight, 2008b).

An international joint degree program is developed in collaboration with two or more partners from different countries, and awards one joint qualification upon completion of the program requirements; an international double degree program awards two individual qualifications at equivalent levels upon completion of the program requirements (Knight, 2008b).

Major Findings from the 2012 Survey

Types of Collaborative Programs

Of the participating HEIs, 75 percent reported international JDDs, compared with 62 percent in 2009. 98 percent of all JDDs are international DDs, above the present global trend of 84 percent (Obst, Kuder, & Banks, 2011), representing an increase for the region in relation with 85 percent in 2009.

A new 2012 finding shows the emergence of the *cotutelle* modality—the French model for cosupervision and coteaching for PhD programs—which has been identified by Knight and Lee (2012) as a developing trend. This new variant was found in such an emblematic institution as the Argentinian University of Buenos Aires (UBA), reporting 140 programs of this sort. In the UBA, all *cotutelles* are in fact doctoral DDs, as the lack of national regulation framework for the recognition of foreign degrees makes the establishment of JDs impossible (M. Tobin, personal communication, December 27, 2012).

Main Rationales

The main rationales for promoting international JDDs in Latin America are to (1) internationalize the curriculum, (2) increase international students' mobility, (3) raise graduate employability, (4) enlarge educational offerings, (5) enhance institutional prestige and profile, and (6) attract foreign students (Figure 18.1). This ranking is almost the same as in 2009, except for the third rationale, which moved up to a higher position, suggesting a growing concern for training graduates with intercultural skills.

FIGURE 18.1: MAIN RATIONALES FOR PROMOTING INTERNATIONAL JOINT AND DOUBLE DEGREE PROGRAMS IN LATIN AMERICA (2012)

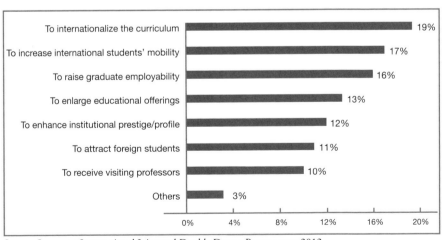

Source: Survey on International Joint and Double Degree Programmes 2012.

Of the remaining HEIs, 25 percent mentioned *not* having JDDs because of (1) lack of faculty members' foreign language proficiency, (2) difficulties in the recognition of qualifications and/or study programs, (3) insufficient financial resources, (4) lack of students' foreign language proficiency, and (5) absence of an institutional policy of internationalization.

Programs per Sector

Although in absolute terms, the 2012 reported international JDDs (99) are less than in 2009 (218), which is related to a smaller sample of respondents, the JDDs ratio per participating HEI in 2012 is higher (3.54) than in 2009 (2.03). Although the proportion of respondents is larger in the public sector (57 percent) than in the private one (43 percent), 60 percent of all JDDs are offered by private institutions, which is nevertheless a lesser amount than 2009 (77 percent). This difference is further evidenced by the ratio per sectors, which is of 6.6 international JDDs per private HEI in contrast with 3.6 per public one. The 2012 survey therefore confirms the leadership of the private sector, which suggests its deep interest in broadening academic offers, in particular at both the bachelor's and master's 5A levels (CINDA, 2011), to recruit fee-paying students stemming from middle- and upper-middle-class families. In contrast, due to their leading position in research, public HEIs are developing more JDDs at the PhD level (Figure 18.4). The private sector's higher involvement in JDDs might be explained by the fact that its management structure gives it more flexibility to establish innovative programs, as the majority of its faculty members are part-time, in contrast with the public sector's larger proportion of full-time tenured scholars. For the same reason, the private sector has also a greater need of international partners to set up new and prestigious programs.

Leading Latin American Countries

The Latin American country leaders in international JDDs are Mexico (47 percent), followed at a distance by Colombia (22 percent), Chile (15 percent), and Brazil (12 percent). These are basically the same findings as in 2009, with the exception of Argentina with fewer programs and Colombia on the rise.

Partner Countries

For 2012, the leading partner countries for Latin America international JDDs are France, the United States, Mexico, Germany, and Spain (Figure 18.2). A comparative analysis with 2009 showed that France, the United States, and Germany have increased their partnerships (by 28 percent, 8 percent, and 4 percent, respectively), while Spain has decreased its participation (by 17 percent).

FIGURE 18.2: LEADING PARTNER COUNTRIES FOR LATIN AMERICAN COLLABORATIVE DEGREE PROGRAMS (2012)

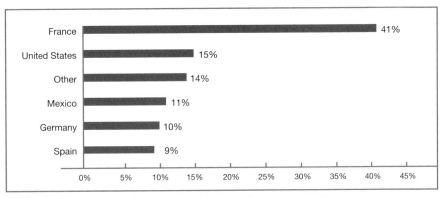

Source: Survey on International Joint and Double Degree Programmes 2012.

Date of Establishment

By 2012, 54 percent of all international JDDs had been implemented during the period 2000–2009, which is similar to the global trend. Nevertheless, a new finding is the steep increase of 39 percent after 2009, compared with the global trend of 10 percent (Obst, Kuder, & Banks, 2011), which can be related to the rising importance of internationalization in the region (IAU, 2010) and with the 82 percent satisfaction level reported in 2009.

JDDs per Level of Studies

Most international JDDs are at the bachelor's level (68 percent Latin America vs. 28 percent globally), followed by masters' (27 percent Latin America vs. 53 percent globally) and PhDs (5 percent Latin America vs. 14 percent globally) (see Figure 18.3 here and Obst et al., 2011). This represents a change from the 2009 survey, where postgraduate JDDs were slightly greater (47 percent) than undergraduate JDDs (44 percent).

FIGURE 18.3: JOINT AND DOUBLE DEGREE PROGRAMS, PER LEVEL
OF STUDY (2012)

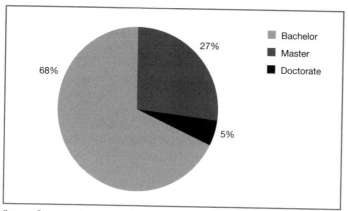

Source: Survey on International Joint and Double Degree Programmes 2012.

The private sector is ahead in both bachelor's and master's degrees, while the public sector is leading in PhDs (Figure 18.4), as it is the sector where by far most research is carried out.

FIGURE 18.4: JOINT AND DOUBLE DEGREE PROGRAMS, PER LEVEL OF
STUDY, PER PUBLIC AND PRIVATE SECTORS

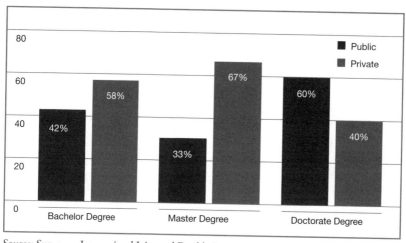

Source: Survey on International Joint and Double Degree Programmes 2012.

JDDs per Area of Studies

Similar to the world trend, the growing areas of interest in Latin America are business and management in first place, followed by engineering. While public institutions are leading in business and management, as well as in the social sciences and humanities, private ones are the leaders in engineering. Additionally, Latin America differs from the global trend with minor percentages in physical and life sciences (6 percent vs. 20 percent globally), law (2 percent vs. 11 percent globally), and medical sciences (2 percent vs. 11 percent globally). There is a noticeable absence of the fields of mathematics and computer science (1 percent vs. 25 percent globally) (Obst, Kuder, & Banks, 2011) in the region, which might be linked with the deficient representation of such fields in Latin America. This could turn out to be, in the end, an area of opportunity for collaborative programs (Figure 18.5).

FIGURE 18.5: JOINT AND DOUBLE DEGREE PROGRAMS, PER SECTOR AND AREA OF STUDY

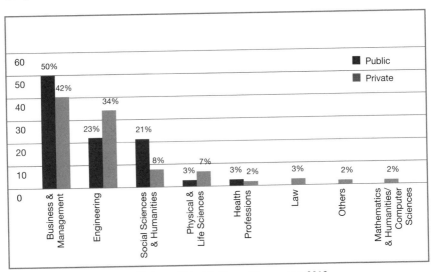

Source: Survey on International Joint and Double Degree Programmes 2012.

JDDs Foreign Language Requirement and Language of Instruction

Of international JDDs offered by private HEIs, 100 percent have a foreign language requirement for graduation compared with 73 percent in the public sector. This is consistent with the Latin America context, where students of the private sector are usually more fluent in foreign languages thanks to their basic education in private colleges, where foreign languages are more extensively taught than in public schools.

With respect to the language of instruction, in 2012 a significant change was noted in relation to 2009, with Spanish (33 percent) and English (32 percent) on an almost equal footing (vs. 61 percent and 22 percent, respectively, in 2009); followed by French (20 percent vs. 8 percent) and German (7 percent vs. 0.3 percent). In contrast, English is globally reported as the most common language of instruction (49 percent) followed at a distance by French (16 percent), German (13 percent), Spanish (8 percent), and Italian (6 percent) (Obst, Kuder, & Banks, 2011). The decreasing use of Spanish is consistent with the rising number of international JDDs with non-Spanish speaking countries, which suggests that the deficiency in foreign language competency in Latin American students and scholars is being addressed by the sector.

JDD Curricular Design and Funding Sources

There is a growing trend of jointly designing curricula by all parties involved (90 percent vs. 79 percent in 2009). In 2012, international JDDs were reported to be funded on an equal level by external resources (37 percent) and partner institutions (36 percent), with a smaller proportion of funding provided by only one institution (28 percent). This is a different response from 2009, where most financial resources were reported to come from both institutions (53 percent), and external funding was almost nonexistent (1 percent). This finding might suggest, on the one hand, increasingly available funding for JDDs at a global scale and, on the other, a better management of internationalization activities in Latin America.

Main Obstacles

The main obstacles reported in 2012 were (1) insufficient financial resources, (2) lack of students' foreign language proficiency, (3) the faculty's lack of foreign language proficiency, and (3) too rigid or inflexible a curriculum (the last two were tied for third place). While insufficient funding unsurprisingly holds the first place in both surveys, the absence of an institutional policy for internationalization has decreased from one of the first positions (19 percent) in 2009 to the last in 2012 (5 percent). This is likely linked with the increasing importance of the internationalization in Latin American policymaking (IAU, 2010). Also noticeable is the higher rank of students' lack of foreign language proficiency in 2012 (20 percent vs. 10 percent in 2009).

Conclusion

The 2012 survey on JDDs brought interesting and positive new findings for the Latin American region: International DDs are definitively on the rise and by far the favorite model of collaborative programs, even above the world average, with HEIs reporting plans to expand these programs in the future. The private sector is still the leader—although in a lesser proportion than 2009, with a 6.6 ratio of international JDDs per private HEI versus 3.6 per public HEI; most JDDs are at the bachelor's level, followed by master's and PhDs, which differs from the global trend where the majority is at master's level; the private sector is leading at both the bachelor's and master's levels, while the public sector is leading at PhD level. The predominant and increasing fields of interest are business and management, followed by engineering, while others areas like law, social sciences, humanities, and medical sciences are decreasing. Noteworthy in Latin America is the scarce number of such programs in mathematics, computer science, physics, and life sciences in comparison with the world trend. The leading Latin American countries in JDDs are Mexico followed at a distance by Colombia—although showing an important increase in recent years—and then by Chile and Brazil. The leading partner countries for Latin American international JDDs are France, the United States, Mexico, Germany, and Spain, with a noticeable increase in France and Germany, although the latter in a lesser proportion, and with Spain in a steeply decreasing trend. By 2012, more than half of all international JDDs were reported to have been implemented between 2000 and 2009, with a sharp increase after 2009, thus confirming the rising trend of JDDs in the region.

The main rationales for JDDs are internationalization of the curriculum and increasing international mobility of students. Noteworthy is the rising graduate employability rationale, which has moved up to the ranking's top positions, suggesting a growing regional concern for training graduates with international skills. A remarkable change in trend is also the increasing use of foreign languages as languages of instruction, with English on an equal footing with Spanish, followed by French and German, in contrast with 2009 where Spanish was by far the dominant language. This might indicate that the deficiency in foreign language competency in students and faculty members is being dealt with, although it is still mentioned as one of the main obstacles for the establishment of JDDs. Further progress includes a growing tendency of a jointly designed curriculum by all parties involved and new modalities of funding that combine external and institutional resources compared with 2009 where external funding was almost nonexistent. To sum up, joint and double degree programs are part of an emerging strategy of the Latin American internationalization process, although perhaps not as dynamic as in other regions of the world.

REFERENCES

Calderón, A. (2012). *Latin American perspectives and drivers for tertiary education development.* London, UK: OBHE.

CINDA. (2011). *Educación Superior en Iberoamérica: Informe 2011.* Santiago, Chile: Author.

Gacel-Ávila, J. (2009). *Joint and double degree programmes in Latin America: Patterns and trends.* London, UK: OBHE.

IAU. (2010). *Internationalization of higher education: global trends regional perspectives: The IAU 3rd global survey report.* Paris, France: IAU.

Knight, J. (2008a). *Higher education in turmoil.* Rotterdam, the Netherlands: Sense.

Knight, J. (2008b). *Joint and double degree programmes: Vexing questions and issues.* London, UK: OBHE.

Knight, J., & Lee, J. (2012). International joint, double and consecutive degree programs. New developments, issues, and challenges. In D. Deardorff, H. de Wit, J. Heyl, & T. Adams (Eds.), *The Sage handbook of international higher education* (pp. 343–357). Thousand Oaks, CA: Sage.

Obst, D., Kuder, M., & Banks, C. (2011). *Joint and double degree programs in the global context: Report on an international survey.* New York, NY: IIE.

Chapter Nineteen

International Joint and Dual Degrees in the United States: A Status Review

Diana B. Carlin, Saint Louis University

A *New York Times* article about the 2011 Institute of International Education (IIE) survey of joint and dual degree programs (Kuder, Obst, & Banks, 2011) described the status of U.S. involvement in such programs this way: "When it comes to academic innovation, Americans have long been accustomed to the traffic being mainly one way.... But the growth of joint- and dual-degree programs in Asia, Australia and above all Europe has left Americans in the unfamiliar position of playing catch-up" (Guttenplan, 2011). The IIE report and others in recent years leave no doubt that U.S. higher education is more follower than leader in the field of international joint and dual degrees. However, interest is growing, and the number of joint or dual degree programs has increased steadily.

This examination of the status of joint and dual degrees in U.S. higher education institutions provides an explanation for the timing of U.S. interest relative to other parts of the world, traces trends in the growth of the degree programs, outlines the facilitators and inhibitors in creating and sustaining degree programs, and summarizes the best practices that can encourage future expansion. This analysis is not meant to be exhaustive in any category given the relative newness of degree adoption and the existing research, but it is intended to provide an overview that places U.S. practices within the larger global community.

Why the Follower Role?

One explanation for the late entry of U.S. institutions into the joint and dual degree arena is simply that the stature of the United States as a world leader in higher education has reduced incentives for institutions to seek such partnerships. The number of international students in U.S. colleges and universities has grown dramatically since the mid-20th century, according to *Open Doors*, reaching an all-time high in 2012–13 of 819,644. Likewise, the number of U.S. students studying abroad has increased annually, with one exception, every year since 1993–94 (IIE, 2013). Thus, joint or dual degree programs were not perceived as necessary to encourage mobility.

A contributing factor to the slower start is not so much what the United States does or does not do to promote study abroad, but what Europe did do to encourage joint and dual degrees through programs such as Erasmus Mundus, SOCRATES, and the Bologna process (Denecke & Kent, 2010, p. 25). For countries outside of Europe interested in increasing their stature as major research universities on the global scene, joint and dual degrees provided a way to both augment their strengths through strategic partnerships and enhance visibility of growing curricular and research excellence. Another disincentive to U.S. participation is the country's decentralized education system and heavy reliance on governance structures that require multiple levels of approval requiring longer periods of time and more complex agreements to enable creation of joint or dual degree programs. The cost of U.S. higher education contributes to the complexity in the absence of formal exchange agreements that maintain balances.

Finally, U.S. students who participate in international experiences tend to do so for short periods of time as a means of enriching their educational experience rather than getting a degree. Many programs are created by universities and are led by their faculty rather than being an immersion into an international university. The 2012 *Open Doors* report indicated that during the 2011–12 academic year, the duration for 59 percent of U.S. students' study abroad experience was for "summer or eight weeks or less." Programs of "one or two quarters or one semester" accounted for 38 percent, and programs of an "academic or calendar year" constituted only about 3 percent (IIE, 2013).

Jane Knight's analysis of the growth of internationalization in higher education noted that the term "double/joint degrees" goes back to the 1980s (Knight, 2010, p. 43), and the 2010 IIE survey found that Italy, Germany, and France "began the majority of their programs" between 1991 and 2000 (Kuder, Obst, & Banks, 2011, p. 6). However, in the past 10 years there has been serious institutional interest in such degrees and discussions at professional meetings, with large numbers of U.S. participants attending.[1] During that time, surveys have provided a snapshot of the growing interest in international collaborations beyond traditional study abroad.

Trends in the Development of U.S. Joint and Dual Degree Programs

Two benchmark studies have been conducted about U.S. involvement in joint and dual degree programs: one by the Council of Graduate Schools (CGS), which looked only at graduate-level programs (study first conducted in 2007), and the other by IIE and the Freie Universität Berlin (first conducted in 2008), of European and U.S. joint and double degree programs.

The CGS study was part of its annual international admissions survey and included responses from 160 colleges and universities. Its major findings included:

- 29 percent of the respondents had one or more collaborative degree programs.

- 11 percent of respondents had one dual/double degree program, and 7 percent had a joint degree program.

- 3 percent had one or more programs that award both dual and joint degrees, and 1 percent had a dual degree and some other type of collaborative degree or certificate.

- Based on the number of international graduate students enrolled, 56 percent of the 10 largest, 48 percent of the 25 largest, and 56 percent of the 50 largest have at least one degree program.

- Most programs were at the master's level.

- European universities topped the partner list, followed by the People's Republic of China, India, South Korea, and the Middle East.

- Business, engineering, and social sciences were the most common master's fields, and engineering and physical sciences for doctoral.

- 24 percent of institutions indicated plans to establish new degree programs within two years (CGS, 2007, pp. 6–11).

A follow-up question in the 2008 survey indicated some changes among the 177 institutions reporting:

- 38 percent of respondents have one or more joint or dual degree programs.

- The share of the 25 largest international receiving institutions rose to 62 percent, with institutions outside the largest 50 going from 22 percent to 33 percent.

- The majority of growth came from dual/double degrees (21 percent), with no increase in joint degrees.

- Of the institutions with joint degrees, 33 percent "double-badged," and 50 percent awarded a diploma with the home university's seal.

- Europe led the list of partners, with Taiwan (8 percent) and Australia (3 percent) registering high enough numbers to be taken from the "other" category.

- The most common master's degree field was business (39 percent), followed by engineering (26 percent), physical sciences (15 percent), and social sciences (15 percent). Doctoral level included physical sciences (19 percent), engineering (11 percent), humanities and arts (8 percent), and life sciences (8 percent).

- 31 percent of respondents indicated plans to develop programs within two years (CGS, 2008, pp. 7–12).

The IIE–Freie Universität Berlin survey had 180 responses (81 U.S.) and took place in spring 2008—approximately the same time as the 2008 CGS survey—but it included undergraduate degree programs as well. The survey looked at partnership relationships for both European and U.S. universities. Major findings include:

- There were 291 degree programs reported by U.S. institutions, with 51 percent at the undergraduate level, 40 percent at the master's, 3 percent doctoral, and 6 percent other.

- U.S. students were less likely to participate than European.

- The top five partner institutions for the United States were Germany, China, France, Mexico, South Korea/Spain (tied); and for Europe, the United States, France, Spain, Germany, and the UK.

- The most popular degree programs for both were business and management and engineering.

- U.S. students were more likely to pay their own tuition, while European institutions drew on university budgets and external sources such as government and foundations.

- The majority of respondents planned to increase their number of programs.

- European universities offered twice as many joint degree programs (either undergraduate or graduate) as their U.S. counterparts, and dual/double degrees were more common overall (Kuder & Obst, 2009).

A third CGS study was undertaken through a REESE (Research and Evaluation on Education in Science and Engineering) grant from the National Science Foundation. Of the 84 institutions surveyed, 43 provided valid responses, representing 168 degree programs. Its major findings were:

- 109 programs were dual master's, 32 were joint master's, 7 were joint doctoral, and 20 were dual doctoral.

- 40 percent of the programs were in business, 31 percent in engineering, and 26 percent in other research disciplines.

- The major funding source was retention of student fees/tuition, university budget, and international sources.

- 65 percent of the respondents indicated that more international students participate than U.S. students.

- 51 percent of respondents indicated that faculty members travel to partner institutions for teaching and research (Denecke & Kent, 2010, pp. 35–43).

The second IIE–Freie Universität Berlin study was a global study conducted in 2011. The report included responses from 245 institutions in 28 countries. The major findings relative to the United States were:

- Dual degrees were more common than joint, with the United States being the top reporting country.

- 50 percent of U.S. programs—either dual or joint—were at the undergraduate level with 36 percent master's, 10 percent doctoral, and 5 percent other.

- The top five partner countries were China, France, Turkey, Germany, and India.

- Business and management and engineering were the most common current and future degree programs, with social sciences, mathematics and computer sciences, and physical and life sciences also being listed frequently.

- Most U.S. universities plan to develop more dual than joint degrees in the future.

- China was the top desired country for future U.S. collaborations, with the United States as the top choice by France, Germany, and Italy.

- 63 percent of U.S. respondents had no specific recruitment measures for the programs, and 65 percent were focusing on international student participants.

- 40 percent of the joint and 45 percent of the dual degree programs had fewer than 15 participants; 53 percent of joint and 25 percent of dual had 16–45 participants; and 7 percent of joint and 29 percent of dual had over 45 participants (Kuder, Obst, & Banks, 2011, pp. 6–7, 11–15).

One growth facilitator was the creation in 2006 of the European Union–United States ATLANTIS Program. Between FY2007 and FY2010, 81 grants were made to U.S. institutions for a duration of four or five years.[2] While development of joint and dual degree programs was not the only goal,[3] many of the grants did result in either undergraduate or graduate degree programs (primarily dual), with the majority at the undergraduate level. Examples include an undergraduate dual degree program in international management between Bentley College (Massachusetts) and the Universiteit van Tilburg (Netherlands), undergraduate dual degree in nursing between Nazareth College (New York) and Semmelweis Egyetem (Hungary), graduate dual degree program in engineering mechanics and materials engineering between the University of Nebraska-Lincoln and the Université de Rouen (France), and a graduate dual degree program in volcanology and geotechniques between Michigan Technological University and Université Blaise Pascal Clermont (France).[4] The United States cancelled calls for additional programs starting in 2011 due to budgetary constraints.

As noted in the 2010 CGS report (Denecke & Kent, 2010), other U.S. government programs that promote international relationships include the National Science Foundation programs PIRE (Partnerships for International Research and Education), and IGERT (Integrated Graduate Education, Research and Training). While government-initiated programs have helped the spread of joint and dual degree programs in the United States, the majority of programs result from existing exchange or other collaborative agreements and are largely initiated by faculty or jointly initiated by faculty/administration (Kuder, Obst, & Banks, 2011, p. 24).

The Whys of International Collaborations

There is hardly a U.S. college or university that does not include some reference to international or global in its mission statement. The importance of preparing 21st-century students to live in a borderless world requires expanded international opportunities, and joint and dual degrees are a means to give students a competitive advantage in their careers. At the graduate level, preparing future researchers for international collaborations is vital given the growth of multinational research projects and publications. The Organisation for Economic Co-operation and Development (OECD) reported that between 1980 and 2001 the percentage of coauthored science articles with two or more countries represented increased from 8 percent to 18 percent (Marginson & van der Wende, 2007, pp. 34–35). A second OECD report showed that between 1985 and 2007 the number of scientific articles with international coauthorship rose from approximately 29,634 to 150,884 (OECD, 2010, p. 32). International relationships to prepare students for careers or expand the research enterprise requires what Nigel Thrift, vice chancellor of the University of Warwick, describes as "networks" that require "deep-seated cooperation … in a partnership that, in the process, changes each of the partners" (Thrift, 2010). CGS recognized that "increased competition for international students. … [and] improvements in technology and communications" (Denecke & Kent, 2010, p. 6) also contribute to increased degree activity. A summary of research conducted on international joint and dual degree programs provides these reasons why U.S. universities want to offer these programs:

- Enhancing campus internationalization efforts, broadening educational offerings, strengthening research collaboration, and raising international visibility/prestige (Obst, Kuder, & Banks, p. 7).

- For both undergraduate and graduate students: personal development and enrichment, enhanced career prospects and increased academic opportunities, and enhanced cultural diplomacy skills (Denecke & Kent, 2010, p. 14).

- For graduate students: enhanced research skills, expanded research networks, access to specialized equipment and expertise, and enhanced "science diplomacy" skills (in science and engineering) (Denecke & Kent, 2010, p. 15).

- Institutions and faculty benefit through increased prestige through globalization, increased recruitment and tuition dollars, sharing world-class equipment and resources, and an enhanced educational climate that results from diverse cultural experiences (Denecke & Kent, 2010, p. 15).

- The public benefits economically through economic, social, and sociopolitical impacts such as increased research productivity leading to patents and job creation, increased revenue from international students, quality of life improvements through research, and science and cultural diplomacy (Denecke & Kent, 2010, p. 16).

Challenges to Development of Joint and Dual Degrees

While there are many reasons for U.S. institutions to continue to play catch-up in offering dual and joint degrees, the complexity of the U.S. higher education system, coupled with differing institutional and legal structures in potential partner countries, complicates degree development. The lack of familiarity among faculty and administrators of the nuances of these degrees is one of the first hurdles to overcome, and it manifests itself in something as simple as defining what constitutes a joint or dual degree. In the absence of university policies, templates, or governing policies for these degrees, such a simple thing as a definition can be a stumbling block. Often the confusion comes from the need to double-count courses for dual degrees, which makes it look like a "joint" venture. The majority of U.S. universities see a joint degree as the issuance of a single diploma that includes courses from both universities but typically requires the same or only a few additional credits as a degree at either university would require. A dual degree, on the other hand, requires work above and beyond what is required for a single degree and may even require two theses, dissertations, or projects. Depending on university or governmental policies, a diploma for a joint degree may or may not be doubled-badged. If not, U.S. universities will indicate the joint nature on the transcript or will issue a certificate from the university that does not issue the actual diploma.

Most of the challenges fall into the categories of agreements, governance/university policies, logistics (i.e., coordination of academic calendars), accreditation, finances, recruitment, quality assurance, and sustainability. The following list contains a summary of the challenges cited by U.S. universities; the surveys cited throughout this chapter, and articles by Tobenkin (2008), Asgary and Robbert (2010), Berka (2011), and Michael and Balraj (2003) provide the basis for this analysis:

- 66 percent of U.S. respondents in the 2010 IIE survey have policies limiting double counting that could complicate negotiations (Obst, Kuder, & Banks, 2011, p. 23).

- Many U.S. students lack language proficiency. While most degree programs are taught in English, language becomes an issue for cultural adaptation for many U.S. students.

- Achieving a balance in programs established by exchange agreements can be difficult, given that there is less interest among U.S. students.

- Funding is one of the most commonly cited challenges, including additional costs for student travel, lack of assistantships at the partner university to compensate for stipend funds at the U.S. home institution, costs of additional time to degree for dual degrees at undergraduate and graduate levels, travel funds for faculty and administrators to visit partner institutions, and lack of scholarships at many institutions.

- There is a lack of clear policies at most institutions to ease the approval process, especially where double counting of credits is involved.

- Challenges for joint degrees are "the duration of degrees in each country, designing the curriculum, and resolving differences in degree requirements. ... for dual degrees resolving differences in academic calendars and resolving cultural issues" (Denecke & Kent, 2010, pp. 45–46).

- Clear outcomes for purposes of quality assurance need to be established.

Best Practices to Promote Degree Development

While challenges exist, they are being overcome or the growth in U.S. degrees would not exist. The chapter in this volume by Mager, Poller, and Girotti provides a summary of recommendations for program development of degree programs based on the JOIMAN (Joint Degree Management and Administration Network: Tackling Current Issues and Facing Future Challenges) project. Shared practices among U.S. universities reflect similar lessons learned. The suggestions in this section were developed from the CGS Graduate International Collaborations Project and a random examination of university websites and presentations at professional meetings that identify good practices along with articles cited in the previous section.[5]

- Have a clearly defined and articulated purpose and goals for the collaboration.

- Know your partner. The most successful degree programs are established with existing partners. This reduces resistance and concerns about quality and comparability of degree programs. In selecting partners, consider familiarity, faculty quality and expertise (especially complementary teaching and research), facilities, student services, curriculum, location, and value added. Use existing agreements as the framework. If it is a new but well-researched partner, have basic agreements in place before finalizing details for the degree.

- The most successful programs are initiated by faculty or through faculty–administrative partnerships. Begin development of degree programs by identifying the strongest existing relationships either for study abroad or research.

- Involve all university units affected by and involved in degree creation and approval in establishing guidelines for degree programs. If guidelines are not in place when negotiations start, make sure everyone is at the table and that the process is recorded and then institutionalized for future use. If intra-university joint or dual degrees exist, use those guidelines as a starting point. Stakeholders include international offices, graduate and/or undergraduate central administrators, research office, representatives of faculty governance committees that review proposals, academic deans, finance offices, registrar, and recruitment and enrollment management.

- Consider the following policy and governance issues: transfer credit limits, articulation agreements, thesis/dissertation supervision, who awards the joint degree and whether it is double-badged, graduate faculty appointments, program approval and review processes, outcomes and target identification, sunset provisions if targets are not made within two to four years, transcripts and diplomas, financial arrangements, management of assistantships, whether new courses are needed, whether additional revenues are necessary, whether policies are in place to accept three-year degrees for programs with Bologna degrees, and how ECTS or other international grading and credit systems are aligned.

- Identify the regional accrediting, state government, university governing board, or professional accreditation policies impact the degree.

- If internships are part of the degree program, know how they are obtained and supervised in both universities, and identify regulatory or legal issues that would prevent certain internships or paid internships.

- Develop a recruitment plan for students at both universities, and establish policies for admission standards and procedures that satisfy both universities' requirements.

- Survey students and faculty at the outset of development to determine if there is sufficient interest among multiple faculty and students to sustain the program.

- Identify seed funding that can provide scholarships to support the first group of students.

- At the graduate level, be aware of restrictions on U.S. students serving as teaching assistants (and determine if they are ineligible for paid work) in order to replace lost assistantship funding at the home institution.

- Include intellectual property and export controls issues in formal documents related to graduate research projects and faculty collaborations.

Conclusions

In the past few years I have been asked to make presentations at several universities on the development of joint and dual international degree programs. I have titled my presentation, "International Joint and Dual Degree Programs: The Wave of the Present." Although U.S. universities lagged behind their international counterparts in establishing these degrees, their popularity is growing, with multiple benefits. Resistance and barriers are declining as more best practices are shared and more institutions and their faculty and students become aware of the unique opportunities.

NOTES

[1] This conclusion is based on a review of agendas of meetings of professional associations such as the CGS and NAFSA: Association of International Educators. In fact, the first major article to appear in NAFSA's *International Educator* was in 2003 on European models, and a report on U.S. trends came out in 2008.

[2] European Union–United States Atlantis Program: http://www2.ed.gov/programs/fipseec/index.html.

[3] According to the EU-Atlantis website, the goals were threefold: (1) joint or dual degree programs including exchanges of students and staff; (2) study abroad programs; and (3) policy-oriented measures including comparative higher education and vocational training issues, as well as promoting dialogue on recognition of qualifications and accreditation. See http://ec.europa.eu/education/eu-usa/usa_en.htm.

[4] For a complete listing, go to https://maps.google.com/maps/ms?ie=UTF8&hl=en&msa=0&msid=10247474677534774421.000470ca2a49 b2d842a8c&z=4.

[5] The following university's websites or conference presentations were examined: The Ohio State University, University of Arizona, State University of New York at Buffalo, Columbia University, Michigan State University, Rutgers University, Cornell University, Washington University, University of Kansas, Texas A&M University, and Saint Louis University.

REFERENCES

Asgary, N., & Robbert, M. A. (2010, June). A cost-benefit analysis of an international dual degree programme. *Journal of Higher Education Policy and Management, 32*(3), 317–325.

Berka, S. (2011, December 30). The University of Rhode Island graduate dual degree program with the Technical University of Braunschweig—Its added value, synergies, and gains for engineering students. *Online Journal for Global Engineering Education, 6*(1). Retrieved from http://digitalcommons.uri.edu/ojgee

Council of Graduate Schools (CGS). (2007, August). *Findings from the 2007 CGS international graduate admissions survey: Phase II final applications and initial offers of admission.* Retrieved from http://cgsnet.org/ckfinder/userfiles/files/R_IntlAdm07_II.pdf

Council of Graduate Schools (CGS). (2008, August). *Findings from the 2008 CGS international graduate admissions survey: Phase II final applications and initial offers of admission.* http://cgsnet.org/ckfinder/userfiles/files/R_IntlAdm08_II.pdf

Denecke, D. D., & Kent, J. (2010). Joint degrees, dual degrees, and international research collaborations: A report on the CGS graduate international collaborations project. Washington, DC: Council of Graduate Schools.

Guttenplan, D. D. (2011, March 28). Dual-degree programs are gathering steam. *New York Times.* Retrieved from http://www.nytimes.com/2011/03/28/world/europe/28iht-educLede28.html?pagewanted=all

Institute of International Education (IIE). (2012, November). *2012 Open Doors Report: 2012 Fast Facts.* Retrieved from http://www.iie.org/en/Research-and-Publications/Open-Doors

Knight, J. (2010). Higher education crossing borders: Programs and providers on the move. In D. Bruce Johnstone, Madeleine B. d'Ambrosio, & Paul J. Yakoboski (Eds.), *Higher education in a global society* (42–69). Cheltenham, UK: Edward Elgar.

Marginson, S. & van der Wende, M. (2007, July 6). *Globalisation and Higher Education* (OECD Education Working Paper No. 8). Retrieved from http://www.oecd-ilibrary.org/education/globalisation-and-higher-education_173831738240

Michael, S. O., & Balraj, L. (2003, November). Higher education institutional collaborations: An analysis of models of joint degree programs. *Journal of Higher Education Policy and Management, 25*(2), 131–145.

Kuder, M. & Obst, D. (Eds.). (2009). *Joint and double degree programs in the transatlantic context: A survey report.* New York, NY: Institute of International Education.

Kuder, M., Obst, D., & Banks, C. (2011, September). *Joint and double degree programs in the global context: Report on an international study.* New York, NY: Institute of International Education.

Organisation for Economic Co-operation and Development (OECD). (2010). *Measuring innovation: A new perspective.* Retrieved from http://dx.doi.org/10.1787/835113070805

Thrift, N. (2010, February 14). The world needs global research cooperation urgently, and now. *Chronicle of Higher Education.* Retrieved from http://chronicle.com.www2.lib.ku.edu:2048/article/Urgently-Needed-Global/64130/

Tobenkin, D. Degrees of success. (2008, May/June). *International Educator,* 36–46.

Chapter Twenty

Canadian Experience with International Joint and Dual Degrees Programs

FRED L. HALL, UNIVERSITY OF CALGARY[1]

Introduction

Joint and dual (or double) graduate degrees are increasingly of interest in Canada. Although *cotutelles* (individualized dual PhDs) have been in existence within Québec for many years, interest in cotutelles in the rest of Canada has increased considerably recently, along with interest in other forms of dual and joint degrees. This chapter describes the Canadian experience with respect to implementation and oversight of the full range of dual- and joint-degree options, including cotutelles, and identifies insights for other universities as they expand this kind of operation. The contents of this report are based on a survey of the graduate dean members of the Canadian Association of Graduate Studies conducted in January and February 2012. (Details of the survey methodology can be found in the original report.)[2]

The definitions for joint and dual degrees used in the survey are consistent with and paraphrased from those in *Joint and Double Degree Programs in the Global Context* (Obst, Kuder, & Banks, 2011).

Although this report presents results in a quantitative way and discusses difficulties encountered, it is well to keep in mind the value of these programs both to the institution and to individuals. The Université de Montréal (UdeM) in its response expressed it this way:

The benefits of cotutelles for UdeM are as follows.

- International experience for students.

- Supervision by two professors is more fruitful for the students' research.

- Fosters collaboration between universities and professors.

- Strengthen ties between universities.

- Additional value for graduate programs.

- Better opportunities to recruit students.

- Students' mobility.

- Students' networking.

The benefits for an individual are expressed in the following quotation:

On a more personal note, my son is a EM [Erasmus Mundus] graduate (MA Euro-philosophie, a French-German program). His personal experience attending 3 universities in 3 countries in 2 years (Toulouse, Prague and Louvain-la-Neuve) is what inspires me to push these types of programs for my university and our students.[3]

Quantitative Results

In all, 64 surveys were distributed, and 48 were returned, for a response rate of 75 percent. Table 20.1 shows the response rate by region of the country, as well as the presence of joint or dual degrees among responders. Québec is underrepresented in the responses relative to the other regions. This might seem unfortunate given its longer history with joint and dual degrees through cotutelle, but in fact there is 100 percent response from the Québec universities other than those in the Université du Québec system. The low response rate for the province arises because only 4 of the 10 within that system responded, but then the system as a whole has only one membership in the Canadian Association for Graduate Studies (CAGS), so perhaps most felt the system as a whole would respond.

Only five universities reported currently having joint degree programs, whereas 21 reported having one or more dual degree programs. Several of the latter had only very recently signed the dual degree agreements, with the result that there are few if any students in their programs as yet. The oldest programs date from 1996 (Montréal, Laval). The next oldest date from 2001 (Ottawa), 2005 (Concordia), and 2006 (Saskatchewan). Cotutelle arrangements occur both as joint degrees and as dual degrees. Of the five universities with joint degrees, two Ontario universities also have one or more dual degrees. Hence a total of 24 of the 48 respondents have one or both of joint or dual degrees.

TABLE 20.1: RESPONSE RATE AND PRESENCE OF JOINT AND DUAL DEGREE PROGRAMS BY REGION

Region	Sent	Received	Response	Joint	Dual
Maritimes[4]	10	8	80%	1	2
Québec	15	9	60%	1	6
Ontario	21	15	71%	3	7
West[5]	18	16	89%	0	6
Totals	64	48	75%	5	21

There is the possibility that universities with fewer international graduate students have less experience with or interest in joint or dual degrees. To check for this, the latest available data on international graduate student numbers were used, from the 2010 CAGS Statistical Report (CAGS, 2010), which represents 2008 enrolments. International master's plus doctoral enrolment ranged from zero to nearly 2,100 among CAGS members. The list of universities was split into three groups using some obvious breakpoints in the distribution of the enrolment: less than 100, 100 to 600, and greater than 600. Table 20.2 shows the response rate and presence of joint and dual degrees by these categories. For the universities with more than 600 international graduate students, 10 of the 13 (77 percent) had one or both joint and dual degrees; for international graduate enrolments between 100 and 600, 13 of 18 (72 percent) had either joint or dual degrees; and for universities with less than 100 international graduate students, only 1 of 17 (6 percent) had a joint or dual degree.

TABLE 20.2: RESPONSE RATE AND PRESENCE OF JOINT AND DUAL DEGREES, BY SIZE OF INTERNATIONAL GRADUATE STUDENT ENROLLMENT

International Enrollment	Sent	Received	Response	Joint	Dual
Large (>600)	15	13	87%	3	9
Medium	22	18	82%	1	12
Small (<100)	27	17	63%	1	0
	64	48	75%	5	21

Of the 48 responses, 19 had definite plans to expand their involvement in joint or dual degrees, and another four expected probably or maybe to do so. Thus, nearly 50 percent of the universities responding are likely to be doing more of this kind of work in the future. Only seven gave a negative response to the question. The remainder did not answer it.

As shown in Table 20.3, the range of countries involved in joint or dual degrees with Canadian universities is broad. As might be expected, France tops the list, and not just with Québec respondents. Of Québec respondents, six of seven had agreements with France; in the Maritimes, two of three; in Ontario, six of eight; and in the West, two of six.

TABLE 20.3: NUMBER OF CANADIAN UNIVERSITIES HAVING DUAL OR JOINT DEGREE AGREEMENTS IN EACH COUNTRY THAT WAS NAMED IN THE RESPONSES

France	16	Congo	1
Germany	8	India	1
China	7	Israel	1
Belgium	5	Italy	1
Australia/NZ	3	Japan	1
US	3	Korea	1
Poland	2	Morocco	1
Portugal	2	Russia	1
Algeria	1	Switzerland	1
Brazil	1	UK	1
Chile	1		

Similarly, the range of disciplines that is represented in joint and dual degrees (including cotutelles) is also wide (Table 20.4). At the level of cotutelle, the choice of discipline can be different for every student. Several universities responded to the question about disciplines to say that a cotutelle is possible in any discipline at the institution. Another listed 27 disciplines in which joint degrees have been awarded. Nonetheless, some patterns are clear in terms of the most popular disciplines. Language and literature, history, and philosophy have been named separately from other humanities disciplines because of the frequency of their mention. In each of these three, the majority of mentions are by French language universities.

TABLE 20.4: NUMBER OF UNIVERSITIES HAVING JOINT OR DUAL DEGREE PROGRAMS IN EACH DISCIPLINARY GROUP

Science	9	Philosophy	4
Engineering	8	Management	4
Law	6	Computer Science	3
Social Sciences	6	Education	3
Language/Literature	5	Health Science	3
History	5	Arts/Humanities	2

Of the 24 universities reporting that they currently have either or both of joint or dual degrees, 16 described cotutelles and 16 described specifically designed multi-university degrees (Table 20.5). Eight universities described both kinds. Of the 16 with specifically designed degrees, the great majority are at the master's degree level, rather than the doctoral level. Several are MBA programs, and several are Erasmus Mundus programs. In general, both the cotutelles and the specifically designed programs report similar comments and advice (discussed below).

TABLE 20.5: UNIVERSITIES WITH COTUTELLE OR SPECIFICALLY DESIGNED DEGREES AS THE JOINT OR DUAL DEGREES

1 = yes 0 = no Blank = not mentioned		
	Cotutelle?	Designed degree?
UBC Vancouver	1	0
Carleton	1	0
Toronto	1	0
Montreal	1	
Sherbrooke	1	
Moncton	1	
Calgary	1	
Memorial	1	
Laval	1	1
Waterloo	1	1
Ottawa	1	1
Concordia	1	1
Simon Fraser	1	1
Western Ontario	1	1
Queen's	1	1
UQ Rimouski	1	1
Guelph	0	1
Saskatchewan	0	1
Alberta		1
Royal Roads		1
Brock		1
Ryerson		1
UQINRS		1
UNB Fredericton		1

With regard to the number of students who have been or are enrolled in joint or dual degree programs, detailed information was not received from all responding universities. Of those for whom these numbers are known, only two (Université de Montréal and Université Laval) have more than 100 students currently registered in these programs (Figure 20.7). Both of these also have well over a hundred graduates from these programs.

Université de Sherbrooke is the only other institution reporting more than 20 registrants. There are also several universities among the 22 reporting joint- and dual-degree agreements for whom the agreements are so new that the first students will not be enrolled before fall 2012.

FIGURE 20.7: NUMBER OF CURRENT REGISTRANTS IN JOINT OR DUAL DEGREE PROGRAMS

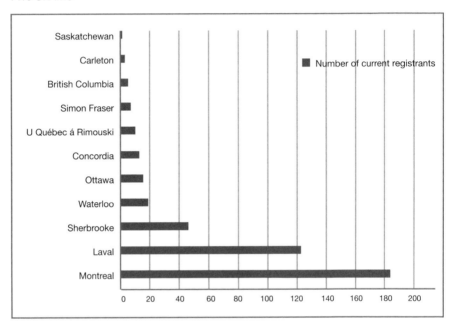

Practical Issues of Concern

Language issues have sometimes been raised as potential problem areas for students in these programs. None of the Canadian universities reported making any special arrangements for students from international partners when on the Canadian campus. At the partner institution, the language of instruction is either that of the country in question, or sometimes English.

Residency requirements for these degrees vary across institutions. Several provinces require that the student spend at least one year at each of the two institutions, but this time need not be consecutive. Other institutions require at least two years at their own campus, but less at the partner institution.

Registration requirements seem reasonably consistent across reporting universities. All who provided an answer to this question require the student to be registered at both institutions.

Tuition fees can be a point of contention. Several universities require students to pay fees in each term only at the institution at which they are present. Other tuition arrangements require the student to pay tuition throughout only to the "home" institution, and not at all to the partner institution. A related issue is that of funding of universities by the provincial government for students in these programs, which varies across the country.

Major Challenges with Joint and Dual Degree Programs

Question 5 in the survey of graduate deans asked, *What have been the major challenges in setting up or sustaining these programs, either for the students or for the institutions? How have you overcome them so far?*

The primary challenge appears to relate to time and effort, first in explaining these types of degrees to colleagues on campus and getting their approval for the concept, then in setting up the initial agreement with another university, and finally in handling the students who are involved in such degrees. Delays with specific agreements include identifying the right person to deal with at the partner institution, and sometimes the degree of complexity even within the Canadian university in terms of the number of different offices that need to be involved in approvals. The advice is to be patient and to follow through on details.

This complexity is also reflected in the variety of agreement templates (for cotutelle, joint, or dual degrees) that exist among different universities, and the fact that each one often insists on using their own, with the result that two mostly parallel documents need to be sent around for approvals.

Another challenge has been dealing with academic terms that do not match well across countries, and the assessment of student fees (other than tuition) that go along with those terms.

Funding is a frequent problem: for travel, for student support, and for the Canadian university if the student is elsewhere.

Identification of Successful Practices

Question 7 in the initial survey asked, *Are there any aspects of your institution's handling of joint or dual degrees that you believe have been particularly successful, and which might be drawn to others' attention as a best (or better) practice?*

The most frequent response is that the establishment of dual and joint degrees works best when this builds upon strong links that have already been established. These can be at the level of the institution, or more frequently at the level of individual researchers who have already established successful research collaborations. In the responses, existing collaboration at the research level is cited more often than institutional level linkages. One reply describes the key as building trust between the two institutions, which would seem to require personal rather than merely institutional relationships.

The second most frequent response is to have clear guidelines and procedures for setting up agreements or cotutelles, even to having a specific template that must be used. In addition, there should be a clear "go-to" person who can deal with the questions and complications that inevitably arise. The intention of these things is to make it crystal clear to those who are interested in a cotutelle, or a joint/dual degree agreement, all that has to be considered and dealt with in order for the program to be successful. Three respondents posted online their procedures or agreement document.[6] These documents are comprehensive and should prove useful not only to those just embarking on such degrees, but also to those who are in the midst of early ones. Having this level of detail is not enough, though: It must be communicated widely and clearly, not merely contained in the minutes of a graduate council meeting.

Other useful suggestions include ensuring that there is a champion for the agreement at the partner institution, and aiming the recruitment (and selection) of top-quality students. One respondent notes that it is important to be flexible in order to provide personalized service to the students, each of whom (in some instances) will be dealing with different bureaucracies at the partner institutions.

An item on which there is mixed opinion is the value of institution-wide agreements. Some respondents recommended keeping specific agreements at the program level, and others have had success with institutional agreements. In both cases, though, some feel it is best to focus on a few carefully chosen partnerships rather than spreading the net widely.

One final item deserves mention here under successes, and that is the multiple university agreements such as those funded by Erasmus Mundus, or the U21 generic statements.[7] Several universities reported considerable success from their involvement in Erasmus Mundus programs.[8] It is worthwhile to look into those possibilities as well.

Words of Warning and Advice

Question 8 in the initial survey asked, *Do you have any advice or words of warning from your experience to offer others who are just starting to develop such programs?*

As in the responses to question 5, the most frequent warning or advice pertains to the time and resource commitment required: for obtaining on-campus support for such programs, for negotiating them with partners, and for managing the students who become involved in them.

A second piece of advice is that these joint degrees are not for everyone.

> There is a lot of interest out there about this option, but some students would be better advised to simply spend some time as a visiting grad student at a second university, rather than establish a formal joint PhD program, given the time and extra academic requirements for many students. The student and their supervisors have to be motivated, engaged, and already collaborative to make these agreements work optimally. In particular, the student needs to take ownership for seeing the agreement through to completion.[9]

And, as pointed out by another respondent, the student needs to be aware that "having two research supervisors may sometimes cause some difficulties."[10]

Advice succinctly put: "Work with institutions with which there is a longstanding collaboration. Less is better."[11]

There is also advice about terminology. Several responses to the survey noted that the terms *joint* and *dual* are defined differently on their campus than in this report. Such definitions can cause problems:

> There was an issue which arose when the joint Canadian-American Master's degree was discussed and developed. The definitions of "joint" and "dual" as defined by the former Ontario Council of Graduate Studies were the exact opposite in the State of New York system. As this issue was not identified early in the process, it led to discussion that ended up being at cross purposes, and a real challenge once the problem came to light. Bottom line: make sure all parties are on the same wavelength in terms of terminology, expectations, and all aspects of program design.[12]

A practical matter brought up regarding implementation of such programs is that design and implementation are often done by different offices: "It is extremely important to have coordination between the people initiating agreements for joint/combined degrees and those who will be implementing or administering the agreements during the entire process."[13]

A survey question not discussed earlier asked whether there was "a separate person or office to assist in handling students taking or interested in joint, dual, or combined graduate degrees," and if so, where. Of the 15 who had such a person or office, 12 said this was within Graduate Studies. The other three said it was in the International Office. If Graduate Studies is not involved early when others handle the students, problems can arise.

Another practical suggestion is to have an example or first proposal under discussion at the same time as some of the key principles will be debated. The specificity assists in resolving the principles.

There is a limit to how much issues such as double-dipping (in the case of dual degrees) can be debated—a strong example is very handy. In our case, the first such proposal went through (ad hoc) approval while the policy itself was being approved (through the same set of committees). We briefly debated the double-dipping issue for the specific proposal, approved the policy shortly there-after, and have not had the debate since.[14]

There is also advice, as in the discussion of successful programs, to rely on individual faculty members, and not the university administration to initiate these activities: "Will-ingness to cooperate must be from the base of faculty members. Implementation of joint programs should not be decreed by the university administration regardless of the aspira-tions and affinities of community stakeholders."[15]

The final word reiterates a number of points that have been stated before, putting many key items together:

Carefully think through the elements required for successful partnership: i.e. mutuality of benefits; commitment (from the top through to the "on-the-ground" administrative supports); and clear (frequent and in-person as much as possible) communication. Flexibility and trust are critical, particularly when working through differences in administrative policy and procedure, which have often been established to meet very localized needs and can frequently be counterproductive when encountering a different educational, cultural, or polit-ical system.[16]

Outlook

Regarding the future, it's fair to say it will be different. The existing focus on France has come in part because of the specific France–Quebec agreement, and in part because France has promoted and funded cotutelles. Table 20.3 shows that the Canadian univer-sities have been reaching out to other parts of the world; that will continue. Simply on the basis of the number of good universities in China, that country is likely to continue to remain high on the list, or maybe even take top spot. In terms of type of program, 17 of the 48 respondents expected to have more joint degree programs in the near future, and only seven expected to have more dual degrees.

NOTES

1 This chapter is an abridged version of a report prepared March 2012 for the Canadian Association of Graduate Studies. The full version appears on its website, at http://www.cags.ca/documents/publications/Best_Practices_Dual_Joint_Degrees.pdf.

2 http://www.cags.ca/documents/publications/best_practices/Best_Practices_Dual_Joint_Degrees.pdf

3 Doyenne Lise Dubois, Université de Moncton.

4 New Brunswick, Nova Scotia, Prince Edward Island, Newfoundland, and Labrador.

5 Manitoba, Saskatchewan, Alberta, and British Columbia.

6 http://www.grad.ubc.ca/forms/joint-phd-agreement
http://www.mun.ca/sgs/Memorial_cotutelle_guidelines.pdf
http://www.sgs.utoronto.ca/Assets/SGS+Digital+Assets/Memoranda/Joint+Placement+Form.pdf
http://www.sgs.utoronto.ca/Assets/SGS+Digital+Assets/Memoranda/Checklist+for+Joint+Placement.pdf

7 See http://www.universitas21.com/article/research/details/109/joint-phdsand the two downloadable "related file" pdfs that are linked at the very bottom of this web page.

8 http://www.algant.eu/, http://www.master-imacs.org/

9 University of British Columbia (Vancouver).

10 Université de Montréal.

11 Université Laval.

12 Brock University.

13 Concordia University.

14 University of Alberta.

15 Institut National de la Recherche Scientifique.

16 University of Manitoba.

REFERENCES

Canadian Association for Graduate Studies. (2010). *39th Statistical report, 1999–2008.* Available with password at http://www.cags.ca/statistical-reports.html

Obst, D., Kuder, M., & Banks, C. (2011). *Joint and Double Degree Programs in the Global Context: Report on an International Survey* (white paper). New York, NY: Institute of International Education. Retrieved from http://www.iie.org/Research-and-Publications/Publications-and-Reports/IIE-Bookstore/Joint-Degree-Survey-Report-2011

Chapter Twenty-One

Employability of Double Degree Graduates: Results of a Franco-German University Survey

JOCHEN HELLMANN AND PATRICIA ROHLAND, FRANCO-GERMAN UNIVERSITY

Every year, around 1,000 students complete binational and trinational degree programs and attain double degrees through the Franco-German University (FGU). They study engineering in Karlsruhe and Metz, law in Mainz and Nantes, political studies in Berlin and Paris, or economics in Tübingen and Strasbourg. No matter what their subject area is, where they study, or what kind of university they attend, all of these graduates have something in common: They speak three or more languages, possess intercultural competence, and have demonstrated resilience abroad through their studies and foreign internships.

The Double Degree Programs of the FGU

The FGU was established through an agreement between the German and French governments[1] in 1997 and began operation in 1999. The primary goal of this international institution is to strengthen relations between Germany and France in the areas of higher education and research.[2] Currently, the FGU cooperates with 180 member and partner universities on both sides of the Rhine River, as well as in several third countries, such Luxembourg, Switzerland, and Poland. Its network comprises every type of institution of higher education: universities, technical universities, universities of applied sciences, *grandes écoles,* and *écoles.* These institutions offer more than 140 degree programs in almost every discipline—engineering, the natural sciences, economics, law, humanities, and social sciences (among others)[3]—in all three Bologna process cycles (bachelor's, master's, and PhD programs). About 5,500 students are currently enrolled in binational or trinational programs.[4] Students in these integrated degree programs receive instruction in two or more countries, and their academic work completed in the partner countries is fully recognized by their home university. Because these programs are based on joint study and examination regulations, students have the possibility of obtaining a double degree (i.e., a joint degree, two equivalent national degrees, or, in the case of trinational programs, three equivalent national degrees) without prolonging their education. The organization of the degree programs is laid out in a cooperation agreement between the partner universities. The duration of study is divided as equally as possible between both partner universities. In the case of trinational degree programs, students are required to study in a third country or complete an internship there. Since the creation of the FGU, about 13,000 students have obtained double degrees. These study programs are not limited to German and French students, but are open to students of other nationalities who speak both languages.[5] The FGU provides financial aid to the enrolled students during their stay abroad, as well as funding to the participating partner universities.[6] The annual budget of the FGU is approximately 13 million euros at this time. Its financial resources are provided in equal parts by the German and French governments.[7]

The FGU Seal of Quality: Evaluation and Regular Quality Control

The degree programs undergo regular quality control by external assessors from both countries.[8] Part of the evaluation involves assessing the practical relevance of the degree programs and the employability of their graduates. The graduates' ability to gain entry into the labor force is an important evaluation criterion for the FGU. Consequently, the binational institution engages in active dialogue with businesses in order to improve the quality of its degree programs with respect to the demands of the working world.

However, are double degree programs an adequate response to the challenges of the market? Can FGU graduates meet the demands of companies that are searching for highly qualified professionals?

Goals of the Survey

To answer these questions and gain more detailed information about the careers of binationally educated students, the FGU conducted a comprehensive survey of its graduates in 2011. The experiences that these double degree recipients have gained and the career paths they've taken are extremely valuable for ensuring the quality of the degree programs and offering students the best conditions for succeeding in the international labor market. Another goal of the survey was to expand the alumni activities. Students who are enrolled at two or even three partner universities frequently regard the FGU as merely a "sponsor." Graduates usually remain in contact with their home universities, which in turn poses a major challenge for the FGU to cultivate a long-term relationship with students and alumni. Conducting the survey offered the FGU a chance to contact its alumni and increase their awareness of the FGU network.

Target Group and Methodical Approach

The FGU contacted all the graduates who had completed their studies since 2000. The survey was conducted from February 1 to March 31, 2011. The data were gathered via various channels. For instance, the FGU sent e-mails to program coordinators—university professors who supervise integrated double degree programs—and alumni organizations in both countries, requesting them to forward the information to the respective target groups. If their e-mail addresses were known, the FGU contacted the graduates directly. In addition to the FGU website, information about the survey was also posted on social networks such as Facebook, Twitter, and Xing. The announcement was supplemented by a contest with sponsored prizes in order to increase the response rate. Participants were required to complete the survey online.

Results

To encourage a high degree of participation, the questionnaire was kept as short as possible—only 10 questions. In addition to general information about the graduate's degree program, the survey focused on evaluating the effect of a double degree on one's success at entering the workforce and on one's professional career.

The FGU received 1,360 valid responses. In view of the 2006 survey, to which only 309 alumni responded, the FGU was especially pleased with the strong response rate. This could be due to a higher level of identification with the FGU thanks to its intensive efforts to foster a closer relationship with its students and alumni.

Over half of the responses were submitted by German participants (~52 percent), followed by some 40 percent by French participants and about 6 percent by alumni of Franco-German nationality. Graduates of other nationalities (predominantly Luxembourgers, Poles, and Bulgarians) accounted for just under 4 percent (see Figure 21.1). With regard to their subject area, most of the surveyed participants (~78 percent) had studied economics, humanities, social sciences, and engineering (see Figure 21.2).

FIGURE 21.1: FRANCO-GERMAN UNIVERSITY SURVEYED PARTICIPANTS, ACCORDING TO NATIONALITY

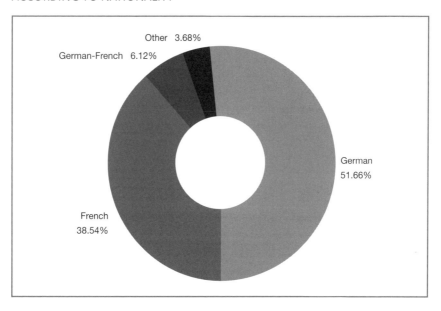

FIGURE 21.2: FRANCO-GERMAN UNIVERSITY SURVEYED PARTICIPANTS, ACCORDING TO PROFESSIONAL FIELD

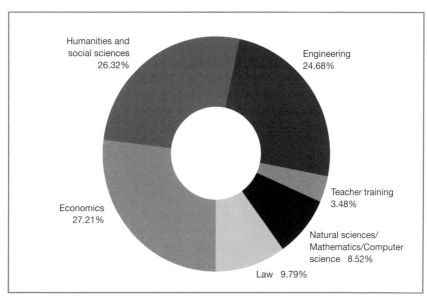

The survey produced the following results: The majority of FGU graduates (~58 percent) regarded their double degree as advantageous for entering the workforce. Consequently, a graduate with a double degree from two countries had a better chance when applying for jobs than a fellow applicant with the same academic qualifications but only a single degree from one country. Furthermore, it is worth noting that engineers evaluated their double degree most positively—a professional field in which such additional qualification is not necessarily expected.

Only about 25 percent of FGU graduates had to look for a suitable position for longer than three months. Around two-thirds of the surveyed participants indicated that they had found a suitable position within three months after graduation, 30 percent of whom were immediately hired following an internship (see Figure 21.3). Not only do internships enable students to gain valuable on-the-job training during their studies, but they also offer companies and institutions the chance to hire these candidates after graduation. This finding emphasizes the importance of compulsory internships and supports the FGU's policy to encourage partner universities to include compulsory internships in their integrated curriculum. A significant majority of integrated degree programs already include a compulsory internship that students are obliged to complete abroad.

FIGURE 21.3: LENGTH OF TIME REQUIRED TO FIND A SUITABLE POSITION

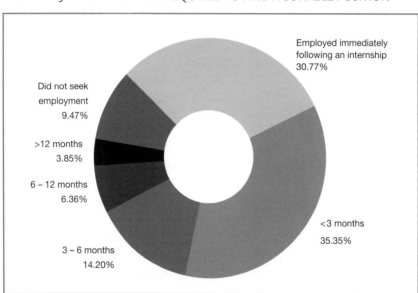

Over two-thirds of the graduates are professionally active in either a Franco-German or international context. Around 32 percent of FGU graduates indicated that their present

jobs were directly linked to Franco-German relations. Of those who were not active in the Franco-German field, more than half (53 percent) were employed in an internationally oriented working environment. As a result, many graduates who had gained bicultural experience during their studies did not return to a purely national working environment. They had gained intercultural experience during their studies that they clearly intended to make use of in their working lives. This trend confirms what the FGU has long believed, namely, that Franco-German degree programs help foster a cosmopolitan mindset in students that can later serve as the basis for working in the international labor market. One of the surveyed participants wrote: "The FGU promotes one's personal and academic development in a unique way. It doesn't matter if you end up working in the Franco-German area later on. What you ultimately learn is how to work internationally."[9]

According to half of the FGU graduates, the double degree had proved beneficial for their professional mobility, for example, transferal to other countries (see Figure 21.4). By studying at two locations, adjusting to a new university system, applying different learning and working methods, and regularly moving between two cultures, the graduates had learned how to quickly adapt to new surroundings. In the words of one respondent: "At all my job interviews, my integrated Franco-German degree program was all I needed to convince them of my mobility and flexibility. This certificate is essential for companies that wish to send their managers around the world."[10]

FIGURE 21.4: DOES A DOUBLE DEGREE HAVE A POSITIVE EFFECT ON PROFESSIONAL MOBILITY?

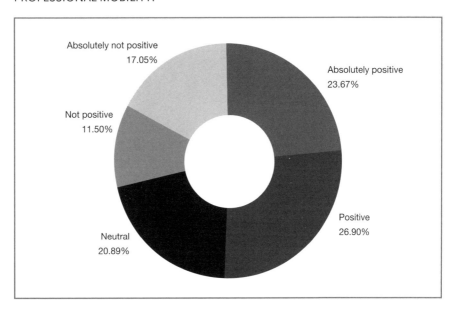

Almost 85 percent of the graduates indicated that they would recommend an integrated Franco-German degree program to future students (see Figure 21.5). This confirms that most graduates are satisfied with their chosen double degree programs despite the challenges and additional effort such programs entail.

FIGURE 21.5: RESPONSES TO THE QUESTION: WOULD YOU RECOMMEND AN INTEGRATED FRANCO-GERMAN DEGREE PROGRAM TO FUTURE STUDENTS?

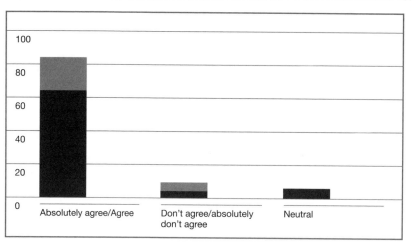

The graduates were slightly less optimistic, however, when evaluating the effect of their double degrees on salary level and career advancement opportunities. More than half of the graduates did not recognize any direct correlation between their salary level and their double degree. In all, 40 percent of the respondents indicated that their Franco-German degree had a beneficial effect on their chances of career advancement. This assessment may seem rather sobering at first, but it is important to keep in mind that many other parameters, such as a company's size and business culture, have a stronger influence on salaries and career opportunities than an employee's university degree. Naturally, there are also differences depending on the employee's professional field.

Integrated Binational Degree Programs from a Business Point of View

According to the majority of FGU graduates, integrated degree programs served as ideal preparation for the international labor market. But to what extent does the labor market share this opinion?

In 2003, a business survey was conducted by the Cologne Institute for Economic Research on behalf of the German Academic Exchange Service (DAAD) with the purpose of assessing double degree programs. The questionnaires were completed by human resource managers and staff responsible for hiring and supervising university graduates in more than 300 companies with over 250 employees.[11] One of the most important findings of the survey was that "in every third company ... , university graduates with a double degree have better chances of getting hired than fellow applicants with a single degree."[12] Furthermore, one in five companies indicated that these graduates entered at a higher position and were paid a higher starting salary. In over 40% of the companies surveyed, employees with double degrees also had better chances at receiving promotions.

In conclusion, FGU graduates and their employers appear to share a positive attitude toward binational, integrated degree programs. This assessment is supported by the extremely low dropout rate among FGU students—only 3% of the students discontinue their studies before graduation.[13]

These findings are very encouraging for the FGU—especially in view of the "Agenda 2020,"[14] which calls for a 100 percent increase of students and doctoral candidates at the FGU by 2020.

NOTES

[1] The "Weimar Agreement" of September 19, 1997.

[2] The FGU is also committed to fostering trinational cooperative projects with a third country.

[3] The most widely represented disciplines are engineering (29 percent), humanities and social sciences (27 percent), and economics (22 percent).

[4] There are 2,524 students in bachelor's programs and 2,994 in master's programs.

[5] The percentage of students of third nationalities has increased from 2 percent in 2001 to 6.4 percent in 2012. For more information, see the annual reports from FGU.

[6] For more information, see the FGU Evaluation Charter, "DFH-Grundsätze der Antragsbewertung und Qualitätssicherung für Studienprogramme." (http://www.dfh-ufa.org/uploads/media/charte_cursus_web.pdf).

[7] The German contribution to the FGU budget is provided by the Federal Ministry of Education and Research (BMBF), the Federal Foreign Office (AA), and the German states. The French contribution is paid by the Ministry of Education and Research (MESR) and the Ministry of Foreign Affairs (MAE).

[8] See the FGU Evaluation Charter, p. 8.

[9] FGU. (2011). "Die Absolventen der Deutsch-Französischen Hochschule. Absolventenstudie 2011," p. 10 (http://www.dfh-ufa.org/uploads/media/DFH_Absolventenstudie_2011.pdf).

[10] ibid.

[11] For more details, see the final report, "Befragung von Personalverantwortlichen zur Thematik: Internationale Doppelabschlüsse 'Doppeldiplome.' Umfrage der IW Consult für den Deutschen Akademischen Austauschdienst," Cologne, 2003.

[12] Joint press release by the FGU, DAAD and the HRK "Doppelt ist besser—Absolventen mit Doppeldiplom

gefragt auf dem Arbeitsmarkt", Berlin, July 5, 2004
(http://www.dfh-ufa.org/presse/pressemitteilungen/pressemeldung/article/doppelt-ist-besser/).

[13] The rigorous demands of double degree programs result in an over-proportional share of ambitious, hard-working students. In contrast to those enrolled in purely national degree programs, the stronger group identity of FGU students helps them overcome difficulties and crises.

[14] See section 3, number 2, of the Agenda 2020, passed by the 12th Franco-German Ministerial Council on February 4, 2010
(http://www.dfh-ufa.org/uploads/media/Deutsch-franzoesische_Agenda_2020_vom_4._Februar_2010.pdf).

Chapter Twenty-Two

Measuring Student Interest in European Joint and Double Degree Programs

ELIAS FAETHE, STUDYPORTALS AND MEGAN BRENN-WHITE, THE BRENN-WHITE GROUP

It is clear that the number of joint and double degree programs offered around the world is growing quickly. What is less clear, though, is whether this is a result of various governmental, regional, and institutional initiatives or a reaction to proven student demand. This information, if available, would be of critical importance to institutions and academic departments with joint programs, as well as staff in charge of developing, managing, and marketing them. In fact, we have found no research on student interest in these specific types of programs, although it certainly may exist.

While it is difficult to pin down cause and effect in the quickly shifting international higher education landscape, the authors realized that there was an existing source of data on both the numbers and types of programs offered, as well as student interest that may be able to help fill in some of the blanks. The website MastersPortal.eu has the largest audience of prospective students looking to study in Europe in addition to the most comprehensive listing of programs.[1] StudyPortals, the parent company, with sites covering all types of degree and nondegree study in Europe, gets roughly three million visits per month.

Methodology

This research focuses on master's programs only, given that data since 2007 on these programs are available, and the 21,020 master's programs listed on the website are thought to cover nearly half of all master's programs offered in Europe. As this study focuses on the data from MastersPortal.eu, all numbers are derived from data of the MastersPortal.eu, unless mentioned otherwise.

Delving into both visitor behavior and changes to the numbers and types of programs listed granted us rare access into both the program offerings and the ways that students search for them. Programs are not automatically listed on the websites at Study-Portals, but can be added at no cost by program administrators. Visitors to the site come from the following regions: 49 percent Europe, 29 percent Asia, 1 percent Oceania, 9 percent Africa and North America, and 3 percent South America.

The data on programs were pulled from the StudyPortals databases. Information on user behavior was based on data from Google Analytics, a free program provided by Google that tracks users via cookies to report on a wide variety of activities such as page clicks, visits, user pathways, source traffic, and the like. Student interest was primarily measured by page views, because the number of views that a particular program or type of program receives would seem to correlate with the level of interest (either because they are selected more from the list of results or students click through the up to five pages within the listing to find more information). In order to understand the data further, we sent e-mail surveys to a handful of students enrolled in joint programs that include stays in Hong Kong, Peru, France, Italy, and the United States. We received six responses that we also considered alongside the quantitative data from the website.

Bologna Process and the Proliferation of Joint and Double Degree Programs in Europe

The growth of joint and double degree programs in Europe has to be tied closely to the "harmonization" of the European higher education system and development of a European Higher Education Area (EHEA) committed to three cycles: bachelor's, master's, and doctoral degrees. This initiative, kicked off with the signature of the Bologna Accords in 1999, made it possible and necessary for European institutions to create new programs at, in particular, the master's level. Where many countries had the first terminal degree end with a master's, the three cycles opened a new phase that has become the locus of full-degree mobility.

Many of these master's degrees were designed with international student recruitment in mind. As we have reported in previous studies, the growth of programs taught in English in continental Europe has been exceptionally fast-paced—from 560 in 2002 to 4,664 in 2011, an increase of 832 percent in just 9 years (Brenn-White & van Rest, 2012). As of October 2012, there were 6,462 master's programs in Europe, outside of the United Kingdom, that were taught in English. While not all joint and double master's degree programs are taught in English, this phenomenon clearly removes at least one barrier to the kind of close and complex interaction between institutions seeking to offer degrees entirely or partially in English. It also, of course, opens up student recruitment to the largest possible group.

Based on the MastersPortal.eu data, the growth of master's programs in Europe has been equally speedy; the growth in program listings was over 250 percent from January 2009 until October 2012. Listings for joint programs at MastersPortal.eu grew from roughly 150 to more than 1,000 in the same time period. Importantly, the joint and double degree master's programs listed on the portal are concentrated in the top five countries: Germany (143 programs), Spain (125), France (110), the United Kingdom (91), and the Netherlands (81).[2]

FIGURE 22.1: GROWTH OF JOINT AND DOUBLE DEGREE PROGRAMS LISTED ON MASTERSPORTAL.EU

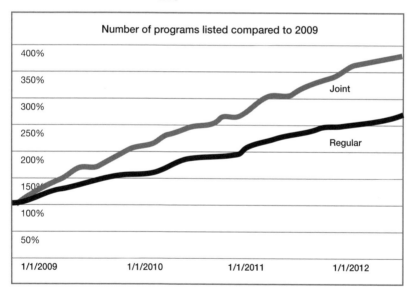

As can be seen in Figure 22.1, the growth of joint and double degree programs listed on MastersPortal.eu has also been impressive, with a steeper trajectory than the growth rate of all programs.

There are also some significant differences in the distribution of disciplines across both regular and joint programs. As Figure 22.2 shows, business and economics programs make up 19.3 percent of single institution programs, but a full 26.1 percent of joint and double degree programs while humanities and the arts programs make up nearly 13.8 percent of regular programs offered but only 8.7 percent of joint and double degree programs, to name just two examples.

FIGURE 22.2: PERCENT OF TOTAL PROGRAMS BY DISCIPLINE AND TYPE

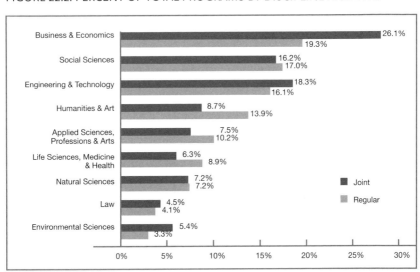

Student Interest and Influencing Factors

To a large extent, a perception of student interest in receiving degrees from more than one institution, along with the kind of cross-cultural perspective and international experience that goes along with it, has led most observers and administrators to assume a high level of interest in joint and double degree programs. For some students, this is certainly the case. "When I found out about the EAGLES program offered through my school, I jumped at the chance to go because it is a three-way exchange, so I got to spend nine months in Milan, Italy, and two months in Madrid, Spain," said Alyssa Bellingham, an engineering student from the United States.

Yet these programs may seem more complicated and more expensive for domestic students—and may or may not be attractive to the international students they also hope to attract. In fact, only one of the six respondents to the e-mail survey had applied for the joint program before they began their master's degree. They all applied and were admitted after spending one semester at one of the partner universities.

It is therefore not entirely surprising that the same factors that affect student interest in one institution's degree program were evident in student interest in joint or double degree programs in general. It is generally assumed that location, reputation, potential career advancement, and cost are four of the most important factors influencing student choice, and this was reflected in our small survey. Before these factors come into play, however, prospective students must qualify to apply by having the right academic background, in addition to language and possibly other skills. What this likely means is that a program that is very narrowly focused will have as small a pool of students to draw from as a joint program as if it were a single institution offering—an MBA will be more popular than, for example, a master's in the business of innovation.

There are many factors that come into play here that could impact student interest. For example, a joint program in a relatively unusual field that is offered by two world-renowned institutions in two desirable locations may receive fewer applicants than a more standard offering at either institution, simply because there is less demand for the topic. Additionally, a joint program between an institution with a strong international reputation and a lesser known one would likely benefit the "weaker" partner more. What we are not sure of is if joint and double degree programs are perceived by prospective students to be as strong as their strongest partner or most desirable location or the weakest partner in the weakest location.

Bellingham said that it was important for her to have a U.S. degree because she was not sure how U.S. employers would value international master's, while Deus Correa Cornejo (enrolled in a double degree program between ESAN University in Peru and IESEG School of Management in France) said, "I believed that a double degree program with a foreign school will provide me better professional opportunities in my home country," reflecting similar (albeit mirror-image) takes on the importance of location and the reputation of the national education systems.

Joint and Double Degree Programs versus Single Institution Programs

In additional to the fact that the growth of listed joint programs on MastersPortal.eu has been faster than the growth of listed single institution programs, joint programs also received 1.72 more page views on average than regular ones. While the information for an average master's program is shown roughly 50 times per month, for a joint program this number is almost 110. Further investigation ruled out the differences in the country or disciplines the joint programs explaining this higher interest. When looking at the interest per program per country, nearly all joint programs receive in total 86 percent more page views (interest) than the regular ones in the top 10 countries with the most joint programs (Table 22.1). This is the same when looking into the differences per discipline. In each discipline the joint programs receive more interest, ranging from 29 percent more in business and economics to 146 percent in the social sciences (Table 22.2).

TABLE 22.1: INTEREST FOR JOINT VERSUS SINGLE INSTITUTION PROGRAMS, BY COUNTRY

Top 10 Countries with the Most Joint Programs	Joint Program Preference
Germany	33%
Spain	31%
France	103%
United Kingdom	35%
Netherlands	−2%
Finland	−35%
Italy	8%
Norway	9%
Sweden	−1%
Switzerland	−14%
Total	86%

TABLE 22.2: INTEREST FOR JOINT VERSUS REGULAR SINGLE INSTITUTION PROGRAMS, BY DISCIPLINE

Discipline	Joint Program Preference
Applied sciences, professions & arts	131%
Business & economics	29%
Engineering & technology	40%
Environmental sciences	82%
Humanities & art	130%
Law	53%
Life sciences, medicine & health	68%
Natural sciences	77%
Social sciences	146%
Total	72%

One potential explanation of this dramatic difference is that the visitors are looking for an international program on a portal that is also international. This group might show a higher preference for joint programs than other prospective students.

Disciplines

Certain disciplines are more or less popular among prospective students overall, so it would follow that the distribution of joint and double degree programs by discipline may impact student interest. We looked into the four countries with the largest numbers of joint and double degree programs listed on MastersPortals to see if the student interest in joint and double degree programs differed from the types of programs offered.

Interestingly, we can see that joint and double degree programs in engineering show a stronger level of interest (representing 25 percent of the total page views) than its percentage of all joint programs offered (18 percent). The reverse is true for business and economics, which represent 30 percent of all joint and double degree programs listed, yet only 20 percent of the overall student interest.

FIGURE 22.3: INTEREST IN JOINT PROGRAMS PER DISCIPLINE AND CONTINENT

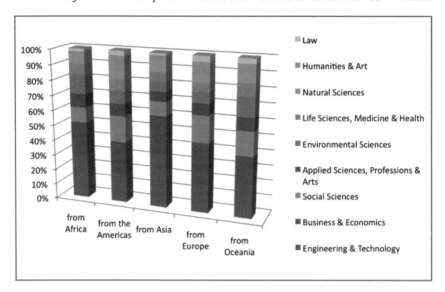

FIGURE 22.4: DISCIPLINES OFFERED AS JOINT PROGRAMS, BY COUNTRY

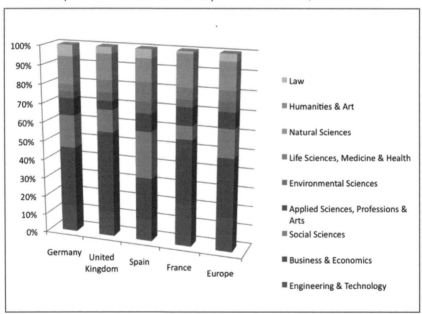

Based on our experience, the development of joint programs seems to be focused on institutions reacting to external opportunities such as funding schemes or an internal drive to create something with a trusted international partner. As with the development of many of the new master's programs, there seems to be relatively little attention paid to prospective student interest and even less concrete research to measure that prospective interest. Looking at these data by discipline can give institutions some idea of where programs may be developing faster than interest—and where there may be opportunities. Since we are looking at pure interest and not actual application figures or numbers of admitted students, it would be imprudent to put too much emphasis on this point, but with a lack of other data, it can at least start to tell a story.

Conclusions

We can already see some ways that student interest in joint programs differs from single programs—and in differences between academic disciplines. The data were based on user behavior and database information at a single website, but the website is the most comprehensive source of information we believe available on a pan-European level. While it is difficult to see evidence of students having sought out joint programs in particular, there seems to be a clear preference for them once they have found them (at least measured in page views per program).

We imagine that there will be continued growth in the number of master's programs in Europe—joint, double, and single institution—as well as in student interest from both domestic and international students in these new offerings.

The real question for the future will be if students and their employers see a major advantage to having earned a joint or double degree. If this is the case, we can imagine that peer-to-peer communications will help drive a greater interest in joint programs that may impact decision making on a dimension outside of the traditional ones of reputation, cost, location, and career impact. It would be interesting to hold those factors equal and compare joint and individual programs within two or three institutions, so we hope that future research might lead in this direction.

NOTES

[1] As of June 26, 2013, 21,020 programs in Europe were listed, and MastersPortal.eu received 1,917,463 visits in May 2013.

[2] A small percentage of these programs have been double-counted; a 10 percent sample showed that less than 5 percent were counted twice.

REFERENCES

Brenn-White, M., & van Rest., E. (2012). *English-taught master's programs in Europe: New findings on supply and demand.* New York, NY: Center for Academic Mobility Research, Institute of International Education.

Chapter Twenty-Three

Accreditation of Joint Programs: A European Approach

Mark Frederiks, Accreditation Organisation of the Netherlands and Flanders (NVAO) and European Consortium of Accreditation

Introduction

Since the late 1990s there has been a substantial increase in the number of higher education programs that are offered jointly by consortia of higher education institutions (HEIs) in various European countries. In 2009 the number of joint programs was estimated to be around 2,500,[1] so the actual number may now be well above 3,000. This high number is a result of initiatives based on both extended cooperation among HEIs in Europe and the implementation of the Bologna process. Subsequent joint declarations of ministers of higher education has encouraged the emergence of new joint programs. The European Commission supports this process through, for example, the Erasmus Mundus program. Joint programs are thought to enhance the mobility of students and staff, facilitate mutual learning opportunities, and create programs of excellence, which can demonstrate the high quality of European higher education. While the political importance of such projects is indisputable, the implementation of joint programs is still hampered by serious problems, especially in the domain of recognition and quality assurance (QA) of such programs. These problems are mainly rooted in the different national laws in Europe and the heterogeneity of QA regimes still existing in the countries concerned.

The European Consortium of Accreditation (ECA)[2] in higher education has been working in recent years on issues concerning the QA and recognition of joint programs in the TEAM II project (2008–2010)[3] and the JOQAR project (2010–2013). JOQAR is the acronym for Joint Programmes: Quality Assurance and Recognition of degrees awarded.[4] The TEAM II and JOQAR projects were funded by the European Commission and involved not only QA agencies but also ENIC-NARICs[5] as project partners. This contribution will particularly focus on the results of the JOQAR project, and especially in the area of QA. The recognition of joint degrees is of course also an important matter, and for the results we refer to the ECA website.[6]

Before looking at the QA results of the JOQAR project, however, we will look at different procedures for accrediting joint programs, specifically through national, joint, and single procedures. Then we will focus on a European approach for single-accreditation procedures, which has been tested through four pilot procedures in the JOQAR project. Mutual recognition of the accreditation of joint programs is an important aid for getting the results of single-accreditation procedures accepted by all agencies and countries that are involved in a joint program consortium. In the context of the JOQAR project, the work on mutual recognition of accreditation results regarding joint programs has resulted in a multilateral agreement that is not confined to European borders. We will conclude with some remarks on how these measures and activities may lead to a new landscape in which barriers for external QA of joint programs are finally removed.

National, Joint, and Single-Accreditation Procedures

There is often confusion about the terminology regarding joint programs. To make it clear from the outset how we understand joint programs in the context of the JOQAR project, we start with some definitions. These definitions are in line with Bologna policy documents and have been agreed upon by ENIC-NARICs (Aerden & Reczulska, 2012, pp. 11–12).

- Joint program: An integrated curriculum coordinated and offered jointly by different HEIs and leading to a (double/multiple or joint) degree.

- Joint degree: A single document awarded by HEIs offering the joint program and nationally acknowledged as the recognized award of the joint program.

- Multiple degree: Separate degrees awarded by HEIs offering the joint program, attesting to the successful completion of this program.

- Double degree: Two degrees awarded by HEIs offering the joint program, attesting the successful completion of this program. Note that a double degree is a specific type of multiple degree.

These distinctions are important: The common characteristic of joint programs is that they are offered jointly, while the degree awarding can be different (double/multiple or joint). Joint degrees are therefore a subset of joint programs.

When accrediting or quality assuring joint programs, several approaches to these procedures are possible: national, joint, and single procedures. These different procedures are explained in the following sections.

National Accreditation Procedure

A national procedure is the classical approach to the accreditation of joint programs. It means that a national agency accredits a joint program offered by one or more HEIs in the country of the national agency. Traditionally only the provision offered by the HEI(s) in the country that falls under the purview of the agency is assessed. As a consequence, the provision offered by the partner institutions abroad is not assessed by the agency, meaning that the assessment is limited to only a part of the joint program. Perhaps the provision offered by the partner institutions is assessed by agencies in their home countries. But even so, assessments of different national parts means fragmentation, which neglects the crucial characteristic of the program, namely, that it is offered jointly. It is of little use to students enrolling in a joint program to know that only one of the consortium partners has been assessed while they are going to receive education from several institutions. The same is true for other stakeholders. When looking at learning outcomes or other aspects of the program, what counts is the totality that is offered, not just what happens to be offered at one location. From the viewpoint of quality, any assessment in any country should therefore cover the totality of the joint program. Fortunately, this has indeed happened in many countries in recent years. However, it poses some new questions, such as how to get a good view on the totality of the joint program, and how to prevent that the totality of the joint program is examined in multiple national procedures by different agencies.

Joint Accreditation Procedure

An answer to the previous questions is to organize a joint procedure of the agencies that will have to assess the joint programs. Certainly, if there are only two agencies involved, or the agencies know each other quite well (e.g., if they are from neighboring countries and have worked together previously), this would be beneficial. The agencies working together can agree on a common assessment framework, for example, by taking one agency's framework and adding additional elements of the other agency, or by agreeing on a new framework that takes the requirements of both agencies into account. They can then jointly install a panel of experts who will make a site visit to one location (although in practice visits to two or more locations also occur) and resulting in one or two panel reports (if the reporting requirements are so different that two reports need to be written). While joint procedures have the advantage that they look at the totality of the joint program, can avoid duplication in national procedures, make it easy to exchange information between agencies, and learn from each other, there are also some drawbacks. Experience has shown that, especially when agencies cooperate for the first time, comparing frameworks and agreeing on the specifics of the procedure mean quite an investment in time for agencies, experts, and the institutions involved. If several locations are visited or multiple reports written, the reduction of costs is limited. In addition, problems in the decision-making phase may loom if the agencies attach different conclusions to the results of the joint procedure. It is possible that the cooperating agencies make different accreditation decisions, which may be detrimental for both the joint program and future cooperation between the agencies. It is exactly for these reasons that another possible approach, that is, a single-accreditation procedure, has been developed and tested.

Single-Accreditation Procedure

In a single-accreditation procedure, only one agency and one assessment framework carry out the procedure. One panel is used for the assessment, and this panel will only visit one location of the joint program. Nevertheless, the aim is that the results of this single procedure will be accepted by the other agencies in the countries where the joint program is offered. Therefore, the panel writes one report that should be the basis for the accreditation decisions of the other agencies. In the TEAM II project, these single procedures were piloted (Braathen, Frederiks, & Harris, 2010). In each of the five single-accreditation pilot procedures, an agency coordinated the procedure. Although there was agreement between the agencies on the essential elements of the procedure, the position of the coordinating agency was so pivotal to the execution of the procedures that various ways of coordinating the procedures also led to different approaches of accrediting joint programs. The following approaches were taken in practice:

- The procedure, criteria, and experts were mainly taken from one country.

- The procedure and criteria were taken from one country but applied by experts from elsewhere.

- A new procedure was developed with "traditional" criteria based on a minimum set plus additional criteria required for another country.

- The procedure was based on one country's practice, but with experts nominated by all and with a new set of criteria specifically developed for joint programs.

Although this variety in approaches suited the aims of the evaluation and formed the basis for some accreditation decisions, it did not result in broad acceptance of the assessment results among other agencies, precisely because of these various approaches. The main conclusion from these pilots was that stronger coordination was needed to carry out successful single-accreditation procedures.

The coordinated single-accreditation approach that was envisaged consisted of three elements. First, there should be a common assessment framework with shared European criteria (the "core"), topped up with necessary additional criteria (the "plus") from the countries of the joint program consortium. Second, there should be a European coordination point that would "bring together QA agencies and help them to apply the single methodology in ways that enable it to be applicable in a variety of situations and in such a way that the outcomes would be acceptable in a maximum number of countries" (Braathen et al., 2010, p. 49). The coordination point should also administer a publicly accessible knowledge base with information regarding QA and recognition of joint programs. Third, the bilateral agreements of mutual recognition of accreditation results should be enhanced with a multilateral agreement for the mutual recognition of accreditation of joint programs. This would facilitate the acceptance of the results of single-accreditation procedures by other agencies. With these TEAM II recommendations in mind, the JOQAR project began.

Single-Accreditation Procedures in the JOQAR Project

An important aim of the JOQAR project was to develop one single-accreditation procedure that could lead to several national accreditation decisions. Through the single-accreditation procedure the joint program is assessed in totality. The results of this procedure—the self-evaluation, the site visit, and the assessment report—are used for accreditation purposes by the relevant national agencies of the higher education systems in which the joint program is offered. An assessment framework[7] has been developed to assess joint programs in one single-accreditation procedure. When developing this framework, ECA's principles for accreditation procedures regarding joint programs[8] were taken into account. The initial framework consisted of two building blocks: the core and the plus. The European shared component covered the essential standards and criteria that needed to be taken into account in all single-accreditation pilot procedures. This shared component was agreed to among agencies participating in the JOQAR project, Working Group 1 of ECA (dealing with mutual recognition and joint programs) and after a two-day workshop with coordinating agencies and coordinators of the Erasmus Mundus programs that took part in the pilots to test the approach.

The national components covered specific national legal requirements. These national components refer to the elements of the assessment criteria and/or the assessment procedure that needs to be included in an accreditation procedure in a specific national higher education system. All agencies in countries of the pilot procedures were asked whether additional national criteria were necessary for them. Some agencies found the shared European criteria sufficient and did not want to include additional criteria. They could also contribute to the single-accreditation procedure in other ways, for example, by proposing an expert or an observer from the agency to the site visit. The simplest way of involving agencies was to inform them about the procedure and the outcomes. In all cases it was made clear at the start of the procedure that there was the hope (and because of the agencies' involvement also the expectation) that the agencies would accept the result of the procedure as the basis for their own decision making.

In each single-accreditation procedure, there was a coordinating QA agency that was responsible for carrying out the procedure. In addition, there was a coordination point that helped to organize and coordinate the procedures. The role of the coordination point was fulfilled by the ECA Secretariat while the main issues were also discussed by Working Group 1 of ECA and the JOQAR Steering Group. The JOQAR Steering Group was also responsible for the selection of the pilot procedures. About 30 Erasmus Mundus joint master programs (the JOQAR project was funded under the Erasmus Mundus Action line 3 program of the European Commission) had indicated that they were willing to participate in the pilots. On the basis of geographical and disciplinary spread, and taking into account a mix of experiences with external QA as well as the representation of JOQAR partners, a selection of four pilot procedures was made. This resulted in the pilot procedures shown in Tables 23.1 and 23.2.

TABLE 23.1: PILOT PROCEDURES: EMQAL AND EMBC

Joint program	European Master in Quality in Analytical Laboratories (EMQAL)	Erasmus Mundus Master of Science in Marine Biodiversity and Conservation (EMBC)
Higher education institutions	University of Algarve, Portugal University of Barcelona, Spain University of Bergen, Norway University of Cadiz, Spain Gdansk University of Technology, Poland Central South University, China	Ghent University, Belgium University of Bremen, Germany University of the Algarve, Portugal University of Pierre and Marie Curie, Paris, France University of Oviedo, Spain University of Klaipeda, Lithuania
Coordinating QA agency	AQU Catalunya (Spain)	AQAS (Germany)
Other involved QA agencies	A3ES (Portugal) ANECA (Spain) NOKUT (Norway) PKA (Poland)	NVAO (Netherlands/Flanders) AQAS (Germany) A3ES (Portugal), AERES (France) SKVC (Lithuania)

TABLE 23.2: PILOT PROCEDURES: EMMIR AND EMLE

Joint program	European Master in Migration and Intercultural Relations (EMMIR)	Erasmus Mundus Master Course in Law and Economics (EMLE)
Higher education institutions	University of Oldenburg, Germany Ahfad University for Women, Omdurman, Sudan Makerere University, Kampala, Uganda Mbarara University of Science & Technology, Uganda University of Nova Gorica, Slovenia University of South Bohemia, Czech Republic University of Stavanger, Norway	Erasmus University Rotterdam, The Netherlands University of Ghent, Belgium Hamburg University, Germany University Paul Cezanne, Aix/Marseille 3, France University of Bologna, Italy University of Vienna, Austria Haifa University, Israel Warsaw School of Economics, Poland Indira Gandhi Institute of Development Research (IGIDR), Mumbai, India
Coordinating QA agency	SQAA (Slovenia)	NVAO (Netherlands/Flanders)
Other involved QA agencies	AQAS (Germany) NOKUT (Norway) ACCR (Czech Republic)	ZEvA (Germany) CHE (Israel) NAAC (India) AERES (France) ANVUR (Italy) PKA (Poland) AQ (Austria)

The writing of the self-evaluation reports by these joint programs, the panel composition by the agencies, and the site visits at one location of each joint program took place in 2012 (with the exception of one site visit in February 2013). There were two workshops with panel chairs, secretaries (who were staff from coordinating agency), and the coordination point. One workshop was held after the self-evaluation was received and was meant to coordinate the issues raised for the site visits. The second workshop was organized after the draft assessment reports were written and was aimed at improving the consistency of these reports. At the time of writing, this contribution to the decision-making phase is still taking place, but it is already clear that in some cases the pilot single-accreditation results have been the basis for decisions made by other agencies.

The pilot procedures were evaluated (Blanc de la Carrere & Frederiks, 2013), which led to a positive conclusion on the use of the standards and criteria in the European shared component. However, with regard to the national additional criteria, it was concluded that these should be removed when assessing joint programs in single-accreditation procedures. The additional national criteria often contradicted other national criteria, and for international experts, the very specific, national criteria were very difficult to evaluate. Agencies and experts agreed that these additional national criteria were not suitable for assessing joint programs and were merely hindering the development of such programs. However, actions from the national governments are required to remove such national obstacles. The pilots have made it explicit where these additional national criteria occur.

Mutual Recognition of Accreditation of Joint Programs

In December 2007 the first bilateral mutual recognition agreements between accreditation agencies were signed.[9] As a consequence of the TEAM II project, the Multilateral Agreement on the Mutual Recognition of Accreditation Results Regarding Joint Programmes (MULTRA) was set up. The essence of MULTRA is that each of the signatory agencies accepts the accreditation results regarding joint programs of other signatory agencies. As a consequence, only one accreditation procedure for a joint program is needed, and other agencies can base their own national decisions on the results of this procedure without setting up their own national procedures. So, whereas in the pilot procedures, each time a consultation with all the involved agencies had to take place to maximize the chances of accepting the results of the single-accreditation procedures, MULTRA does not require this anymore, because the signatory agencies have already agreed to accept the results of the procedure by one of the other agencies.

MULTRA was first signed in December 2010 and has been expanded with new agencies ever since. In the JOQAR project eight new agencies, including two in Latin America, indicated their willingness to join MULTRA. These agencies had all been reviewed externally, which is an admission requirement for MULTRA. The external review mostly used the Standards and Guidelines for Quality Assurance in the European Higher Education Area (ESG). However, an external review against criteria that are comparable to the ESG is also possible; for example, the two Latin American agencies had been reviewed against the Guidelines of Good Practice of the global network of QA agencies INQAAHE.[10] The second admission requirement is that the applicant agency has to undergo an observation. This means that two observers from agencies that have already signed to MULTRA must observe a procedure of the applicant agency and write an observation report. This observation report forms the basis for the decision making by the MULTRA signatories on the admittance of the new agency. This procedure ensures that not only formal requirements, as in the ESG, are fulfilled, but that there's also evidence on how the agency conducts a procedure in practice. The likelihood of acceptance of decisions of other agencies is very much increased because the MULTRA procedure actively involves agencies in expressing their trust in other agencies. The observations were evaluated positively and led to some minor recommendations on improving the observation procedure (Blanc de la Carrere & Frederiks, 2013).

MULTRA is currently signed by agencies in Austria, Colombia, Costa Rica, Denmark, France, Germany, The Netherlands and Flanders, Poland, Slovenia, and Spain.[11] There is an interest from agencies in other countries to join MULTRA.

Conclusions

Joint programs are on the rise, but they are still hindered by many obstacles regarding national QA requirements and by difficulties in the recognition of degrees awarded by joint programs. The JOQAR project has focused on these issues and arrived at solutions, both in the recognition area (especially when awarding joint degrees) and in the QA area. It has been argued that the difficulties stemming from national QA requirements can be solved by introducing single-accreditation/QA procedures. In these single procedures there is one shared European framework with agreed-upon standards and criteria, with one assessment procedure comprising an international panel (for which experts can be nominated by the agencies in the countries where the joint program is offered), with a self-evaluation report written by the joint program according to the European framework, and with a site visit at one location of the joint program but with representation of the other locations in the interviews; and this results in one assessment report written by the panel.

On the basis of this assessment report, all the agencies in the countries where the joint program is offered can make their national decisions. Thus, only a single procedure instead of multiple procedures is needed. One agency can carry out the single procedure, for which it can receive support by the coordination point provided by ECA. The coordination point can train experts for single-accreditation procedures, explain the methodology of the European assessment framework, and help to bring agencies together (e.g., in the decision-making phase). Making such decisions will be much easier if the agencies have already agreed to accept the results of accreditation procedures of other agencies. It would therefore be desirable if MULTRA could be expanded with more agencies.

MULTRA and organizing single-accreditation procedures are in line with the aim of the ministers in the Bucharest Communiqué "to recognise quality assurance decisions of EQAR-registered agencies on joint and double degree programmes" (EHEA Ministerial Conference, 2012, p. 2). MULTRA even enhances the ambition level of the ministers because it is also open for non-European agencies that are not listed in European Quality Assurance Register (EQAR) but have been reviewed against international QA standards comparable to the ESG. Moreover, because an observation of a real-life procedure is a requirement for admittance to MULTRA, trust among agencies is built—trust that is needed to recognize the results and decisions made by other agencies. After all, the accreditation of joint programs is a national responsibility, and there is nothing in the Bucharest Communiqué that suggests otherwise. By giving their support to MULTRA, single-accreditation procedures, and a European assessment framework with shared standards and criteria, the ministers can attain their goals regarding the QA of joint programs without giving up their national sovereignty in the field of joint programs.

However, to successfully carry out single-accreditation procedures, the ministers would have to remove obstacles in national laws that have been defined for national purposes but are not suitable for assessing joint programs. Such obstacles include different specifications regarding the credits needed for thesis work or modules, national requirements for some categories of academic staff, the duration of the program beyond the requirements of Bologna (e.g., the requirement in some countries of a 300 ECTS total duration for bachelor's and master's degrees), among other things. Such additional specific national criteria not only hamper the accreditation and QA of joint programs, but in some cases also make it impossible for joint programs (and especially joint degrees) to exist at all. An important recommendation from the JOQAR project addressed to governments is therefore to remove these specific national and legal criteria aimed at national and not joint programs, thereby honoring the commitment of ministers to "dismantle obstacles to cooperation and mobility embedded in national contexts" (EHEA Ministerial Conference, 2012, p. 5).

NOTES

[1] http://www.ehea.info/Uploads/Documents/Stocktaking_report_2009_FINAL.pdf

[2] http://www.ecaconsortium.net/

[3] Transparent European Accreditation decisions & Mutual recognition agreements II (TEAM II). http://www.ecaconsortium.net/main/projects/team-ii-

[4] For a description and outcomes of the JOQAR project, see: http://www.ecaconsortium.net/main/projects/joqar

[5] ENIC: European Network of Information Centres, NARIC: National Academic Recognition Information Centres, http://enic-naric.net

[6] In collaboration with ENIC-NARICs, an ECA report has been published dealing with questions such as: How should a joint degree be awarded in such a way that it will recognized? How can the design of the joint degree and the diploma supplement facilitate access to the labor market? (See Aerden & Reczulska, 2012.)

[7] http://www.ecaconsortium.net/main/projects/joqar/achievements-joqar

[8] http://www.ecaconsortium.net/main/documents/main-documents

[9] http://www.ecaconsortium.net/main/documents/mutual-recognition-agreements

[10] International Network for Quality Assurance Agencies in Higher Education: http://www.inqaahe.org/main/professional-development/guidelines-of-good-practice-51

[11] The formal signing is expected in the second half of 2013.

REFERENCES

Aerden, A., & Reczulska, H. (2012). *Guidelines for good practice for awarding joint degrees*. The Hague, Netherlands: ECA. Retrieved from http://www.ecaconsortium.net/main/documents/publications

Braathen, K., Frederiks, M., & Harris, N. (2010). *How to assess and accredit joint programmes in Europe. Methodologies tested and proposed by the TEAM 2 project*. The Hague, Netherlands: ECA.

Blanc de la Carrere, T., & Frederiks, M. (2013). *Single accreditation of joint programmes: Pilots evaluation report*. The Hague, Netherlands: ECA.

EHEA Ministerial Conference. (2012). *Making the most of our potential: Consolidating the European Higher Education Area. Bucharest Communiqué*. Bucharest, Hungary.

Chapter Twenty-Four

Quality Assurance of Joint Programs in the Arab Region

NADIA BADRAWI, ARAB NETWORK FOR QUALITY ASSURANCE IN HIGHER EDUCATION (ANQAHE)

The Arab region is composed of 22 countries. The culture of quality assurance started spreading in 2000. By 2004, five countries, namely, the United Arab Emirates (UAE), Egypt, the Kingdom of Saudi Arabia, Jordan, and Palestine, were working on developing their quality assurance organizations. These countries discussed the different ways of collaboration and decided to establish a network for quality assurance bodies. The Arab Network for Quality Assurance in Higher Education (ANQAHE) was established in 2007 with seven full members; currently (2013), there are 12 full and five affiliated members in ANQAHE.

In this region all the quality assurance agencies are governmental. Most of these countries can be categorized as developing countries; however, some aspects differ, such as population size and the educational economic position of each country, which usually reflects the governmental education funding. Some countries have developed a quasi-independent quality assurance organization; others have developed an organization affiliated with their ministries of higher education, and a smaller percentage have not yet started to work on establishing quality assurance agencies.

Many of the Arab countries support partnerships with foreign education in the form of joint degrees, dual degrees, branch campuses, franchised programs, or other informal collaborations with cross-border higher education institutions. Most of the Arab countries' governments differentiate between the recognition and licensing of any new program and quality assurance and accreditation, regardless of whether the programs are national or cross-border.

ANQAHE has sent a survey to its entire full and affiliated membership to assess the situation of quality assurance and/or accreditation of joint or double degrees in these countries. ANQAHE has received replies from 9 of a total of 17 requests. According to the survey responses, the political force of the government plays a major role in the approval and motivation of the higher education institutions in developing any foreign programs, whether joint or double degree program, branch campuses, franchise programs, or any other informal affiliation like mutual agreement between two universities. In most of these countries, in order to start a joint or double degree program, there should be prior approval from either the ministry or the higher education council of the country. A higher education institution cannot offer such a degree without clear permission from higher education authorities, or this degree will not be recognized in the country.

In Palestine, there are two quality assurance bodies, one in the West Bank and a newly developed one in Gaza. In the West Bank, the authority does not initiate such programs; it has rejected all attempts by local universities to offer joint degrees, and it does not have any policies or procedures to support joint programs in the country. If such degrees are programs are in effect, they exist by mutual agreement between universities but are unrecognized by the ministry of higher education. In other countries like Egypt, Lebanon, Kuwait, Oman, Qatar, Bahrain, and Yemen, these degrees do exist and are recognized by the higher education authorities. In Egypt, there are no real branch campuses, although there are universities that carry the name of foreign countries like the British University, the German University, the French University, and recently the Russian University. Each of these universities are affiliated with a foreign university from its country name, and they all award their degrees from Egypt. Many of them offer joint or double degrees, or they are licensed to apply a curriculum, or their programs are validated by their respective universities. On the other hand, Egyptian universities export branch campuses in other Arab and African countries like Lebanon and Chad. Moreover, Egypt has many joint programs, especially with Germany, organized by German Academic Exchange Service (DAAD) and franchise programs with many countries like United Kingdom, the United States, and France.

In Lebanon, there are one joint degree and five double degrees, as well two branch campuses, affiliated with French universities. The degrees awarded from these universities in Lebanon are given from the native country universities. In UAE, there are seven joint degrees and one double degree, in addition to 29 branch campuses and five collaborative hybrid programs. In Yemen, there are a number of joint and double degrees and three branch campuses in collaboration with other Arab, Asian, and African universities. In Kuwait, there are no joint degrees, but there are four branch campuses, and a fifth branch is expected to open in 2015; there are five affiliated programs, and another eight are expected in 2013–2015. All branch campuses awards are given from the local universities.

In Oman there is only one joint degree. Private colleges are expected to have an affiliation agreement with international universities in order to be licensed and recognized. Accordingly, there are affiliation agreements for 20 higher education institutions with international universities in Oman. In Bahrain, there are no joint or double degrees, but there is one branch campus. In Qatar, there are no joint or double degrees, but the government supports branch campuses with highly ranked universities.

In most of the Arab countries, there is no special law to regulate the joint or double degrees, but there are policies and procedures that should be considered to recognize the degree. Most of the Arab countries each have an equivalence committee affiliated with its ministry of higher education to recognize foreign degrees; this committee meets regularly under the umbrella of the UNESCO convention on recognition of qualifications to harmonize their recognition standards and processes. The governments usually encourage these degree programs to be affiliated with reputable universities. They usually do not limit the partner countries, except rarely; for example, UAE do not allow joint or double degree or branch campuses with India. Other countries have the same policy with Israel.

As a result of this survey, the Gulf area in the Arab region invests in branch campuses more than joint or double degrees. They have a lot of good practice in this domain, they attract highly ranked universities, and they invest financially in supporting these branch campuses. In the Gulf countries, the branch campuses are accredited either from the native country or directly from the Arab country. In general, the composition of the external panel usually includes more than one international reviewer. As a result, the accreditation given has a more or less international background. In Bahrain, Oman, the Kingdom of Saudi Arabia, UAE, and the non-free zone of Europe, the accreditation decision is made by the national quality assurance body. In Lebanon, although the final degree is awarded from the native university, there is always quality control from the country over the branch university. In the free zone of UAE, the decision is made by the quality assurance agency of the native country.

In a conference in Egypt organized jointly by DAAD and ANQAHE in 2012, the process of accreditation of joint or double degrees was discussed intensively in world café sessions. There were about 80 participants from 13 countries from the Arab region and Germany. This discussion paved the way for joint accreditation for these programs. The participants concluded that there are many steps that need to be considered when accrediting a joint or double degree. Involvement of stakeholders (faculty, students, labor market, and quality assurance agencies) is a major step in accrediting such degree. Building trust and confidence between the two institutions offering these degrees takes time, and both institutions should work hard to reach the expected level of trust. The period of the accreditation procedure would be 6–12 months, including initial quality review plus final review. The participants pointed out that additional standards and requirements should be taken into consideration when accrediting these degrees.

The differential points between joint and double degree programs and standard programs include risk assessment, student support systems, faculty collaboration, and accessibility to learning resources. The role of different quality assurance agencies is an important factor in the accreditation process, given that sometimes problems are encountered because of different national regulations, which is why early cooperation between the two partners is necessary. The presence of more than one quality assurance agency in the country and the selection of the partner quality assurance agency are other factors to keep in mind to ensure successful outcomes.

During this conference, there was also time to discuss the role of peers, selection criteria, nomination of peers, cultural awareness, and exclusion criteria of the peers, and the presence of students in the panel. There was a consensus concerning the development of a peers' database to facilitate the process of accreditation. A debate on the method of report writing was sparked regarding how to satisfy quality assurance agencies of both countries involved in the accreditation of the joint/double degrees, while bearing in mind the different or conflicting agency policies. There was discussion about follow-up visits after accreditation. Finally, the ultimate outcome of this conference will be a joint report and decision signed by the DAAD and ANQAHE.

In Egypt, the development of new joint programs has been expanding. The recognition of these programs begins with the approval of the Supreme Council of Universities, before students can be accepted into the joint degree program. The accreditation of the program by Egyptian law takes place after the first graduation cycle. In Egypt there is a proposed strategy, to have a mutual agreement between the Agency for Quality Assurance through Accreditation of Study Programmes (AQAS) from Germany and the quality assurance and accreditation agency in Egypt to accredit German/Egyptian joint degrees. The two quality assurance agencies would first agree on the standards and the process needed to accredit the program. This mutual agreement would include the main items of accreditation, principle namely, the information sharing and transparency, the evaluation processes, and the accreditation decision. Moreover, it would include the composition of the panel with an equal number of reviewers from both sides. The role of ANQAHE in this domain can be significant. The goal is to work for a single accreditation process for joint/double degrees and simplify the procedures between agencies. ANQAHE can develop an awareness program for accreditation of joint degrees, highlighting the difference between recognition/licensing and quality assurance, overcoming the existing national barriers in the recognition and accreditation of joint programs in the Arab region, exchanging information and ideas between the agencies, facilitating selection of partners between agencies, and building trust between quality assurance agencies. These are the necessary components of a successive accreditation. ANQAHE could also develop a code of practice for coordination between accrediting agencies and establish a database for reviewers. All of these efforts would help to strengthen the capacity of the national quality assurance agencies by working to reduce border restrictions and enhancing mutual understanding and recognition.

About the Contributors

Nadia Badrawi is an expert in quality assurance and accreditation in higher education. Badrawi is currently the president of the Arab Network for Quality Assurance in Higher Education (ANQAHE), as well as a board member of the Advisory Council of the CHEA International Quality Group (CIQG), the Quality Assurance Commission of the Association of Arab Universities, the Global Pediatrics Education Consortium (GPEC), and the National Medical Sector Committee for Planning and Development in Egypt. Badrawi was the chairperson of the National Quality Assurance and Accreditation Committee in Egypt. She disseminated the culture of quality assurance in higher education at regional and national levels. She was the chairperson of the Pediatrics Department Cairo University. Badrawi is also the main author of four quality assurance and accreditation books and two pediatrics and neonatal books. She has also published many papers in national and international journals in the fields of medicine and education.

Diana Bartelli Carlin has served as associate vice president for graduate education at Saint Louis University since June 2011. She chairs a faculty governance committee charged with reviewing program development and approval for international joint and dual degree programs, and oversees all international initiatives for the Office of Academic Affairs. She has presented at professional meetings and U.S. campuses and has written on international joint and dual degrees. Prior to her position at Saint Louis University she was graduate and international dean at the University of Kansas and was the Council of Graduate Schools dean in residence and director of international outreach. Her academic field is political communication and she has authored numerous books, chapters, and articles on political campaigns and women in politics. She works in new democracies on election and civil society projects. She received a Ph.D. in speech communication from the University of Nebraska–Lincoln.

Megan Brenn-White is managing director of The Brenn-White Group, a New York City–based company that helps universities and higher education organizations reach their international goals by providing marketing, strategy, and communications services. Brenn-White has been writing about and presenting on topics related to internationalization and international marketing to university administrators and faculty around the world for over a decade. Before founding The Brenn-White Group, she served as deputy director of DAAD New York (responsible for marketing the German higher education system in North America), executive director of the Hessen Universities Consortium New York Office, and director for international partnerships at Parsons School of Design. In addition to her work in international education, Brenn-White has held senior positions in marketing and content at major international websites. She holds an AB in government from Harvard College and an MSc in European studies from the London School of Economics.

Stephen Connelly is an international education specialist with over 20 years of experience in the field. From 2010 to 2013, he was deputy vice-chancellor (international and development) at RMIT University. Prior to joining RMIT he spent five years at Swinburne University of Technology as pro vice chancellor (international) and later deputy vice chancellor (development and engagement). He spent seven years at La Trobe University as director of international marketing and then director of the International Programs Office. He was president of the International Education Association Australia (IEAA) from October 2008 to October 2012 and has been a board member since 2005. He has lived and worked overseas in Germany and Malaysia, and has qualifications from Monash University, the University of Melbourne, and the Australian Institute of Company Directors.

Elias Faethe has worked in the field of higher education for three years. He works at StudyPortals, a company providing an overview of study options in Europe, where he is the liaison person for universities in the DACH (Germany, Austria, and Switzerland) region. He also researches the behavior of millions of visitors to StudyPortals, and has been involved in preparing various articles, including an IIE Briefing Paper, "English-Taught Master's Programs in Europe." He has led efforts at StudyPortals to research new European trends in student mobility, particularly in the context of increasing study abroad demand from countries including Spain, Italy, Greece, and Portugal. He holds a degree in engineering and management (Dipl.-Wi.-Ing.) from the University of Bremen.

Manar Fayyad is a professor of analytical and inorganic chemistry at the University of Jordan, a position she has held since 1978. She was the director of the Water and Environment Research and Study Center at the University of Jordan from 1999 to 2007. Her research interests lie in the areas of water resources management, water quality, and environmental pollution. She is a member of several committees related to higher education and water management. Fayyad is the Jordanian coordinator for the seventh year of Integrated Water Resources Management, a bicultural master's program executed in collaboration with Cologne University in Germany and funded by DAAD. She has coordinated several projects related to water management and water education. Fayyad supervised about 70 students at the master's and Ph.D. levels. She is the author of about 75 articles and books, in addition to numerous research reports. A Jordanian native, she received her Ph.D. in chemistry from the University of Bonn in 1978.

José Pissolato Filho has been a professor of engineering since 2005 at the Department of Energy and Control, Unicamp, which he joined in 1979. He started to get involved with international education when he pioneered the establishment of double degrees with French institutions in 1998. Over the years he has been responsible for several double degree programs. Since 2009, he has been an advisor of the Unicamp International Relations Office. His main research interests are high voltage engineering, electromagnetic transients, and electromagnetic compatibility. He was born in Campinas, São Paulo, Brazil, and received a Ph.D. in electrical engineering from Université Paul Sabatier, France, in 1986.

Mark Frederiks is coordinator of the International Policy Department of NVAO, the Accreditation Organisation of the Netherlands and Flanders. He is also the coordinator of the

European Consortium for Accreditation in higher education (ECA), and for five years served as administrator at INQAAHE, the worldwide network of quality assurance agencies. Before joining NVAO in 2003, he worked for five years with HBO-raad, the Netherlands Association of Universities of Applied Sciences. In 1998 he was a consultant on higher education with PricewaterhouseCoopers Management Consultants. In 1997 he was based in London as a research fellow with the Quality Support Centre at The Open University UK. He worked with the Center for Higher Education Policy Studies (CHEPS) at the University of Twente as a researcher and research trainee from 1991 to 1996. Frederiks obtained his Ph.D. from the University of Twente in 1996.

Jocelyne Gacel-Ávila is a tenured professor and researcher at the University of Guadalajara, Mexico, where she was in charge of the international office for 25 years. Considered a world expert on internationalization of higher education, she is a member of the Mexican National System of Research and the author and editor of more than 14 books and 70 scientific publications. Her many professional roles include vice-president of the Governing Board of the IMHE Programme, member of the Expert Group for the Reviews on Higher Education in Regional and City Development of the OECD, vice-president of CONAHEC Board of Directors, president of the Mexican Association for International Education, and others. Gacel-Ávila is founding director of the journal *Educación Global* (AMPEI) and a member of the editorial advisory board of the *Journal of Studies in International Education* (SAGE). She received the CONAHEC Award of Distinction 2010 for outstanding contributions to academic collaboration in North America, and the AMPEI prize 2006 for her contribution to Mexican higher education internationalization. Fluent in French, Spanish, English, and German, Gacel-Ávila received her Ph.D. in higher education and her Master of Arts from the University of Paris.

James Garton is a Melbourne-based consultant in the areas of strategic planning and transnational education. He was formerly director, international partnerships & quality, at Swinburne University, Melbourne, and has worked in transnational education and related fields for more than 20 years. His experience includes planning, developing, and reviewing transnational education programs; strategic planning and policy development; quality assurance; teaching in overseas universities in Asia, the Pacific, and the Middle East; and intercultural research on multicultural communities in Australia.

Francesco Girotti has been working at the European Programs Unit within the International Relations Office at the University of Bologna since 2004. His main expertise is the management of higher education, including international projects focusing on student mobility, joint degree development, and structural and policy measures. In recent years, he has focused on the promotion and implementation of European higher education programs, specifically in connection to Erasmus Mundus. Girotti has been the project coordinator of the JOIMAN Structural Network on Joint Degree Management and Administration, and was intensely involved in the JOI.CON training project. In the frame of both projects, he authored several publications and was invited to present project results at acclaimed panels such as the EAIE sessions. Girotti has been nominated by the European Commission as an external member of the steering committee of the EMQA project for the evaluation of the quality of Erasmus

Mundus programs. He also chairs the task force on joint degrees in the Utrecht network, which includes 31 European universities. A native of Italy, he graduated in international politics at the University of Bologna and received a master's degree in European policies and programs.

Allan E. Goodman is the sixth president of the Institute of International Education, the leading not-for-profit organization in the field of international educational exchange and development training. Previously, Goodman was executive dean of the School of Foreign Service and professor at Georgetown University. He is the author of books on international affairs published by Harvard, Princeton, and Yale University presses. Goodman served as presidential briefing coordinator for the director of central intelligence in the Carter Administration. Subsequently, he was the first American professor to lecture at the Foreign Affairs College of Beijing, helped create the first U.S. academic exchange program with the Moscow Diplomatic Academy for the Association of Professional Schools of International Affairs, and developed the diplomatic training program of the Foreign Ministry of Vietnam. Goodman has a Ph.D. in government from Harvard, an MPA from the John F. Kennedy School of Government, and a BS from Northwestern University. He also holds honorary degrees from Chatham, Susquehanna, and Toyota Universities; Dickinson, Middlebury, Mount Ida, and Ramapo colleges; and The State University of New York. He has received awards from Georgetown, Johns Hopkins, South Florida, and Tufts universities, and the Légion d'honneur from France. He was awarded the inaugural Gilbert Medal for Internationalization by Universitas 21 in May 2012.

Fred L. Hall, currently retired, was vice-provost (graduate education) and dean of graduate studies at the University of Calgary from August 2007 through July 2011. Prior to 2007, he had been the dean of graduate studies at McMaster University in Ontario for eight years. For the whole of his 35-year career at McMaster he was appointed jointly between geography and civil engineering, with a focus on urban transportation. He is author or coauthor of roughly 80 peer-reviewed journal articles, as well as numerous conference papers and several book chapters, primarily in the areas of freeway traffic flow theory, freeway operations and quality of service, and earlier on the impacts of transportation noise on residential communities. From 2005 on, he also conducted research on aspects of doctoral education. Hall holds a Ph.D. in geography from the University of Chicago.

Jochen Hellmann has been secretary general of the Franco-German University since February 2009. Between 2001 and 2008, he was head of the International Department at the University of Hamburg. His main fields of study are international comparison of university systems, with an emphasis on the European dimension, mobility, university reforms, and modernization of university administration, as well as the introduction of the bachelor master system. Hellmann was department head for the promotion of "Germany as a destination for research and studying" at the German Academic Exchange Service (DAAD) from 1998 to 2001, and senior officer for research promotion and European mobility programs in Hamburg from 1993 to 1998. Prior to this, he was an officer at the European Liaison Bureau at the University of Hanover, and worked as a lecturer in German language and literature at Sorbonne University in Paris. He was educated at the University of Hamburg in arts in Romance and German languages and literature, where he was awarded a Ph.D. in 1991.

Elena Karpukhina is professor and vice rector of the Russian Presidential Academy of National Economy and Public Administration. Her professional interests include global education and international strategic alliances. Karpukhina is the author of various books, book chapters, and articles, and has helped to promote double degree programs with European universities in Russia. From 2004 to 2008, Karpukhina was a member of the Strategic Committee of the BRIDGE project, a double/joint UK–Russia degree program initiative. She is well known for her expertise as a consultant for the Ministry of Education and Science of the Russian Federation, the UNESCO Institute for Education, the Delegation of the European Commission to Russia, and the World Bank on the issues of lifelong learning, adult education, mobility of students and academics, and the Bologna process. Karpukhina has been a visiting professor at numerous European and American Universities. She is a native of Russia and received a Ph.D. in economics from Lomonosov Moscow State University.

Jane Knight, Ontario Institute for Studies in Education, University of Toronto, focuses her research on the international dimension of higher education at the institutional, national, regional, and international levels. Her work in over 65 countries with universities, governments, and UN agencies helps to bring a comparative, development, and international perspective to her research, teaching, and policy work. She is the author of numerous publications on internationalization concepts and strategies, quality assurance, institutional management, trade, education hubs, and cross-border education. Knight is the cofounder of the African Network for the Internationalization of Education and sits on the advisory boards of several international organizations, universities, and journals. In 2010 the University of Exeter awarded her an Honorary LLD; in 2011 she was the recipient of the Outstanding Researcher Award from the European Association for Institutional Research; and in 2013 she was awarded the Gilbert Medal from Universitas 21 for her contribution to higher education internationalization.

Matthias Kuder works with the Centre for International Cooperation at Freie Universität Berlin, a unit focusing on strategic internationalization. He is in charge of developing strategic partnerships with universities abroad and heads FUB's network of liaison offices, with representation in New York, Brussels, Moscow, São Paulo, Beijing, New Delhi, and Cairo. Kuder is coauthor of the international survey report "Joint and Double Degree Programs in the Global Context" (2011), and coeditor of the book *Joint and Double Degree Programs: An Emerging Trend for Transatlantic Exchange* (2010). In 2012, he was appointed as a member of the Center for International Partnerships in Higher Education Advisory Group at the Institute of International Education, New York. Before joining Freie Universität, Kuder worked as a consultant with Lemmens Media, specializing in services for higher education institutions. He also served with the Science and Technology Section of the Canadian Embassy in Berlin. Kuder studied at Bonn, Toronto, and Berlin, and holds a master's degree in North American studies and political science.

Alessia Lefébure serves as the director of the Alliance Program at Columbia University and is also an adjunct professor at SIPA, the School of International and Public Affairs. An expert on global higher education and international affairs, she has been in charge of the academic and external relations with the Asia Pacific region at Sciences Po where she served as the director of the Beijing Office between 2011 and 2006, than as the director of the Centre for Asia and the Pacific between 2006 and 2011. She has lectured and taught at Sciences Po in Paris and at Tsinghua University in Beijing on topics related to comparative higher education policies. Her most recent publication is a chapter in the book *China Innovation Inc.*, published in Paris by les Presses de Sciences Po (2012). She is native of Italy, and completed her academic studies in Italy (LUISS, Rome), the United Kingdom (East Anglia University), and France (Sciences Po, Paris).

Nina Lemmens studied art history and worked as a freelance journalist for 10 years during her time at university. After finishing her Ph.D. at the University of Bonn, she worked as personal assistant for an MP in the German parliament for one year. Lemmens joined the German Academic Exchange Service (DAAD) in 1997 and since then has held numerous positions, including director of the DAAD London office (2000 to 2006) and director for the Asia-Pacific Department in the Bonn head office (2006 to 2009). In July 2009, she took over the directorship of the Department for Internationalization and Communication at DAAD in Bonn. As of January 2014, Lemmens will be the director of DAAD's New York office.

Liu Jinghui began her appointment as secretary-general of the China Scholarship Council in 2008. She simultaneously serves as the president of the China Association for International Education and chairperson of the board, Dongfang International Center for Educational Exchange. Prior to this, from 2001 to 2008, Liu was the counselor and minister counselor in the Education Section of the Chinese Embassy in Berlin. Liu was the secretary-general and deputy director-general at the Central Institute for Vocational and Technical Education from 1990 to 2001, and worked in the Department of International Cooperation and Exchanges, Ministry of Education of P. R. China from 1980 to 1990. Liu studied German language and literature at the University of Heidelberg, Germany, and received her Ph.D. in education from Humboldt University, Germany.

Tabea Mager has been working in the fields of student recruitment and joint program management at Leipzig University since 2009. As coordinator of JOI.CON, she centrally managed the training and dissemination project on joint program management, and also edited the project publication. Currently she advises academic staff at Leipzig University on the process of implementing joint programs at the bachelor's and master's levels. In this context, Mager draws from her experience in the administration of several Erasmus Mundus programs and networks. She has furthermore participated in the JOIMAN network as part of the work groups dealing with financial issues and with cooperation outside the European Union and in other LLP networks such as EMQT (Erasmus Mobility Quality Tools). A native of Germany, she graduated from Leipzig University in the fields of cultural studies, journalism, and English studies.

Xavier Prats Monné is the deputy director-general for education at the European Commission (EC). He is responsible for the European Union's policies and programs in the fields of education and training, and represents the EC at the European Institute for Innovation and Technology (EIT). He previously served as director for EU employment policy and one of the five founding members of the Impact Assessment Board reporting to the EC president, director of the European Social Fund, deputy chief of staff of the EC vice-president for foreign policy, counselor to the EC commissioner for regional policy, and assistant to the spokesman under President Jacques Delors. He holds degrees in social anthropology from the Complutensis University of Madrid, Spain (Licenciatura), in development from the International Centre for Advanced Mediterranean Agronomic Studies (DESS, Paris), and in European affairs from the College of Europe in Bruges, Belgium, where he graduated first in the Class of 1981–82.

Claire Morel has worked for the past 17 years in the field of international cooperation in education and training. Before joining the European Commission, she worked at the European Training Foundation, an agency of the EU based in Turin, on the modernization of vocational education and training systems in the Eastern neighboring countries. She then moved to DG Education and Culture (DG EAC) of the European Commission where she worked for Tempus, a program for higher education modernization, dealing mainly with Central Asian countries, and as an information officer. She is now deputy head of the unit for international cooperation and programs in DG EAC, and her work concentrates on international policy dialogue in education and training, in particular with the EU's neighboring countries, and preparing the next generation of EU international education programs.

Daniel Obst is deputy vice president of international partnerships at the Institute of International Education (IIE) in New York, one of the largest and oldest not-for-profit organizations in the field of international educational exchange and development training. Obst oversees all the activities of IIE's network of 1,200 member institutions, publications and higher education services, IIE's Center for International Partnerships in Higher Education, and strategic communications. Obst recently coedited several books, including *Developing Strategic International Partnerships, Joint and Double Degree Programs: An Emerging Model for Transatlantic Exchange*, and *Innovation Through Education: Building the Knowledge Economy in the Middle East*. In 2013, Obst was appointed to serve on the U.S. National Commission to UNESCO. Obst received his BA in international relations from the George Washington University and holds a master's degree in European studies from the London School of Economics.

Svend Poller has been directing the International Centre at Leipzig University since 1992. In this context, he has steered the International Center through reorganization processes and taken responsibility for strategic changes. These included fostering the implementation of joint programs as part of advanced internationalization in higher education. The JOI.CON training project was initiated on the base of Poller's commitment to the topic, and carried out under his leadership. Prior to JOI.CON, he had assumed responsibility over the JOIMAN network as the leader of the work package "Financial Issues in Joint Degree Programs," and was engaged in similar LLP networks such as EMQT: Erasmus Mobility Quality Tools. He coauthored several publications related to these projects and was invited to present project results in Europe and South Africa. Poller is a member of various advisory boards to the German Academic Exchange Service (DAAD) and presided over the Utrecht Network, a network of 31 European universities, from 2010 to 2012. A native of Germany, Poller graduated from Leipzig University and received a Ph.D. in linguistics.

Lars Ribbe is a professor for integrated land and water resources management at Cologne University of Applied Sciences. After research stays in the United States, Sri Lanka, India, Syria, Brazil, Cuba, and Chile, he became director of the Institute for Technology and Resources Management in the Tropics and Subtropics (ITT) in 2009. In this capacity, he coordinates several research projects in Asia, Africa, and Latin America, and heads the Centre for Natural Resources and Development, an international network of 11 universities fostering scientific exchange and collaboration related to the MDG 7. Furthermore, he is the coordinator of the interfaculty research cluster NEXUS-Water Energy and Food Security at Cologne University of Applied Sciences. Ribbe promotes the concept of enquiry-based learning throughout the different master's courses offered at the ITT and in collaboration with partner universities in Mexico, Jordan, and Vietnam. He obtained a degree in chemistry at Bremen University, a master of engineering at Cologne University of Applied Sciences, and a Ph.D. at Jena University in hydro-informatics.

Patricia Rohland has been working for the Franco-German University (FGU) for 12 years. Since 2010, she has been head of the department for external relations and in charge of public relations, alumni relations, and partnerships with the business world. She previously worked for six years in the field of public and press communication and for two years in the area of alumni relations and private public partnerships for the FGU. During her binational Franco-German studies in cross-cultural communication and political sciences, she gained professional experience in the binational, European, and international fields through internships at institutions including the German Academic Exchange Service (DAAD), New York; the Information Office of the European Parliament, Paris; the Information Center of the German Embassy in France (CIDAL), Paris; and the Franco-German Youth Office (DFJW), Paris.

Dorothea Rüland has been secretary general of the German Academic Exchange Service (DAAD) since October 2010. Before coming back to DAAD, she was director of the Center for International Cooperation at the Freie Universität Berlin for two years. During her time at DAAD from 1980 to 2008, Rüland was responsible for several regions of the world. In 2004 she was assigned deputy secretary general of the DAAD. From 1999 to 2004 she was in charge of diverse DAAD activities in Asia, Africa, and Latin America; from 1994 to 1999 she was head of the office in Indonesia. She is a member of several national and international associations and administrative boards. Rüland studied German literature, history, and musicology at the University of Freiburg.

Christoph Steber started his work in international relations at the Technische Universität München (TUM) in 1990 at a time when the internationalization of universities was just beginning. As director of the International Office for more than 15 years, he was responsible for the international strategy, network, and exchange programs of TUM. Today, TUM has the highest number of ERASMUS students in Germany and offers the most double degree courses. Recently, Steber became a consultant to the president for international recruitment. Steber has taught culture and civilization at Ecole Centrale Paris, where he worked as professeur invité in 2003/04. He published a book about the history of the Bavarian dukes and their relation to Munich and wrote for several newspapers. He studied history in Vienna and Munich, where he received an MA.

Dorothy Stevens is deputy director of the Postgraduate and International Office (PGIO) at Stellenbosch University, South Africa, where she plays an institutional role advising on matters relating to postgraduate student success and international student enrollment. In addition to having a general overview of many aspects of international education, she has developed specific skills and experience in the establishment of joint degree programs between Stellenbosch University and foreign universities, including related policy development. She is a member of the International Education Association of South Africa (IEASA), which plays a national role in policy-making that affects international education. She has offered training workshops on credential evaluation and has presented at conferences on the topic of joint degrees. She holds an Honours degree in industrial sociology from the University of the Witwatersrand (WITS).

Bernard C. Y. Tan started his tenure as vice provost (education) of NUS in September 2012. Prior to this, he was associate provost (undergraduate education), executive council chairman of NUS Teaching Academy, head of the Department of Information Systems, and assistant dean of the School of Computing. He is a professor of information systems, and his research focuses on social media, virtual communities, and Internet commerce. He has won the NUS Outstanding Educator Award and the NUS Young Researcher Award. Bernard is a fellow of the Association for Information Systems, and served as that organization's 15th president. He has served as senior editor of *MIS Quarterly*, senior editor of *Journal of the Association for Information Systems*, and as department editor of *IEEE Transactions on Engineering Management*. He has been a visiting scholar at Stanford University. A native of Singapore, Tan received a Ph.D. in information systems from NUS.

Mareike Tarazona has been working as a researcher at the German Institute for International Educational Research (DIPF) since September 2008. Since February 2011 she has been predominantly researching indicators for the National Education Report, a report elaborated by a consortium of independent scientists. Before joining the DIPF she lectured at the University of Flensburg on topics such as regional development and education and development, both focusing on Latin America. Besides lecturing, her tasks included administration of research initiatives at the Center of Education Research at the university. Her research interests are organization and administration of education institutions, education in Latin America, and returns on education. She holds a Ph.D. in business administration/economics from the University of Flensburg.

Leandro R. Tessler joined Instituto de Física "Gleb Wataghin," Unicamp in 1991, where he has been an associate professor since 1999. He has authored or coauthored more than 50 research papers on experimental condensed matter physics, as well as three book chapters and many articles about higher education in magazines and newspapers. Tessler was dean of admissions and director of international relations at Unicamp. He is a frequent consultant for the Brazilian Ministry of Education. Before joining Unicamp he was a CNRS researcher at ISMRa, Caen, France. He was a visiting scholar at Ecole Polytechnique, Palaiseau, and at the University of Wisconsin–Madison. His research interests include access, affirmative action, internationalization of higher education, and rare-earth doped nanostructured semiconductors. He is a native of Brazil and received a Ph.D. in physics from Tel Aviv University in 1989.

Christian Thimme is head of the division for internationalization of higher education at the German Academic Exchange Service (DAAD). Before he joined the DAAD in 2001, Thimme worked for the European Bureau for Project Support in Bonn, where he was the coordinator of the European program Youthstart, a strand of the European-wide Employment Initiative, which supports innovative projects in all EU member states. Prior to this, he was a DAAD lector for German language and history in the French university Blaise Pascal in Clermont-Ferrand. Thimme studied history, sociology, and German as a foreign language, and holds a Ph.D. in German as a foreign language.

Joern Trappe is scientific researcher at Cologne University of Applied Sciences. After research stays in Botswana and Jordan, he started to work for the Institute for Technology and Resources Management in the Tropics and Subtropics with a research project on optimizing water allocation in Upper Egypt. Since 2009, he has been coordinating the German-Jordanian master's program Integrated Water Resources Management in cooperation with the University of Jordan. His focus area is the management of water resources. Trappe received a degree in Geoecology at Technical University of Braunschweig and a master of science at Cologne University of Applied Sciences.

Diana Yefanova is a researcher and practitioner in international education currently based at the University of Minnesota. In the course of her professional career, she worked in international student admissions and counseling, as well as with program evaluation and assessment projects in higher education and international development. Her main research interests are international cooperation in higher education, intercultural competence development, and curriculum internationalization impacts on school and society. She is from Russia and has lived in the United States and Japan. She holds a doctorate in comparative international development education from the University of Minnesota, where she also served as instructor and study abroad adviser.

Takako Yuki is a research fellow at Japan International Cooperation Agency (JICA), Tokyo, Japan. She specializes in education policies and development, public finance, and gender. She has managed research projects on higher education in East Asian countries, and basic education in the Arab region and West Africa. She has also published articles and lectured at universities on these topics. Previously, she worked at the World Bank and managed education projects and analytical work programs in Yemen. She was research associate at Research Center for Advanced Science and Technology, University of Tokyo. She received her master's degree from Cornell University and her Ph.D. from the University of Tokyo.

IIE Information and Resources

About the Institute of International Education

The Institute of International Education, founded in 1919, is a world leader in the exchange of people and ideas. IIE has a network of 30 offices and representatives worldwide and 1,100 college and university members. In collaboration with governments, corporate and private foundations, and other sponsors, IIE designs and implements programs of study and training for students, educators, young professionals, and trainees from all sectors with funding from government and private sources. These programs include the Fulbright and Humphrey Fellowships and the Gilman Scholarships, administered for the U.S. Department of State, and the Boren Scholarships and Fellowships administered for the National Security Education Program. IIE's publications include the *Open Doors Report on International Educational Exchange*, supported by the Bureau of Educational and Cultural Affairs of the U.S. Department of State, as well as *Funding for United States Study,* the *IIEPassport Study Abroad* print and online directories, and the StudyAbroadFunding.org website. **www.iie.org**

THE CENTER FOR INTERNATIONAL PARTNERSHIPS IN HIGHER EDUCATION

The IIE Center for International Partnerships in Higher Education draws on IIE's wide-ranging network of more than 1,200 colleges and universities and extensive expertise in international education to provide administrators, policymakers, and practitioners with the resources and connections to develop and sustain partnerships around the world. Major initiatives of the Center are the International Academic Partnerships Program and the IIE Global Partner Service. The Center also produces timely policy research and convenes international education leaders in conferences and workshops.

WEBSITE: www.iie.org/cip

THE CENTER FOR ACADEMIC MOBILITY RESEARCH

The IIE Center for Academic Mobility Research brings together the Institute's in-house research expertise with leading minds from around the world to conduct and disseminate timely and relevant research and policy analysis in the field of international student and faculty mobility. The Center provides applied research and program evaluation services to domestic and international governmental agencies, nongovernmental organizations, corporations, and foundations. The Center's in-depth books and reports are key reference resources.

WEBSITE: www.iie.org/mobility

RECENT IIE PUBLICATIONS

- A Student Guide to Study Abroad (2013)
- A Process for Screening and Authorizing Joint and Double Degree Programs (2013)
- English-Taught Master's Programs in Europe: A 2013 Update (2013)
- Women in the Global Economy: Leading Social Change (2013)
- New Frontiers: U.S. Students Pursuing Degrees Abroad (2013)
- The U.S. Community College Model: Potential for Applications in India (2013)
- Investing in the Future: Rebuilding Higher Education in Myanmar (2013)
- U.S. Students in China: Meeting the Goals of the 100,000 Strong Initiative (2013)
- Expanding U.S. Study Abroad to Brazil: A Guide for Institutions (2012)
- Latin America's New Knowledge Economy: Higher Education, Government, and International Collaboration (2012)
- Developing Strategic International Partnerships: Models for Initiating and Sustaining Innovative Institutional Linkages (2011)

WEBSITE: www.iie.org/publications

DAAD Information and Resources

About the German Academic Exchange Service (DAAD)

The German Academic Exchange Service (DAAD) is the largest funding organization in the world supporting the international exchange of students and scholars. Since it was founded in 1925, more than 1.5 million scholars in Germany and abroad have received DAAD funding. It is a registered association, and its members are German institutions of higher education and student bodies. Its activities go far beyond simply awarding grants and scholarships. The DAAD supports the internationalization of German universities, promotes German studies and the German language abroad, assists developing countries in establishing effective universities and advises decision makers on matters of cultural, education and development policy. DAAD relies on a global and constantly expanding network of 15 regional offices and 55 information centers to carry out its international work on all five continents.

WEBSITE: www.daad.de

Structural Programs

Funded by the German Federal Ministry of Education and Research, the DAAD supports the implementation of international study programs at German universities. Internationally oriented courses of study with firmly established windows for mobility are at the core of this group of programs, and their central element is the mutual recognition of coursework. These programs' main funding goal is to promote the internationalization of German universities and the academic mobility of German students. The programs in particular are: International Study and Training Partnerships (ISAP), BACHELOR PLUS – Program to establish four-year bachelor's degree programs with an integrated year of studying abroad, and the Integrated International Degree Program with Double Degrees.

International Study and Training Partnerships (ISAP)

By supporting International Study and Training Partnerships (ISAP), the DAAD aims to encourage German and international universities to establish long-term cooperative agreements. This program supports groups of highly qualified German and international students who wish to complete part of their degree program at the partner university and receive full recognition of their academic achievement abroad. The German universities should also strive to create a basis for a long-term mutual exchange by offering attractive courses of study for foreign students. Credit transfer agreements and joint development of curricula should promote the internationalization of the participating universities as well.

WEBSITE: www.daad.de/isap

BACHELOR PLUS – Program to establish four-year bachelor's degree program with an integrated year of international study

The four-year bachelor's degree programs, funded by the DAAD under this scheme, enable students to complete a one-year study visit abroad. Such programs allow students to gain special interdisciplinary competence and/or professional qualification without increasing the length of their undergraduate study. After completing the programs, students receive a bachelor's degree from their home university, whereby the qualifications acquired abroad are indicated in their certificate, diploma supplement or additional documents from their home or partner university. By helping to establish four-year bachelor's degree programs, the DAAD wishes to promote mobility among undergraduate students and to increase the academic and intercultural benefit of international study. Furthermore, by supporting this rare study model, the diversity of the degree programs at German universities is increased.

WEBSITE: www.daad.de/bachelorplus

Integrated International Degree Program with Double Degrees

The program supports courses of study which are offered alternately at German and international universities and conclude with the conferral of two national degrees (either a joint degree or double degree, conferred by both partner universities). Such degree programs promote further internationalization of German universities and strengthen the exchange of instructors and students.

WEBSITE: www.daad.de/doppelabschluss